PROFITABLE SERVICE MARKETING

PROFITABLE
SERVICE MARKETING

EUGENE M. JOHNSON
EBERHARD E. SCHEUING
KATHLEEN A. GAIDA

DOW JONES-IRWIN
Homewood, Illinois 60430

© DOW JONES-IRWIN, 1986

ISBN 0-87094-613-7
Library of Congress Catalog Card No. 86–070516

Printed in the United States of America

1 2 3 4 5 6 7 8 9 0 K 3 2 1 0 9 8 7 6

To our parents
who helped us grow in love
Elizabeth and Willis Johnson
Lore and Helmut Scheuing
Georgine and Fred Gaida

Preface

The September 27, 1985, issue of *The Wall Street Journal*—chosen for its convenience, not for any other significant reason—featured articles with the following headlines: "Jump in Local Rates Since AT&T Breakup Is Spurring Protests"; "Philadelphia Electric Seeks 9.4% Rate Boost"; "Proposed Federal Rules May Limit Interest Charges on Credit Cards"; "Travel Agencies Change Tactics to Keep Clients"; and "American Airlines Expected to Be Fined $500,000 after FAA Maintenance Probe." These articles reflect the scope and importance of marketing to service businesses in the 1980s. Marketing has moved from the "nice to know" category of information to the forefront of service management.

The growing significance of service marketing is demonstrated in a number of other ways. The first major conference devoted strictly to the marketing of services was held in 1981 by the American Marketing Association. This conference is now an annual event. The AMA has also formed a separate Services Marketing Division and the AMA's president has identified service marketing as a major focal point for the future development of marketing. Leading service industry trade associations such as the Bank Marketing Association and the Financial Institutions Marketing Association have seen their memberships grow. Major colleges and universities have begun to offer undergraduate and graduate courses in service marketing.

This book also represents a milestone in the development of service marketing. Ten years ago it is unlikely that there would have been sufficient demand to justify publication of a book on service marketing. As services have grown in importance in the economy—they now account for more than half of all consumer expenditures in the United States—the interest in service marketing has increased tremendously. This interest has also been spurred by many other factors: deregulation of the airlines, financial services, telecommunications, and other major service industries; important social, cultural, and demographic changes that have increased the demand for household cleaning, child care, fast-food, entertainment, and other consumer services; dramatic technological changes that have altered the ways in which financial, transportation, communications, data processing, and other leading service businesses meet the needs of their business customers; and changes in the professions and their codes of ethics that have forced firms in the medical, legal, accounting, and other professions to concentrate more on marketing.

The purpose of this book is to help service managers learn how their businesses can grow and prosper through the application of modern marketing concepts and practices. It analyzes the nature of services, the service environment, the service marketing management cycle, and the service marketing mix. A central theme of our discussions will be the concept of evolution and continuing innovation. The marketplace is dynamic. Each element affects other elements with which it interacts. Service businesses, too, must be dynamic if they are to be successful. It is not sufficient to introduce a service, and then expect continued customer patronage. As needs change, so must services continually change in line with marketplace demands.

Our coverage of service marketing will identify a number of major issues and trends that will confront service managers in the coming years. These include the following:

- Greater emphasis will be placed on marketing research to identify buyers' service needs.
- A major response to changing needs will be greater service innovation and differentiation.
- Changes in service marketing organization and distribu-

tion structures will be made so that customers' needs will be better met.

- Customers will be involved more efficiently in the creation and marketing of services.
- Improved internal marketing efforts will be implemented to ensure that consistent service quality is maintained.
- Deregulation and increased competition from goods marketers will require that marketing continue to grow in stature in service businesses.

The authors gratefully acknowledge the contributions of those people who have assisted us in the preparation of this book. Gert Greene, Lisa Hayes, Geraldine Lang, Christina Vitez, Joan Zanni, George Maggiore, and Dorothy Canner have helped us in the preparation of the manuscript. Our appreciation goes also to the many academic and business colleagues who have provided us with ideas and suggestions throughout our years as teachers, researchers, and consultants in service marketing.

Eugene M. Johnson
Eberhard E. Scheuing
Kathleen A. Gaida

Contents

PART ONE

SERVICE MARKETING
AND ITS ENVIRONMENT

CHAPTER 1

Service Marketing—Challenge and Opportunity

The United States is a service economy. Seven out of 10 members of the labor force work in industries ranging from financial services to nonprofit institutions. The output of the service sector represents a steadily growing share of the gross national product—currently about two thirds. Services' share of U.S. exports is also constantly expanding. It includes travel-related services, telecommunications, consulting, design, training, advertising, banking, insurance, health care, and franchising of food-service establishments, to name but a few.

Clearly, service firms are a vital part of the U.S. economy. Their number and importance reflect an advanced stage of economic development—the postindustrial society. They are a major source of employment, economic stability, and growth. Their size can range from a one-person professional office to a multinational organization employing in excess of 100,000 people.

Managing service firms—as opposed to manufacturing establishments—poses some unique challenges. Since their output is largely intangible, image and reputation are a significant concern for service businesses. Airlines, for instance, aim to convey an image of friendliness ("the friendly skies of United") or competence ("the most experienced airline in the world"). Since demand often fluctuates substantially during the course of a day, week, or year, capacity is often designed to accommodate

peak demand, resulting in a substantial underutilization of resources during off-peak periods. Hospital and inner-city hotel
bed counts drop markedly on weekends, leading to incentives for
weekend admissions and budget-priced miniweekends to improve utilization.

THE CHALLENGE OF COMPETITION

These and related challenges will always be part of the service
management scene. However, something dramatically new has
occurred over the past decade or so in many service industries:
the age of competition has arrived. Service industry managers
must engage in a carefully planned, strategic marketing effort
or see the fortunes of their firms seriously suffer. Not that service providers didn't have competitors before. They did—since
many service businesses are relatively easy to start up due to
limited capital requirements. But in the past, most service firms
did not really compete. They just simply "were there," waiting
for business to walk through the door. Churches, dentists,
banks, museums, airlines, hospitals, and many others had the
attitude that they had something valuable to offer and the public should come and ask for it under its own initiative. To many,
it was unthinkable to use such crass commercial tools as advertising or selling to stimulate demand, and price wars were un-
heard of.

In part, this perspective was due to professional ethics—
medical societies and accounting associations prohibited their
members from advertising. In part, prices were fixed by agreement—local lawyers agreed on minimum fees and airlines had
rate-setting cartels. In part, government regulation protected
industry members against the rigors of unbridled competition—
thanks to the Civil Aeronautics Board, domestic airlines did not
have to face any significant new entrant for decades, and AT&T
all but owned the telecommunications market.

But the rules of the game have changed. Deregulation has
opened previously closed industries to hordes of aggressive new-
comers. The skies are abuzz with upstart airlines, who often
started with only a single leased plane and gate. In four years,
People Express has become one of the nation's largest carriers,
simultaneously making Newark Airport one of the busiest.
Court decisions have struck down restrictive rules, and an over-

supply of legal and health care professionals has forced some of them to advertise their services. Industry definitions have been blurred—banks, insurance companies, and brokerage houses are invading each other's turf, creating financial service power-houses and nationwide networks in the process. Even complete outsiders have joined the game: Sears Roebuck & Co. has made a major commitment to financial services and is now introduc-ing its own general-purpose credit card, Discover, in direct com-petition with Visa and MasterCard. Financial supermarkets of the future will thus include such diverse players as Merrill Lynch, Citibank, Prudential-Bache, American Express, and Sears. Since the breakup of the Bell System, MCI—a virtual unknown just a few years ago—has become the nation's second largest long-distance carrier. And a change in government reim-bursement practices has wreaked havoc with a cost-plus ori-ented health care system.

THE NEED FOR MARKETING

Where many service enterprises formerly had no competitors, they now have competition—vigorous competition—and face the need to be competitive themselves. This is where marketing comes into the picture. Marketing aligns a service firm's offer-ings with the requirements of the marketplace. But service firms must realize that marketing is more than selling. Instead of merely pushing services that a company is willing to provide, marketing creatively interprets customers' needs and develops appropriate benefit packages. Even when the necessity to ac-tively market is recognized, however, there is often a great deal of resistance to actually making the necessary changes to adapt the organization to meet customers' needs.

When hospitals and banks first discovered marketing, for example, they typically created a single-person position and ap-pointed a long-term employee to fill it. In many instances, they coyly referred to this person as the "director of development" or "director of new business development," instead of using the word *marketing* in the title. By institutionalizing a marketing unit within the organization, these institutions might have felt that they were now engaged in marketing. Such thinking, though, was erroneous on three counts. First, the person so ap-pointed usually knew nothing about marketing and tended to mistake advertising or new account premiums for marketing. Second, these hospitals and banks had created a scapegoat, a person to blame if things did not go right. Third, and worse yet, by charging one person with the responsibility, they thought that nobody else would have to worry about marketing. This is one of the biggest errors any service enterprise can commit. One of the basic tenets of this book is that although one person ultimately has to pull it all together and make it all happen, *in a service firm everybody is engaged in marketing*. It is a fundamental mistake to think that marketing is basically a functional department. No, marketing is essentially *a way of thinking* and of orienting an entire business to serve its customers well.

As an example of how service firms adopt and adapt to the marketing concept, Kotler has traced the evolution of marketing practices in banks.[1] Until the 1950s, bankers were simply supplying needed services and did not have to worry about marketing. Bank buildings looked like temples and tellers worked in cages. Marketing arrived in the late 50s in the form of advertising and sales promotion to attract savings funds. But competitive imitation made one bank look like another, and retaining the newly acquired depositors proved more difficult than anticipated. So bankers learned to smile (just like health care professionals are now attending seminars on smiling or "bedside manners"), and banks became friendlier places at which to do business.

When all banks had become friendly, pacesetters began offering new services to create a differential advantage. Innovations can be copied quickly in financial services, however, and competitive advantages tend to be short-lived. The number of services provided mushroomed to over 100 for the average commercial bank. Look-alike banks discovered that they had to position themselves in the marketplace by zeroing in on a specific target group and its needs. But the real essence of marketing is present only in those banks that systematically apply cycles of marketing analysis, planning, and control to achieve carefully selected marketing objectives.

---

[1] Philip Kotler, *Marketing Management,* 5th ed. (Englewood Cliffs, N.J.: Prentice-Hall, 1984), pp. 27–28.

EXHIBIT 1-1   The Selling Concept

$$\textbf{Seller} \xrightarrow[\text{Selling}]{\text{Service}} \textbf{Buyer}$$

MARKETING FOR SERVICE FIRMS

Modern marketing practices have developed over the past quarter century in response to profound changes in the business environment such as those just described. Although variations exist, marketing as practiced today by service firms basically reflects two perspectives: the selling concept or old view, and the marketing concept or modern view. As Exhibit 1-1 illustrates, the *selling concept* represents a one-way street where the service seller decides what to offer in the marketplace and then uses promotional pressure to get the buyer to buy this service. Conspicuously absent is any input from the marketplace. This input is considered unnecessary in a sellers' market where demand outstrips supply or, of course, in a monopoly situation where the buyer has no other choice, such as used to be the case for telecommunications services. The seller concentrates on the quality of the service offering and pays little attention to the buyer. The Bell System used to be technology driven, paying little heed to the needs of specific customer groups. Similarly, some hospitals became forbidding fortresses of medical technology, featuring the latest equipment yet neglecting the emotional needs of their patients.

In contrast, the *marketing concept* focuses on the needs of the buyer. As shown in Exhibit 1-2, the marketing concept establishes a circular relationship between buyer and seller, placing the buyer at the heart, not at the end, of the marketing process. Marketing begins with marketing research, designed to find out what the buyer needs or wants. Once this marketplace input is clearly understood, the service seller develops and offers a problem solution that delivers the desired benefits.

The difference between the old and new concepts can be summed up this way: Under the selling concept, sellers attempt to create markets for existing services; under the marketing concept, they create services for existing markets. Properly practiced, marketing research identifies need gaps in the mar-

---

EXHIBIT 1–2   The Marketing Concept

Marketing research

Seller   Buyer

Problem solution

ketplace, that is, needs that are not being adequately satisfied by currently available services. The service marketer can then design a benefit bundle that fills this gap and thus addresses an existing market. As the example of People Express demonstrates, no-frills, low-cost air transportation was such a need gap. Similarly, medical drive-ins—low-cost, short-wait, no-appointment emergency-care facilities located in shopping centers—appear to be filling a gap between the family physician and hospital emergency rooms.

Marketing can thus be defined as *satisfying the needs of chosen customer groups at a profit.* It helps assure the best utilization of a service firm's physical, financial, and human resources by offering only services that the market truly needs or wants. The select groups of prospects that it has chosen to serve are called *target markets.* Persons responsible for directing and implementing a service firm's marketing effort are referred to as *service marketers.* They employ marketing research, that is, careful analyses of special market studies and secondary market data, to sharpen managerial decision making and improve the fit between the firm and its markets. Marketing research is an integral part of and a vital ingredient in the marketing concept because it provides the tools necessary for listening to the demands of the marketplace. A service enterprise that attunes itself to the needs of its chosen audiences is more likely to meet with lasting success than its less sophisticated competitors.

Profit orientation of a service business means that it can serve specific needs and target markets in the long run only if these needs and markets offer enough substance and adequate rewards. A low-price policy may not be the most sensible approach, particularly if prospects judge the quality of a service by its price, in the absence of tangible value indicators. For instance, while a client may visit a storefront legal clinic to have a will drawn up, an affluent defendant in a murder case will prefer high-priced legal talent. Similarly, modestly priced business consulting services may suggest a lack of competence or confidence.

The pursuit of profit, however, must be tempered by the overriding consideration of achieving long-term customer satisfaction. Profits will continue to accrue to a service firm only if there is a solid foundation of customer satisfaction. This perspective might suggest forgoing short-term opportunities to charge higher prices if such prices might discourage buyers from repeat purchasing. Sustained success in a competitive buyers' market such as banking, insurance, or hospitality requires a systematic, planned, strategic approach to marketing. *Marketing planning* means setting marketing objectives and deciding on ways to attain them.

THE SERVICE MARKETING MANAGEMENT CYCLE

But marketing planning is only part of the broader task of *service marketing management,* which involves the analysis, planning, organization, implementation, and control of the firm's marketing resources and activities to achieve customer satisfaction and satisfactory profits. The activities constituting the key responsibilities of service marketing management generally occur in the same sequence in a repetitive fashion. As a result of the sequential nature of these activities, one can refer to a cycle of service marketing management, with all activities held together by the structure of the organization, as shown in Exhibit 1–3.

The analysis dimension of the cycle calls for the investigation and interpretation of environmental and market conditions and trends as well as of the firm's own resources and capabilities. These resources may be equipment or people. Equipment-based services include automated delivery systems such as electronic data bases, automated teller machines (ATMs), and electronic diagnostic systems, and range all the way to sophisti-

EXHIBIT 1-3 The Service Marketing Management Cycle

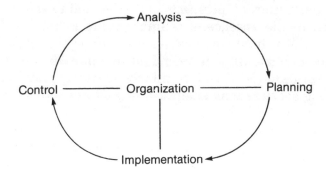

cated medical equipment operated by highly skilled technicians or even professionals. Many services, however, are people based, involving unskilled labor such as in building maintenance, skilled labor such as registered nurses, or professionals such as engineers. What is said of advertising agencies applies to many other service businesses as well: "Our assets walk out the door at night." Needless to say, many services combine equipment and people, with the former enhancing the latter's productivity, for example, a personal computer used by a pharmacist to keep track of patient records.

In addition to examining the environment at large and assessing the firm's internal resources, the analysis function also encompasses marketing research, that is, the creative interpretation of the needs and wants of the firm's chosen customer groups. This factual and creative input forms the basis of strategy development in the planning phase. Here, specific objectives are set for the planning period (usually a year) and the ways to achieve them are chosen. Detailed tactical planning concerning the use of the marketing mix is then followed by the implementation of the marketing plan. In the control stage of the cycle, planned and actual results are compared. Once the reasons for any deviations have been determined, necessary plan revisions or appropriate corrective actions can be undertaken. Organization is needed to hold the marketing effort together and drive it smoothly and successfully.

But the entire marketing effort of a service firm is of little avail unless it penetrates the organization and enjoys company-wide support. Service marketing management must employ an integrated approach, proceeding in a logical fashion and creating a basic system that is internally consistent, coordinated, flexible, and dynamic. As stated earlier, service marketing will not succeed as a department or function alone. Rather, it must be adopted and implemented as the philosophy of the entire company, aligning the firm's capabilities with the demands of the marketplace and educating all employees to the fact that they are involved in marketing and that their behavior and performance directly affect the success of the company.

THE MARKETING MIX

In the attempt to achieve the firm's marketing objectives, service marketers have to carefully orchestrate the tactical elements of the marketing plan. The *marketing mix* involves the integrated utilization of four Ps—product, price, promotion, and place. These vital tools for the implementation of the firm's marketing strategies can be described as follows:

Product—the offering; a benefit bundle providing a problem solution or want satisfaction; insurance companies or banks refer to policy or account types as products.

Price—the amount of money in exchange for which the seller is willing to perform the service; the cost to the buyer; rarely referred to as price—instead, words like premium, tuition, rate, fee, retainer, honorarium, fare, interest, and charge are used.

Promotion—informative and persuasive messages to encourage target market members to purchase the firm's services; this includes advertising, personal selling, sales promotion, and public relations.

Place—the service delivery or distribution system; this covers such considerations as number of service outlets, facility locations, and design.

All of these elements must be combined into a cohesive package by the astute service marketer. Because of their crucial importance to the success of the service marketing effort, each of these tools is treated in a separate chapter in this book.

EXHIBIT 1–4   Goods versus Services

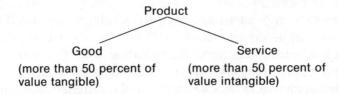

Product

Good
(more than 50 percent of
value tangible)

Service
(more than 50 percent of
value intangible)

THE NATURE OF SERVICES

But what, after all, is a service? And how does its marketing differ from that of a manufactured good? A service can be defined as an *activity* performed for another person or firm. In the case of a good, title to and physical possession of a tangible item are transferred to the new owner. Service buyers, in contrast, often literally have nothing to show for their purchases and walk away empty-handed. This is the case for such services as electronic banking, air travel, computer training, or attendance at a concert. In many instances, it is therefore useful to think of a service as an *experience,* although this experience may actually last longer than so-called durable goods, for example, education, surgery, or a trust, as opposed to a car or a washing machine.

The experiential aspect of services points up the fact that they are largely *intangible.* As a matter of fact, services can be described as purchases in which more than 50 percent of the total value acquired is intangible in nature. The opposite, of course, is true for goods, so that the following picture emerges (see Exhibit 1–4).

This places a fast-food meal squarely in the middle. In many people's opinion, half of the value received is speed and predictability. In contrast, a dinner at an expensive restaurant qualifies more clearly as a service. Although food and drinks are served, ambience and the style of cooking play a greater role.

As these examples indicate, tangible elements are always involved in the production and consumption of services to one degree or another. They are basically used in two ways: as support goods or as facilitating goods. Support goods are employed by service performers in the delivery of a service: the physician's stethoscope, the software designer's computer terminal, the motel room's furnishings, or the day-care center's toys. Facilitating goods are acquired and/or used by the recipients of services: students' notebooks, depositors' passbooks, cardholders' credit cards, or passengers' tickets.

Goods can play a role in service delivery in yet a different way. They can be made available for temporary use at a fee, in other words rented, leased, or loaned. In this case, possession of a good but not its ownership is transferred to a service buyer for a specified period of time. Car rental and equipment leasing are worldwide industries as are bank loans, illustrating the ease of exporting many services.

UNIQUE CHARACTERISTICS OF SERVICES

There are several characteristics that set services apart from goods and make their marketing more challenging. These include intangibility, perishability, simultaneity, and heterogeneity.

Intangibility

The first, and most obvious, feature of services is their *intangibility*. They go out of existence at the very moment that they are rendered, although their effects may last for some time. Because of the lack of tangibility, service marketers find it very difficult to differentiate their offerings. To consumers, a savings account at bank A is the same as a savings account at bank B, provided that they are both federally insured. A homeowner's policy issued by one company is interchangeable with one written by another insurer, so that the premium charged becomes the main selection criterion.

To the average person, intangible services are very abstract and thus difficult to describe and understand. This, in turn, makes it hard to demonstrate, illustrate, and promote services. Since the service itself cannot be shown, an airline finds itself restricted to picturing aircraft, in-flight settings, or destinations in its advertisements. Only rarely can a service be tried on a limited basis, as is frequently done with trial-sized packages of grocery products. Speed-reading and similar educational institutes at times offer free initial sessions of their courses and sign up recruits then. Airlines hope to convert nonflyers by offering them "fear-of-flying" classes that culminate in a short sight-seeing flight.

But by and large it is impractical if not impossible to provide a service on a limited basis. Potential buyers cannot examine samples and must therefore rely on the recommendations of others with appropriate knowledge and/or experience in their attempt to assess the quality of a service offering. This is why the hospitality industry courts travel agents and invites them on free trips. Similarly, patients are referred to physicians by other physicians or health care professionals.

In many instances, service buyers will rely on the tangible aspects of a service that they are able to experience directly when making their selection decision. As stated above, this includes support goods and facilitating goods. *Support goods* are the equipment used by service performers in delivering a service. These tangible goods must, accordingly, be in place before a service can be performed. As such, they may limit the capacity of the service firm or the level of sophistication of the services offered. Conversely, they can add value to or enhance a service. Many university courses, for instance, are still taught in the form of blackboard lectures, while most industrial training and seminar programs use a variety of audiovisual media to present the subject in a more dynamic manner. Ophthalmic surgeons make extensive use of laser technology in treating their patients.

While support goods are sometimes consumed during the production of a service—jet fuel, chalk, accountant's pads—they are never acquired by the service buyer. The opposite is true for *facilitating goods,* which are acquired and/or used by a service buyer. The recipient of a facilitating good may own it, for example, the home computer used in electronic banking or the manual given to a workshop attendee, or may use it for a time under certain specified conditions, for example, a guest towel for a hotel's swimming pool or a credit card that remains the property of the issuer. Facilitating goods can help to make a service more appealing to buyers since the buyers can see, feel, and show a physical symbol of their purchase. Because it reduces the frustration of empty-handedness, such tangibilization of an intangible service can be a powerful tool for attracting patronage. Educational institutions award diplomas or certificates, insurance companies issue policies, banks provide passbooks, consultants submit reports, and airlines give out in-flight magazines and slippers.

Perishability

The second unique characteristic of services is their *perishability,* a feature that is closely related to intangibility. As mentioned before, services go out of existence the very moment that they are created. This means that they cannot be stored but rather have to be produced on demand. Service marketers thus lose the valuable buffer function of inventory that decouples production and consumption from each other and allows a goods producer to manufacture for inventory during slow times and draw on inventory during periods of peak demand. Since they are intangible, services cannot be owned, distributed, or resold. Since services are perishable, unhappy customers cannot return them for a refund—in extreme cases, the only meaningful recourse is a malpractice suit. Conversely, a service provider may have limited recourse in the event of nonpayment. Once services have been rendered, they cannot be repossessed.

Excess capacity not profitably utilized in service production is lost forever, as, for example, empty seats on an aircraft that go to waste as soon as the flight takes off. This is why airlines sell remaining seats at much lower rates to standby passengers and even overbook planes in anticipation of no-shows. Many service establishments such as telephone companies, resort operators, and utilities use off-peak price promotions to improve capacity utilization during slow times. Fast-food chains have introduced breakfast menus to get more mileage out of their facilities.

In contrast, too little capacity to meet demand results in lost revenues. A bank that can't handle the lunchtime crowd permanently loses customers. This problem can be alleviated by employing part-time help during peak times or installing automated teller machines. And the capacities of different parts of a service operation have to be properly balanced. People Express has the flight crews and planes it needs but its reservation system is severely strained. Adding extra rooms to a hotel is useless if the pool, restaurant, or bar cannot accommodate the additional guests.

Simultaneity

The third unique characteristic of services is *simultaneity*, which describes the fact that services are produced and consumed at the same time. Goods are generally produced, then purchased, and then consumed. Services, on the other hand, are typically first purchased or contracted for, and then produced and consumed simultaneously. This feature limits the geographic area that a particular service firm can cover, with important implications for the service delivery system. Service performer and service buyer usually have to interact and, accordingly, be in the same place at the same time.

This can be accomplished in one of three ways. First, the buyer may travel to the service facility, as is the case for a student, depositor, or restaurant patron. Second, the performer may visit the buyer's premises, as in the case of home care, temporary services, or consulting. As these examples indicate, physical proximity is essential to the successful delivery of services. Trading areas of individual facilities are limited by the amount of travel that either party will tolerate. The location of facilities thus becomes a key marketing decision in the successful operation of many service firms. Branch location/convenience is typically the overriding consideration for depositors in choosing banks.

A third delivery option that is occasionally applicable is the concept of performing certain services in transit while the performer and buyer are jointly traveling to a particular destination. An example of this system is a "classroom on wheels," where university-sponsored courses are offered to commuters while they travel on the train to or from the office. Other examples include continuing education cruises for physicians with on-board seminars, or paramedic treatment of accident victims during ambulance transportation.

Simultaneity may result in mutual dependence through the close relationship that may develop between service performer and customer. This can lead to a personal following. A beauty salon patron or advertising account may not really patronize the salon or agency as a whole, but rather a specific stylist or account executive, and will follow this person to a new affiliation. It also means that the seller is often unable to perform the service without the presence and active participation of the buyer—students will not learn if they do not attend and study, and patients may not recover if they do not follow their doctor's advice. Conversely, buyers of services may not be able to consume them without the presence and active involvement of the service performer, for example, when a concert has to be canceled because the artist falls ill or a closing cannot take place if the attorney is absent.

Heterogeneity

The fourth unique characteristic of services is *heterogeneity*, or variability of output, which manifests itself in three ways:

1. The quality of service performance varies from one service organization to another. Not all universities or hospitals are held in equally high regard, and airlines and hospitality chains differ in the levels of service provided.
2. The quality of service performance varies from one service performer to another. A seasoned attending surgeon will bring more experience and skill to an operation than will a resident, and airlines always use their most experienced captains to pilot jumbo jets.
3. The quality of service performance varies for the same service performer from one occasion to another. A seminar leader will achieve varying results, depending on audience response and cooperation.

Whatever its nature, the variability of service output makes it difficult for a service firm to establish and maintain performance standards and thus guarantee quality continuously. To ensure consistent quality, service firms have to select and train their employees carefully and exercise tight quality control. Multisite operators such as McDonald's Corporation practice quality control through periodic field inspections. They send teams on unannounced visits to check each unit for quality, service, friendliness, and cleanliness. Other service providers such as hotels, restaurants, and airlines employ "mystery shoppers" who visit their facilities unbeknownst to the employees, conduct business as usual, and rate both the condition of the facility and the performance of the employees. One bank president plays "mystery shopper" himself: Convinced that branch employees do not know him by sight, he stands in line to cash a check and to evaluate teller competence and friendliness.

In a very real sense, the employees of a service firm *are* the organization, and their attitude on the job is as important as their skills. Because of this, enlightened service firms endeavor to instill a sense of excellence, self-worth, and accomplishment in their performers to keep motivation and morale high. Airlines and hotels issue attractive uniforms to their customer-contact personnel and conduct "employee of the month" contests. Fast-food chains, however, experience big problems in motivating their employees and holding on to them. Their operating environment is characterized by near minimum wage pay levels and the monotony of standard operating procedures that govern every move and deliberately leave counter workers little if any discretion. Personnel turnover at individual outlets, accordingly, often reaches 100 percent.

In human-intensive professional service firms, the composition of the work force makes or breaks the company, and the caliber and effort of each employee become essential to the organization's success. Accordingly, the arrival or departure of a single person can make a substantial difference in the reputation of the firm and the kind of clients it is able to attract and serve. Individual professionals often develop their own followings, which they may take with them when they change affiliation or go into business for themselves. This is a frequent occurrence in the advertising business where talented people often break away to form their own agencies, usually taking key accounts with them.

This high mobility of top service performers is a by-product of the fact that some services are vitally dependent on the person and skill of a specific service performer. In order for such a firm to keep talented individuals, it may have to make them partners, as is done in law practices, accounting firms, and investment banking houses.

Wherever nonstandardization could prove detrimental, a stabilizing influence can be exerted through the use of the latest and most sophisticated equipment to assist or supplant people in the performance of services. Diagnostic equipment in the medical field or in automotive care, for instance, removes a great deal of the variations inherent in human judgment by substituting objective analyses for subjective conjecture. Modern technology brings other economic and psychological benefits as well. Proper, up-to-date equipment can facilitate and expedite service production greatly, simultaneously impressing both clients and workers with its complexity, speed, and precision.

Buyer participation in service production introduces an element of great uncertainty into the service equation. In some instances, greater buyer involvement is desired and beneficial: Salad bars have become very popular, and self-ticketing of airline passengers is being tried in some places. Self-service islands at gas stations are also attracting a lot of business. But in many instances, different levels of understanding, skill, and cooperation on the part of service buyers result in output heterogeneity because the buyers themselves frustrate the service firms' attempts to control their production. In spite of the efforts of a service business to hire only well-qualified personnel and train them appropriately, the involvement of buyers in the production of services may render it all but impossible to standardize the outcome of and bring assembly line efficiency to the service production process. For example, a bank customer who incorrectly completes a deposit slip will require special attention from a teller, which will slow down the transaction.

In many instances, though, output heterogeneity is deliberate and strategic. Hospitality chains, for example, have found that travelers' needs differ and have therefore diversified into different types of accommodations: To attract different kinds of guests, Marriott has built Courtyard Motels and Holiday Inns has opened Crowne Plaza hotels. Instead of creating separate subsidiary organizations, other service businesses choose to offer different levels of service to different classes of customers within the same facility. Airlines differentiate between economy and first-class passengers on the same plane, hotels offer private elevator and concierge service to club members, and car rental companies provide preferential treatment to a select group of patrons, as do banks in their private banking or trust departments.

SERVICE MARKETING STRATEGIES

Keeping in mind the unique characteristics of services, the question arises as to how service firms should strategically deal with their challenges and turn them into opportunities. For each characteristic, there are several potential strategic actions and resulting benefits, as suggested in Exhibit 1–5. Each action can be carried out separately or in combination with others for maximum benefit.

Since a service is largely intangible, it cannot be examined on its own merits, separately from the organization delivering it, as is the case for goods. A service business is often built on a bond of trust in the integrity and stability of the serving institution. This is evident when the public loses faith and, for example, stages a run on a bank's deposits. Similarly, in its attempted rebirth under Pritzker ownership, Braniff was not able to instill sufficient confidence in travel agents and travelers to allow it to successfully function again as a scheduled airline. Accordingly, a service firm is often well advised to communicate how long it has been in business, satisfactorily serving the needs of its chosen clientele. Lufthansa, for instance, consistently directs its advertising to business travelers, using the results of passenger surveys. A quality image, fine reputation, and predictable performance make a powerful blend when a firm attempts to overcome the drawbacks of intangibility. As a matter of fact, a case could be made that predictability is the key to growth in chain operations. Patrons do not necessarily receive a better service, but they know what to expect—the predictable hamburger or the predictable motel room, reproduced time and time again with cookie-cutter precision. Holiday Inns uses predictability as a theme when it advertises "no surprises" or its "no excuses room guarantee." It is further beneficial to present a customer with an impressive document of some sort, such as an attractive card, certificate, or passbook, to manifest the occurrence, completion, or continuance of a service relationship. It pays to create a first-class impression of a service.

Demand often occurs in bursts for service businesses, but demand that goes unsatisfied now is often lost forever because the customer uses another source or gives up. While regulated service firms such as utilities are required by law to have adequate capacity to satisfy any reasonable demand level, even nonregulated service providers may find it to their advantage to follow this rule or at least have the option of expanding.

Although the physical facilities should be spacious and carefully appointed, generous full-time staffing can result in a great deal of unabsorbed overhead during slow or idle times. Here,

---

EXHIBIT 1–5   Strategic Responses to Unique Service Characteristics

---

Characteristic	Strategic Action	Benefits for Company
Intangibility	Stress quality image, fine reputation.	Relieves prospect anxiety and uncertainty.
	Emphasize predictable satisfaction.	Builds confidence.
	Offer some tangible element.	Reduces frustration of empty-handedness.
	Give your service a first-class ticket.	Reflects and enhances experiential aspect.
Perishability	Have adequate capacity "in place" to satisfy demand.	Enables flexible response to demand fluctuations.
	Employ part-time help during peak time.	Keeps fixed salary costs manageable while satisfying demand.
	Use a reservation system.	Improves capacity utilization.
	Make waiting enjoyable.	Keeps patrons happy.
	Encourage service consumption during off-peak times.	Levels out load factor.
Simultaneity	Locate close to consumption centers.	Responds to customer need for convenience.
	Utilize alternate facilities.	Permits servicing several trading areas.
	Travel to clients or provide transportation for clients.	Overcomes constraints of rigid centralization.
	Delegate part of production task to buyer.	Increases buyer involvement; reduces seller cost.
Heterogeneity	Hire the best.	Outstanding performance stimulates business.
	Standardize, program, and package services.	Controls output variability.
	Utilize latest equipment.	Impresses customers and employees, expedites production, and improves performance.
	Train, motivate, and reward service performers.	Provides personal reasons and tools to excel.

Reproduced with permission from *Marketing Update,* Issue 22 (New York: Alexander-Norton, Inc., 1981).

cross-training of a core crew of full-time employees and the planned use of well-trained part-timers can produce useful economies and considerable scheduling flexibility.

Where capacity is limited, as in a restaurant, hotel, or aircraft, even in a doctor's office, a reservation system can alleviate overcrowding. The problem then is what to do about no-shows, that is, people who make a reservation but do not show up. Airlines usually impose no penalty but try to cope with no-shows by systematic overbooking. Restaurants have no recourse, but will assign a table to another patron after a reasonable grace period. Unless guaranteed by credit card, hotels will reassign rooms after a specified check-in hour. And doctors may charge for an office call if a patient makes an appointment but does not appear.

Where waiting is more or less unavoidable, background music, magazines, television, toys, mirrors, and refreshments make the time go by faster and more pleasantly. Some airport lounges offer personal television sets, and airlines make magazines or even movies available on board for long flights. Restaurants often encourage patrons to wait in the bar, thus generating extra revenues and keeping the patrons happy. The promotion of off-peak consumption can be used to deflect excessive demand from peak periods to periods of underutilization as well as to attract additional price-sensitive business during these times and thereby smooth out the fluctuations of the demand curve. A multitude of service providers use time-of-day or time-of-year pricing to achieve this purpose. Airlines have "red eye" midnight specials, restaurants have luncheon menus, hotels have miniweekends, movie theaters have matinees, and telephone companies have night rates. Some utilities are experimenting with off-hours residential rates to even out the load factor.

Service firms engaged in the production of convenience services can improve their success by locating where customers live and opening up (or buying) branch locations. Banks have found that in order to attract deposits, their branches have to be easily accessible. In professional service firms, key professionals can maximize the use of their talents by alternating between different offices. Physicians and orthodontists, for instance, are known to follow this procedure, thus effectively enlarging the geographic area that they can serve.

In the case of shopping or specialty services such as advertising or consulting, a service performer has to be ready to travel to the client. Conversely, a sponsor must at times provide limousine service for a prominent speaker or popular artist, or a gambling casino for a high roller, or a bank for a wealthy investor. Letting consumers do part of the work themselves can actually be fun, increase involvement and satisfaction, and save money. This can be done by having customers interface with and operate machines such as automated teller machines, ticket-writing equipment, or vending machines dispensing travel insurance or traveler's checks. While it is common for hospitals to serve patients their meals in bed, some have successfully experimented with cafeteria-style arrangements for their noncritical patients. Motels and no-frills airlines have their customers handle their own baggage. Car rental firms compete effectively with taxis and services providing chauffeur-driven limousines.

Since for human-intensive service firms the employees *are* the firm, it pays to hire the best personnel available. Multisite operators have to ensure homogeneity of service delivery by standardizing and planning, to the minutest detail, site selection, facility layout, service mix, and operating procedures. Utilizing the latest equipment to aid or replace humans in the performance of services can also act as a stabilizing influence. Finally, careful training and attractive incentive systems can substantially reduce performance heterogeneity. McDonald's operates "Hamburger University" to train managers and franchisees who, in turn, train their people in standard operating procedures.

SUMMARY

People responsible for marketing in service businesses— whether formally charged with this task or just informally concerned about the long-term viability and growth of the organization—are beginning to grasp the seriousness of the challenge in an increasingly competitive environment, as well as the attractive opportunities inherent in service marketing.

Every service organization—profit-oriented or nonprofit, one-person operation or national chain—has to examine its corporate mission vis-à-vis its chosen clientele. It must then develop a marketing program specifically tailored to delivering satisfaction to this target group while at the same time providing for the steady growth of the organization. It is time that service marketers face up to this challenge by applying the ingenuity and sophistication developed in packaged goods marketing to the unique conditions of service businesses.

CHAPTER 2

The Service Marketing Environment

Service marketers design their firms' marketing efforts to be carried out and succeed in a given *marketing environment*. The latter could be defined as all the forces outside a service marketer's control that affect the success of the company's marketing activities. Because environmental forces are largely *uncontrollable,* they have to be taken into account when formulating marketing strategies and tactics. Service marketers have to carefully scan the environment to understand the nature and relevance of environmental parameters and adapt their firm's marketing activities to them.

Another consideration to keep in mind is that environmental forces are *dynamic* in nature. They are subject to frequent, sometimes discontinuous, changes that render yesterday's marketing responses inappropriate, if not fatal, today. To protect itself against detrimental environmental changes and to be in a position to capitalize on emerging opportunities, a service firm has to engage in continuous *environmental monitoring*. This enables it to read evolving trends early on and have enough lead time to develop appropriate responses. Environmental developments can accordingly be seen to represent either threats or opportunities, depending on management's perspective. After all, it has been said that a problem is a brilliantly disguised opportunity (John W. Gardner). In other words, what is one firm's problem is another firm's opportunity.

The interdependence of marketing environment and strategy may be exemplified by the situation in the airline industry after deregulation. The labor costs of unionized nationwide carriers such as American Airlines had grown to substantial levels, with some senior captains earning more than $150,000 per year. Considering this fact to be a problem that artificially inflated airfares, low-cost upstart airlines saw an opportunity to enter the market with a low-price strategy and take business away from the established carriers. Taking up the challenge, the established carriers struck back with selected discount fares and two-tier wage structures that compensated new hires at substantially lower levels. Continental Airlines even went so far as to declare bankruptcy in order to abrogate existing labor contracts and slash labor costs. The strategy worked, and Continental has since flown back to solvency.

The service marketing environment can be said to consist of five major sectors. (A sixth sector, the natural environment, tends to affect services businesses less than goods manufacturers and comes into play primarily when the location of service facilities has to be decided upon.) The five sectors are:

1. The economic environment, which concerns the ways in which scarce resources such as personal income are used.
2. The social environment, which deals with the shifting values, preferences, and behavior patterns of constituent groups of American society.
3. The legal environment, which refers to the laws and regulations governing service businesses, for example, banking laws or professional licensing requirements.
4. The technological environment, which includes the equipment used to enhance or replace human labor in the production of services, for example, personal computers or automated teller machines.
5. The competitive environment, which examines the nature and types of competition for various service enterprises, for example, low-cost carriers or in-store service departments.

As shown in Exhibit 2–1, these sectors of the service marketing environment both influence and are influenced by a service business. Being surrounded by and dependent on the envi-

EXHIBIT 2–1   The Service Firm and Its Marketing Environment

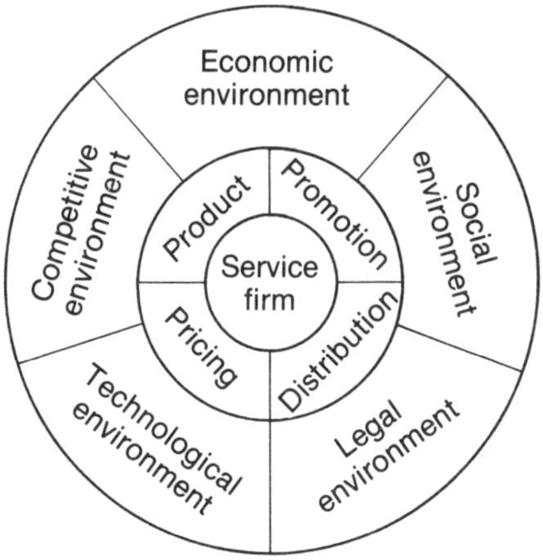

ronment, a service business uses its marketing mix to achieve its marketing objectives within this setting.

THE ECONOMIC ENVIRONMENT

In the decades since World War II, the economies of the United States and other advanced nations have undergone extensive social and economic transformations. One significant change has been an increased rate of spending for services. In the years following World War II, service expenditures accounted for approximately one third of personal consumption expenditures; now, they account for about one half of household expenditures. This figure is expected to rise still higher, at the expense of purchases of manufactured goods. Approximately one half of a family's service expenditures are for shelter and household operations. Education, medical and dental care, transportation, and banking and insurance also account for significant portions of consumers' expenditures for services. However, as discussed later in this section, the growth in service expenditures has not been confined to consumers; business and government service purchases have escalated sharply as well.

Economic Thought Concerning Services

Economists have postulated several reasons for the ever-increasing expenditures for services in our economy, and the resulting shifts in employment. These reasons are based, in large measure, on the increased affluence and consequent preference for leisure time associated with a mature economy and the resulting by-products of economic growth in service industries.

One economic concept often used to explain the growth of services is Engel's Law, first presented over 100 years ago by the German statistician Ernst Engel. According to Engel's studies of spending behavior, as a family's income increases:

1. The percentage spent on food decreases.
2. The percentage spent on housing and household operations remains about the same.
3. The percentage spent on other purchases increases rapidly. These other purchases include, to a great extent, such services as education, health care, recreation, entertainment, and transportation.

Studies of sales and income statistics in the United States confirm that the pattern of growth for services follows Engel's law. In general, as their incomes rise, people will spend a higher proportion of them on services.

A second theory that explains the growth of services has been advanced by the Australian economist Colin Clark, who views the economic development of a nation as a three-stage process. Clark's theory cites an agricultural orientation as the first and most primitive stage in this process. Whether engaged in farming, fishing, hunting, trapping, or grazing, society depends directly on the use of natural resources. As the economy becomes more advanced, society moves away from this direct dependency to an indirect reliance on available natural resources. The ability to convert coal, gas, and hydroelectric power into energy, for example, contributed significantly to the Industrial Revolution that swept the United States and other Western nations during the last century. Jobs soon shifted to manufacturing, since workers who had been replaced by machinery on the farm were now needed to keep the factories operating. As machinery becomes more and more refined, requiring fewer workers, the economy shifts into the third, and most advanced, stage. Here, the majority of the labor force is engaged in the production of services—building and construction, transportation and communications, commerce and finance, public administration and defense, and personal and professional services. Clearly, the United States economy is at this advanced stage of economic development.

Yet another explanation for the growth of services has been presented in a study conducted by the General Agreement on Tariffs and Trade (GATT) secretariat. This study reported that 19 million new jobs were created in the United States between 1970 and 1980, an increase of 24 percent. Eighty-seven percent of these jobs were in the service sector, and many of these were with small firms that employ fewer than 20 people. Why were these jobs primarily in services, and not in manufacturing? First, the worldwide trend toward protectionism has made it more difficult to penetrate foreign markets, making manufacturing less appealing to potential entrepreneurs. While services may be geographically concentrated, goods manufacturers must rely on larger markets to produce profits. Second, many large manufacturers have begun to contract for service activities, thus providing greater opportunities. Additionally, the initial capital costs per employee are much lower in service industries. Finally, government policy is cited as a contributing factor, since economic uncertainties adversely affect manufacturers to a greater degree than service providers. The study thus contends that there is more to the emergence of a service economy than the maturation of American enterprise.

Service businesses are also less subject to the fluctuations of the business cycle than are goods manufacturers. In an advanced, affluent economy like the United States, most durable goods purchases are replacement purchases, not first-time purchases. For instance, most new car buyers are replacing an existing vehicle rather than shopping for their first automobile. Replacement purchases, however, are generally postponable, because instead of being replaced, many durable goods can be repaired. This is evidenced by the sharp drop-off in durable goods purchases during recessions, accompanied by marked increases in the sales of replacement parts and home improvement materials.

Service purchases, on the other hand, due to their intangible, experiential nature, often cannot be postponed indefinitely.

Personal services, such as haircuts or medical care, are typically inevitable. Financial services, such as banking and insurance, are needed in good as well as in bad economic times, as are telecommunications services. Pleasure travel can be curtailed but business travel tends to be less flexible. Even movie theaters are little affected by economic fluctuations—in bad times, they provide an escape from harsh realities.

Increased consumer spending for services is undoubtedly due to a combination of advanced economic development, increased affluence, a growing preference for leisure time activities, larger numbers of dual-career and singles households, government policy, and interactions with other nations. Psychological and sociological factors, however, must also be taken into account. The desires for personal service, convenience, and service differentiation are three important consumer service needs that must be recognized. These and other facets of buyer behavior are considered in the next chapter.

The Growth of Business Services

Perhaps even more spectacular than the growth of consumer expenditures for services has been the increased spending for business services. Servicing business customers has itself become big business, and companies in the business service field range from suppliers of temporary help to highly specialized consulting firms.

Some business services are part of the economic infrastructure, making possible economic development and growth. Electric power and telecommunications were necessary aids to production processes, and goods had to be shipped, insured, financed, and distributed. Dun & Bradstreet, for example, widely known today as a credit rating service and provider of many other specialized business services such as computerized data bases, was formed in 1841 to provide eastern manufacturers with business and credit information about businesses in the West.

In recent years, business service companies have prospered primarily for two reasons. First, business service firms frequently are able to perform a specialized function more efficiently than would the purchasing company itself. Telephone companies, for instance, routinely "farm out" to outside concerns the task of telephone interviewing to measure customer satisfaction with their services. Rapidly growing firms providing economical services include companies that offer maintenance, cleaning, and protection services for office buildings and industrial plants. In particular, the demand for protection specialists such as the William J. Burns International Detective Agency, and Brinks, Inc., has increased as the nation's crime rate has soared.

Second, many companies are unable to perform certain services for themselves. Marketing research studies, for example, often require impartial outside experts. Also, the increasing need for specialization in modern business management has led to the development of expert business services, such as data processing specialists and firms that specialize in designing and conducting sales incentive campaigns.

The Problem of Inflation

While inflation has affected all aspects of the economy, service industries have been particularly hard-hit. The rapidly escalating cost of energy has caused tremendous problems for transportation and utilities, among other industries. These costs must ultimately be passed on to both consumers and industrial users in the form of higher prices for services rendered. The high cost of labor in many service businesses also contributes to the inflationary trend. Providers of professional services—physicians, lawyers, accountants, and consultants—are engaged in people-based services and command higher salaries than wage earners in capital-based manufacturing businesses. These personnel costs must also be borne by service purchasers. Finally, productivity growth to compensate for inflationary pressures is more difficult to obtain in service businesses than in manufacturing enterprises.

THE SOCIAL ENVIRONMENT

The *social environment* may be defined as the cultural and interpersonal values, attitudes, and behavioral patterns that comprise a society's unique way of life. Social changes have affected service marketing in a number of ways. There is evidence, for example, that the tastes of U.S. consumers have shifted to a preference for various nonessential, or "luxury," services as status symbols. Travel, culture, fitness, personal care, and higher education have to some extent replaced durable goods as status symbols in the minds of many consumers.

Other social trends have affected the demand for services. These trends include a growing emphasis on security, which has expanded the market for insurance, banking, and investment services; greater stress on health and physical fitness, which has led to a greater demand for dental, medical, and hospital services, and exercise centers; the changing attitude toward credit, which has expanded the demand for the services of banks and other lending institutions; and the growing use of professional counselors to cope with the personal and business pressures of modern society. It is also interesting to note that there is now a broad spectrum of services closely related to an individual's life cycle. From birth (obstetrical services) through childhood (educational services) to adulthood and old age (health care), and finally death (funeral services), the list of services goes on and on. As new consumer needs emerge in our fast-paced, action-oriented society, the quantity and types of services available will increase further.

A detailed discussion of social change and corresponding growth of services is beyond the scope of this book. To illustrate the impact of social change and its interaction with other components of the environment, we shall briefly describe two issues—the two-paycheck family and the "me generation."

Two-Paycheck Families

The changing role of women in society has had an impact on various aspects of the U.S. economy, including the service market. Due to economic pressures and the desire of many married women to pursue a career, there has been a tremendous increase in the number of two-paycheck families. In over half of the families in the United States, both spouses are employed—a situation that is expected to continue.

Service marketers must be aware of the implications of the two-paycheck family, including the following:

1. Families, especially those in the growing 35 to 44 age group, will enjoy a higher standard of living, with more discretionary income for entertaining, travel, dining out,

and other luxury services. Two-paycheck families eat out an average 7.4 meals per week.

2. Working wives create a greater demand for convenience and time-saving services, such as fast foods, dry cleaning, laundry, and other personal care services.

3. Banks, dry cleaners, and other service retailers have been forced to revise their hours of operation to meet the changing needs and schedules of the many women who are now part of the labor force.

4. The growing sophistication of the American public— thanks, in part, to the increasing numbers of women who work outside of the home and use these services, as well as to the availability of mass media—has resulted in a demand for greater quality in services offered for consumption.

The "Me Generation"

The study of lifestyle trends has become important to many service marketers. *Lifestyles* are distinctive modes of living, often associated with particular age groups and/or generations. One of the strongest lifestyle trends has been the emergence of the "me generation." This expression has been used to describe those people, often young and affluent, who are concerned with self-satisfaction and living for today. The service marketer should be aware that the "me generation" may lead to the following:

1. Overall, a greater use of services to save time and labor.

2. More frequent purchases of entertainment and travel services to increase self-satisfaction, to satisfy the desire for change, and to provide an escape from the perceived boredom and frustrations of everyday life.

3. Greater use of financial services, especially credit, to purchase luxury and enjoyment-related services.

4. Increased purchases of health and exercise services to enhance health, physical appearance, and longevity.

5. Greater need for conveniently located service establishments, due to the desire for quick and easy access, as well as immediate satisfaction.

THE LEGAL ENVIRONMENT

The legal environment of service marketing is made up of laws, government regulations, and court decisions. These legal constraints limit the marketing activities of service businesses. In fact, many service firms are regulated more closely than most other forms of private enterprise. Hospitals in New York City for instance, have to satisfy the requirements of no fewer than 160 regulatory bodies. Many service organizations are subject to some special form of government regulation above and beyond the usual taxes, antitrust laws, and restrictions on promotion and price discrimination. The number of service organizations subject to such regulations, however, is decreasing as the move toward deregulation gains momentum. Examples of regulatory restrictions include the following:

- A long-distance telecommunications firm must gain the approval of the Federal Communications Commission (FCC) before rate changes can be made.
- Local providers of public transportation must obtain approval by the public service commission before adding or dropping routes.
- Funeral directors, barbers, and cosmeticians must be licensed to practice in most states.
- Telecommunications companies, utilities, insurance companies, and banks are also subject to various types of restrictive legislation, such as plain-English laws, limits on interstate banking, and restrictions on engaging in other businesses.

The Scope of Regulation

The scope of regulation for many service industries is vast. At the federal level, several government agencies are charged with the responsibility for regulating the activities of service firms, including the Securities and Exchange Commission, the Federal Communications Commission, the Federal Reserve System, and the Comptroller of the Currency. State and local regulations affect the activities of such service industries as banking, insurance, education, medicine and related health services, and real estate. Many personal and business services are also restricted at state and local levels by special fees or taxes and certification or licensing laws. Law, medicine, nursing, hair care, funeral directing, accounting, teaching, and engineering are among the professions subject to various state and local restrictions.

In addition to these restrictions, many professional services are regulated internally by industry associations. These groups may set standards for members of the profession in terms of entrance requirements for new members, educational qualifications, certification and/or licensure requirements, ethical standards and fair practice, pricing and promotional activities, or other aspects of work performance. Even though they may not be an official arm of the government, these associations often have the force of law, since violators may be subject to a variety of penalties—perhaps even revocation of the license to practice, if the charge is severe enough.

An example is the American Institute of CPAs (AICPA), the self-regulating body of the accounting profession, which was created in an attempt to stave off government regulation. Only under pressure from the SEC, the Department of Justice, and the Federal Trade Commission, did the AICPA update its Code of Professional Ethics in 1978 by repealing Rule 401 ("Encroachment") and deleting that portion of Rule 502 ("Advertising and Other Forms of Solicitation") that forbade direct, uninvited solicitation of specific potential clients.[1] Meanwhile, competitiveness in this formerly gentlemanly profession and the aggressive search for new clients have reached such proportions in public accounting that Mark Stevens felt moved to entitle a recent book on the subject *The Accounting Wars.*

Rathmell defines this regulatory situation in terms of three distinct levels.[2] In the case of *restricted* services, performance of the service without the direct sanction of the state is illegal. Examples of restricted services are the medical and legal professions. *Semirestricted* services are those in which anyone can practice, but only those who successfully complete a prescribed program of study and pass a qualifying examination can claim to be certified members of the profession. Accountants, engi-

---

[1] John G. Keane, "The Marketing Perspective: The CPA's New Image," *The Journal of Accountancy,* January 1980, p. 60.

[2] John M. Rathmell, *Marketing in the Service Sector* (Cambridge, Mass.: Winthrop Publishers, 1974), pp. 45–46.

neers, funeral directors, and architects are among the professionals working in semiregulated industries. The third group, *nonrestricted* services, includes those with no established criteria, such as standards of performance or codes of conduct, that must be adhered to by members. Examples of this last group include professional consulting, marketing research, and advertising.

Implications for Service Marketers

Government regulation has many implications for service marketing. Two, in particular, stand out. First, excessive regulation has quite possibly been one reason for the lack of marketing innovation by service businesses. Prior to passage of the Airline Deregulation Act, which ultimately dissolved the Civil Aeronautics Board, no new nationwide carrier had entered upon the scene in several decades. Routes and fares were severely regulated and all changes were subject to cumbersome government approval. The marketing options generally available to the business community, such as aggressive price competition, service diversification, and promotion, are limited by government restrictions for certain service industries. In many states, current banking laws prohibit banks from establishing or acquiring branches in other states and sometimes even in the same state, or from engaging in such nonbanking activities as insurance.

With Citibank leading the charge, however, these restrictions have successfully been challenged on a variety of fronts. State governments have permitted out-of-state money center banks to take over failed thrifts. Nationwide electronic banking networks have been established. Retailers (Sears, J. C. Penney) as well as money market funds (Dreyfus) have been permitted to buy banks. Ironically, in anticipation of an invasion of their territories by Citibank, bankers in several northeastern states have been able to persuade their legislatures to let them branch out into adjoining states by keeping large money center banks out. Citibank has also solicited credit card holders nationwide and established loan-generation offices in major cities across the United States.

A second implication of government regulation is the fact that service businesses must concentrate much of their marketing efforts on the pursuit of favorable regulatory treatment and/

or the prevention of unfavorable actions and restrictions. Service businesses do this directly by lobbying legislators, members of regulatory agencies, and other government officials. Industry trade and professional associations, such as the U.S. League of Savings Institutions, have active lobbying organizations, as do many individual service businesses.

Service businesses also try to influence regulation indirectly through their efforts to create and maintain a favorable public image. Utilities, transportation companies, telecommunications firms, and other regulated service firms direct a major part of their marketing efforts toward maintaining consumer satisfaction and holding back government intervention. To do this, they must maintain a favorable public image, since any large outburst of public displeasure will almost certainly lead to government action. The outcry in many states over electric utilities' adjustment charges, for example, has resulted in public hearings and legislative action. Utilities have tried to offset this negative publicity by informing their customers of the steps they have taken to conserve fuel.

The Move toward Deregulation

One of the most important legal issues confronting the service marketer today is deregulation—the move toward lessening restrictions on service industries. Deregulation allows greater freedom in making and altering marketing decisions, more competition, and the occurrence of the "natural selection" process in the marketplace. From its gradual beginnings in the late 1960s and early 1970s, deregulation has gained considerable momentum in the service sector. Table 2–1 provides a listing of some of the major stepping-stones toward deregulation in this country. Further changes are expected as the results of deregulation are examined over time.

The case for deregulation has not been made easily. Confusion and conflicting arguments have dominated the movement. Supporters favor competition, support natural regulation by the marketplace, and seek to decrease the scope of government control because of its alleged inefficiency, cumbersomeness, and disadvantages to the consumer. Opponents, however, view competition as disruptive and dangerous, and favor increased government control of various service industries. A third group as-

---

TABLE 2–1 The Move toward Deregulation in the United States

Year	Decision
1968	The Supreme Court permits non-AT&T equipment to be connected to the AT&T system.
1969	The Federal Communications Commission (FCC) allows MCI to connect its long-distance network into local phone systems.
1970	After a decision by the Federal Reserve Board, banks are free to set their own interest rates on deposits of more than $100,000 with maturities of less than six months.
1974	The Justice Department files an antitrust suit against AT&T.
1975	The Securities and Exchange Commission (SEC) orders brokers to cease commission fixing on stock sales.
1977	Merrill Lynch introduces its Cash Management Account, designed to provide greater competition with commercial banks.
1978	The Airline Deregulation Act of 1978 reduces the Civil Aeronautics Board's control over fares and market entry and ultimately puts the agency out of business.
1979	AT&T is permitted to sell nonregulated services, such as data processing, following an FCC decision.
1980	The Depository Institutions Deregulation and Monetary Control Act puts commercial banks and savings institutions on equal footing with respect to the services they may offer, and provides for the elimination of interest rate controls (Regulation Q).
1980	The Staggers Rail Act allows railroads to set their own rates, thus allowing them to compete with one another and with trucking and barge lines.
1980	Sears Roebuck & Co. offers insurance, banking, and brokerage services to its customers.
1984	AT&T divests itself of its local phone companies.
1985	The Supreme Court permits interstate banking on a regional basis.

SOURCE: Adapted from "Special Report: Deregulating America," *Business Week,* November 28, 1983, pp. 80–82.

serts that the interests of the consumer should dictate the prevailing climate toward deregulation. Basically, then, disagreements abound among all affected parties concerning the proper position to be taken on the issue of deregulation, including the industry itself, with major companies reversing their positions from time to time. American Airlines, for instance, first opposed deregulation, then advocated it, and now favors reregulation.

Deregulation has resulted from a fundamental lack of satisfaction with the regulatory system, which imposes a structure on an industry unlike that which would be expected to occur naturally. The move toward deregulation is generally supported by service industry leaders and some of the smallest firms in an industry; it is generally opposed by firms in the middle of an industry. Leaders may see a chance to increase profits, while small firms may attempt to be acquired by larger concerns.

Deregulation is not sudden, but usually follows a lengthy transitional period during which corporate attitudes and strategies may be adjusted gradually. Once deregulation is enacted, however, changes in the industry occur rapidly. Firms that have not properly adjusted their strategies can then face serious difficulties. Service marketers engaged in industries where regulatory policies may be subject to changes must attempt to anticipate and prepare for such changes as early as possible. Keeping abreast of industry trends and maintaining flexibility are the two best ways to prepare for the conditions that deregulation may bring.

Supporters of continued regulation cite the following objectives of the regulatory process:

- Protection of consumer rights, the underprivileged, and the small business owner through cross-subsidization (this was the case for telephone service where high business telephone rates subsidized low residential customer rates).
- Improvement of the quality of life via legislation (guaranteed access to residential telephone and electric service).
- Prevention of monopolies (actually, the government granted monopolies but prevented their abuse through regulatory commissions).
- Control over prices to protect the interest of the consumer and to prevent unfair trade practices by requiring government approval of prices and price changes.
- Prevention of service disruption through competition (routes could not be abandoned without government approval).

Opponents of regulation, however, mention the following as problems with the regulatory process:

- Lack of concern for the consumer, since the focus is on regulatory agencies.
- Lack of innovation and contentment with the status quo.

- Collaborative agreements with competitors to dictate volume and price to the consumer (rate cartels in the transportation industry).[3]
- Inertia—Price adjustments are time-consuming (a typical utility rate case takes one year), costly, and risky (the commission tends to grant less relief than requested).

Supporters of deregulation cite the many positive results that have been achieved where deregulation has taken place. Chief among these is the return to a competitive marketplace. Innovation, increased productivity, and reduced prices have all been achieved as a result of deregulation in several major service industries. And these benefits are dramatically different from the grave problems predicted by opponents of deregulation. Long-distance airline fares, for example, are roughly half of what they were seven years ago; trucking rates have decreased approximately 30 percent since 1980; and discount brokers may save clients 60 percent on commission costs.[4] Far from suffering, some of the major service industries in the United States— banking, telecommunications, trucking, and the airlines—are reaping profits while contributing to the overall health of the nation's economy and to the welfare of the consumer. The trend is expected to continue as deregulation affects still more industries.

Implications of Deregulation for Service Marketers

The dire predictions of opponents of deregulation have not come to pass. While some newly deregulated businesses have been poorly managed by short-sighted executives and have suffered in their new competitive environment, well-managed, marketing-oriented businesses have survived and prospered. In the long run, deregulation will lead to stronger service industries and greater customer satisfaction. The most important change to be considered by service marketers in newly deregulated industries is increased competition for the service buyer's dollar.

---

[3] Thomas S. Robertson, Scott Ward, and William M. Caldwell III, "Deregulation: Surviving the Transition," *Harvard Business Review,* July–August 1982, p. 4.

[4] "Deregulating America," *Business Week,* November 28, 1983, p. 80.

New services (products), competitive prices, creative promotional techniques, and more convenient methods of distribution (place)—the four Ps of the marketing mix—must all be developed and coordinated to meet the changing demands and challenges of the marketplace. The astute service marketer will recognize these new requirements and respond appropriately with carefully developed marketing programs.

While much of this discussion has centered on the positive aspects of deregulation, it would be well to acknowledge those who hold the opposing viewpoint. Despite many glowing reports of increased profits and overall satisfaction with the process of deregulation, there is a groundswell of disenchantment that continues to build. In the airline industry, for example, with its recent rash of disastrous crashes, some would advocate a return to the "good old days" of regulation. Increased operating costs and labor problems have plagued many established airlines with large fleets, especially in the face of competition from small carriers, smaller aircraft, and lower labor costs. The Airline Deregulation Act of 1978 contains a provision that allows for the reestablishment of the Civil Aeronautics Board (CAB), should the need exist. While it is unlikely that such a move will actually take place, it is essential that service marketers be aware of the existence of discontent among members of the air travel industry.

A similar problem, but with a slightly different twist, is apparent in the telecommunications industry. Here, however, it is the general public, and not the service providers, who have voiced their displeasure. Many feel that deregulation has actually led to less efficient service at a higher price. Efficiency and accuracy are essential ingredients for success in this industry; those who would be industry leaders must be willing to provide both at an equitable price.

Other Legal Issues

While deregulation has been the major focus of our discussion concerning the legal environment, other issues have also influenced the nature of service marketing. One of the most important is the Supreme Court decision that removed the ban on advertising by professional service providers. Its primary effect has been the advent of competition in previously noncompetitive industries. The implications of this legislation will be discussed in our consideration of the competitive environment.

THE TECHNOLOGICAL ENVIRONMENT

For service businesses, the technological environment manifests itself primarily in the form of increasingly sophisticated equipment (support goods) used in producing and delivering services.

This equipment can facilitate the job of the service worker, for example, diagnostic equipment in an automobile repair shop. It can make service performance more accurate, for example, laser devices in ophthalmic surgery or computers in the cockpit of jumbo jets. It can expedite service delivery, for example, account inquiry terminals in bank branches or electronic card readers at check-in counters. Or it can replace human service performers altogether, placing the burden of activating and directing the machine exclusively on the service buyer, for example, automated teller machines, automated airline ticketing machines, or in-home banking by personal computer.

Productivity in Service Industries

As in manufacturing firms, equipment can often be used in service industries to reduce heterogeneity and at the same time increase the rate and quality of the output. In manufacturing businesses, automation and robotization have displaced workers no longer needed to operate equipment, thus contributing to the shift of workers to service industries.

Unfortunately, the productivity increases evident in the manufacturing sector have not yet been duplicated in the service sector. In fact, some observers blame the national slowdown of productivity on the shift to a service economy, suggesting that low-paid, less productive service workers are holding back overall productivity gains. While others argue against this view, the criticism of productivity rates in the service sector continues.

What are the reasons for the lower level of productivity in service industries? Part of the problem is undoubtedly due to the heterogeneity of output and lack of standardization that characterize service operations. While manufacturing of goods often involves the use of machinery and other technology to increase productivity rates and maintain standardization of output, many service industries are human centered, and thus subject to fluctuations in productivity and other problems of human origin. In an effort to reduce the problems associated with productivity and to find an alternative to the rising minimum wage, many service providers have turned to nonpersonal ways to deliver their services. Many service workers have been displaced through increased buyer involvement, self-service options, or the trend toward increased use of technology. Direct long-distance dialing, automated bank teller machines, and computerized reservations systems are just a few of the ways in which service businesses have used technology to improve productivity. A relatively new use of technology is demonstrated by the business of providing computerized home-shopping services. A variety of banks, publishing houses, and retail chains have begun to introduce service systems that enable consumers to make purchases, complete and verify bank transactions, view catalog selections and order merchandise, retrieve information on a variety of topics, and even buy and sell securities—all in the comfort of their own homes. Home-shopping services are presently in place in selected cities and will become more widely available within the next few years, once the cost of the systems to consumers is reduced from current levels. Industry consultants are optimistic about the success of this new means of performing services; predictions of expected revenues by the mid-1990s range from $4 billion to $30 billion.[5]

Industrialization of Services

Levitt states that part of the productivity problem in service industries may be due to the erroneous assumption that service is synonymous with servitude, or the one-on-one relationship of performer to buyer. Services are presumed to be performed under loosely controlled, variable conditions; service providers are assumed either to behave ritualistically (not rationally) or to simply obey orders—not to reason or think independently. Increases in productivity are supposedly tied to the performance of the worker, not to the methods by which the task itself is performed. As long as these attitudes persist, Levitt contends, im-

---

[5] Martin Mayer, "Coming Fast: Services through the TV Set," *Fortune,* November 14, 1983, p. 55.

provements in productivity levels will be impossible to achieve.

We must begin to think in industrial and technical terms so that service delivery can be improved. One way is to substitute machinery, tools, or other tangible equipment for people. Examples include airport X-ray surveillance equipment, automatic car washes, and electrocardiograms. A second approach is to substitute a preplanned system for an individualized service. Examples of this approach include prepackaged vacation tours, fast-food restaurants, and mutual funds. Finally, some service businesses have combined equipment with a preplanned system to provide an efficient, quick service—for example, the fast, specialized auto repair services provided by Midas and similar companies.[6]

One caveat should be mentioned here. While increased use of technology may improve both the quality and quantity of output in service industries, the problem of depersonalization may occur. For example, the American Medical Association has become concerned that some physicians are relying too heavily on medical technology and neglecting the personal aspects of the doctor-patient relationship. Astute marketers will attempt to "humanize" technology in order to overcome consumer resistance and gain acceptance.[7]

THE COMPETITIVE ENVIRONMENT

The competitive environment for services is a paradox. While deregulation has stimulated price competition and changed the competitive environment for many service businesses, much competition still comes, not from other service businesses, but from the goods sector, from government services, and from "do-it-yourself" services.

---

[6] Theodore Levitt, "Production-Line Approach to Services," *Harvard Business Review,* September–October, 1972, pp. 41–52; and "The Industrialization of Services," *Harvard Business Review,* September–October 1976, pp. 63–74.

[7] Naisbitt has emphasized the necessity to restore the "human touch" to high tech interactive situations with his concept of "high tech–high touch." See John Naisbitt, *Megatrends* (New York: Warner Books, 1984), pp. 35–52.

Competition among Service Providers

Historically, many forms of internal competition have been almost nonexistent in some service industries:

- Price competition has been severely limited by regulation and trade practices in transportation, telecommunications, and in business, legal, and medical services.
- Many important service providers, including hospitals, educational institutions, and religious and welfare agencies, are not operating for profit in the business sense.
- Many service industries are difficult to enter.
- A major financial investment may be necessary (utilities).
- Special education or training may be required (professions).
- Government regulations may restrict operations (telecommunications, banking).

One example of the changes wrought by deregulation may be found in the legal profession. Prior to 1977, when the Supreme Court ruled that lawyers could advertise their services, lawyers were only permitted to accept cases referred through social contacts or professional reputation. Now, however, the environment has changed drastically. Firms of all sizes—from corporate giants to small practices—have found themselves facing increasing competition from their peers. Gone are the days when marketing was looked down upon. At the 1985 convention of the American Bar Association in London, England, which drew 12,000 U.S. lawyers, a well-attended workshop was called "Marketing of Legal Services." External consultants and internal marketing specialists are being used more frequently as the need for their expertise becomes more pronounced. The trend toward increased competition is not restricted to the legal profession, however. Health care professionals and other service providers have also begun to use paid advertising and a variety of public relations techniques. This trend is expected to escalate in the future, as the potential benefits of these activities become more widely felt in service industries and as competition from group practices, prepaid plans, and the like becomes more severe.

Competition from Goods

Direct competition between goods and services is inevitable, since competing goods and services often provide the same basic benefits. A woman may go to a hair stylist for a permanent, or she may choose to purchase any one of a number of home permanents on the market and apply it herself. Likewise, consumers may either go to a gym or health club, or they may purchase athletic equipment for use in the home.

Competition between goods and services has become greater in recent years because manufacturers who recognize the changing desires of consumers are building services and added conveniences into their products. Examples include wash-and-wear clothing, which has rendered some laundry and dry cleaning services unnecessary, and television, which competes with motion pictures and other forms of entertainment. Consumers and businesses now often have a choice between goods and services that perform the same general function, for example, a telephone answering service or an answering machine. Further, because the low productivity of some service businesses has resulted in their charging high prices, services have suffered even more from sales lost to less expensive products, such as home barber kits, washing machine repair kits, and a variety of other do-it-yourself items.

Competition from Do-It-Yourself Products

The preceding examples of products point to a unique feature of the competitive environment for service marketing. In most cases, the purchaser of a good has only two choices—buy the product or forgo satisfaction. However, there is another alternative—the do-it-yourself product—available to the service buyer, which further complicates the service marketer's task: Not only must buyers' normal reluctance to act be overcome, but also buyers' willingness to perform the service for themselves must be discouraged.

A consumer is more likely to perform a service if the skill required is relatively low and/or time can be saved. A homeowner, for example, will perform minor repairs on a home rather than go to the trouble and expense of hiring a repair person. Texts, courses, and other study materials, such as home repair books, and products, such as tools and repair kits, have made it easier for consumers to perform services for themselves.

Competition from Retailers and Manufacturers

The entry of retailers and manufacturers into consumer and business service markets has also increased the intensity of competition for the service dollar. Sears Roebuck & Co., J. C. Penney, and other large retailers are providing services such as optical centers, automobile repair facilities, and beauty salons that go far beyond traditional department store offerings. As in many other facets of retailing, Sears was a leader in the trend to diversify into services with its entry into insurance (Allstate) and other consumer services. In recent years, Sears has evolved into a full-service provider of consumer financial services with Allstate (insurance), Coldwell-Banker (real estate), Dean Witter (brokerage), and a large California savings institution. Sears and other large-scale retailers have discovered that technological advances have made mass merchandising of consumer services possible and profitable.

In a related development, large manufacturers have begun to offer spin-off business services to other businesses. For instance, Du Pont, Dow, Alcoa, and other companies noted for their technological expertise market analytical services and facilities, pollution control systems, and related products or services to other companies. These large manufacturers see the special needs of other businesses as an opportunity to profit from their own investments in research and development.

Competition from Government

An expanded range of services is now provided by the various levels of government. Some services, such as highways and many welfare programs, can be provided only by government agencies, but many government services compete with privately produced goods and services. Often, the consumption of government services is mandatory, for example, contributory social insurance and compulsory education. Whether or not they are mandatory, government services limit the consumption of privately produced goods and services.

Some government services, such as the U.S. Postal Service, compete directly with private enterprise. When this occurs, service managers often feel that they are at an unfair disadvantage. Government services and those that are subsidized by the government present a unique competitive situation, since such organizations do not necessarily include the full cost of providing the service in their fees. Consequently, marketing efforts may be directed at limiting the scope of government services or reducing the level of government subsidies. This may involve lobbying and other direct cr indirect efforts to sway public opinion.

International Competition

Many services have become international in scope. Accounting, insurance, advertising, project engineering, consulting, and even fast foods are now international industries, with offices in the United States and abroad. As other industrialized nations become more service oriented, they will export their services to the United States as well. For this reason, trends in services that occur in other advanced nations should be monitored in an effort to keep abreast of, and perhaps ahead of, developments that are occurring elsewhere. Also, the United States must modify its international trade legislation and policies to give American service industries more flexibility to compete in international markets.

SUMMARY

Service marketing managers are confronted with a number of forces that must be taken into account when planning the firm's strategies. These environmental considerations fall into five categories: economic, social, legal, technological, and competitive. While some of these may be more important in certain service industries than in others, it is nonetheless essential that each of these sectors be carefully assessed by marketing managers on an ongoing basis to help determine trends that may have an impact on their businesses.

CHAPTER 3

Service Buyer Behavior

As the general affluence of the American consumer increases, and as services become more accessible through a combination of advanced technology and more intense competition, the number and types of services purchased will undoubtedly increase. To the astute marketer, then, one fact should be apparent. Those who understand the behavior patterns of actual and potential customers will be better able to provide acceptable service packages designed to meet buyer needs. Much information has already been compiled on the topic of buyer behavior. Most of this material, however, is related to the purchase of goods, not services. The unique characteristics of services, outlined in Chapter 1, point to various differences in buyer behavior.

There are many reasons why service buyers do what they do. Some of these reasons may be economic; others may be caused by the buyer's demographic profile; still others may be psychological in nature. Since the service field is characterized by frequent introductions of new services, it is helpful to develop an understanding of the process by which new services are accepted or rejected by their intended audience. This chapter will describe the nature of buyer behavior in regard to various types of services and the implications of these behavior patterns for service marketing planning and strategy.

EXHIBIT 3–1 The Purchasing Cycle

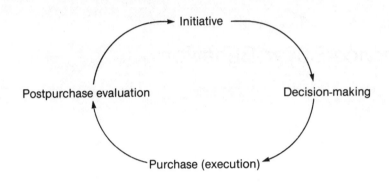

THE PURCHASING CYCLE

The act of purchasing is actually just one stage in a more complex and comprehensive process known as the *purchasing cycle*. The cycle, depicted in Exhibit 3–1, demonstrates the importance of planned behavior in the selection of a product or service to be purchased. The stages in the cycle may be explained as follows:

1. *Initiative stage.* The purchasing cycle begins when a triggering force, or stimulus, alerts the potential customer to the fact that he or she either needs or wants a particular product or service. The stimulus may be internal; that is, it is initiated by the consumer in response to a perceived need or desire. On the other hand, the stimulus might be external, created by an outside source—in this case, a service firm. The customer may see an advertisement, designed by a firm to encourage consumers to purchase one or more of its services. In either case, the consumer perceives an unfulfilled need that leads to the decision-making stage.

2. *Decision-making stage.* Once a need or desire has been established, the consumer must consider which available product or service will best satisfy this need. During this second stage, the consumer develops objectives, gathers relevant information, assesses alternatives, and decides on the "best" course of action. As we will see later in this chapter, the degree of concentration and energy expended during this stage will depend on the relative importance of the need or desire in the eyes of the consumer.

3. *Purchasing stage.* It is here that execution, or a response to the initial stimulus, occurs. The selected option is implemented as the purchase takes place. The purchase of a service involves an interaction between provider and client. We have already discussed the fact that consumers participate in the service purchase, due to the simultaneity of production and consumption that characterizes service industries. As a result, there is much opportunity for subjectivity in service purchases. It is essential that the consumer be pleased with the purchase, since repeat business or patronage will be decided on the basis of treatment received during this stage. The initial visit to a physician, for example, may lead to return visits and possible recommendations. Should the experience be negative, however, the patient will be unlikely to seek out that physician in the future.

4. *Postpurchase evaluation stage.* Once the purchase has been completed and the consumer has experienced the product or service, the actual results are compared with the expected objectives. This feedback sets the stage for further action, when necessary.

PURCHASING SERVICES VERSUS PURCHASING GOODS

The differences between purchasing goods and purchasing services are apparent even from this preliminary discussion. A tangible physical product, such as a gold watch in a jeweler's showcase or on a friend's wrist, can serve as a powerful purchasing incentive due solely to its visibility. Services, however, are not tangible, making it difficult, if not impossible, for potential consumers to view them and decide to purchase them on that basis. Service buyers must rely much more heavily on word-of-mouth advertising during the decision-making stage of the purchasing cycle. Trial sizes, samples, and other such materials available to purchasers of goods have little meaning in the service arena. Thus, subjectivity becomes a more crucial factor in service marketing, since many of the objective means of assessing a product and its ability to satisfy needs and/or desires are unavailable. Service marketers, then, must attempt to make other factors work to their advantage in making the services offered by their

---

EXHIBIT 3–2 Roles in the Buying Process

Informer ———→ Influencer ———→ Decider ———→ Buyer ———→ User

---

firms known to the public. If possible, the reputation of the firm should be promoted by renowned experts, famous celebrities, or satisfied customers. In addition, both new and established firms can "concretize" or "tangibilize" their service offerings in an effort to increase the number of tangible clues that can be used by consumers during the decision-making stage of the purchasing cycle.

A second, and perhaps more important, difference between goods and services purchasing becomes apparent after a consideration of the various roles played in the purchasing cycle. In the goods sector, five distinct roles have been identified (see Exhibit 3–2):

Informer—secures initial factual information that serves as a stimulus to initiate the buying process.
Influencer—adds persuasive or influential data to the factual information. The influencer may have a personal interest in the purchasing decision (advocate influencer), or may be completely objective or neutral (independent influencer).
Decider—makes the actual buying decision, based (at least in part) on data provided by the informer and the influencer. The decision includes a choice of: timing, budget, brand, and store and/or provider.
Buyer—executes the purchasing decision in accordance with instructions.
User—derives intended benefit from the product.

When goods are purchased, it is possible that five separate individuals or groups may become involved, each assuming a separate role. On the other hand, one individual may assume more than one role (the user, for example, may also be the influencer) or even all five roles. When this model is applied to service buying, however, it is most frequent that at least two roles—buyer and user—would have to be assumed by the same person, due to the simultaneity of production and consumption, and the importance of buyer participation that characterize service industries. An exception occurs when individuals buy services for others, such as parents for children. Buyer and user are then different persons, although both may become involved in the service delivery process. Conversely, it is often the case that the last three roles (decider, buyer, and user) merge into a larger role carried out by a single person.

Two major exceptions to this pattern should be noted however: third-party purchases and right-to-performance purchases. The first instance may be illustrated by the purchase of life insurance. The buyer—the person who pays the premiums—may also assume the role of decider, choosing the company, the type of insurance, and the amount of coverage. This person is not, however, the beneficiary or user of the service that is purchased. Similarly, brokers may decide on and purchase stocks for their clients without being the beneficiaries (users or title holders) of the purchase. In the second instance, right-to-performance purchases, a service may be contracted for now but not actually consumed until a later date. Advance purchases of concert tickets, theatre tickets, or travel services are examples of this type of service purchase. Here, buyer and user may be separate persons, or cancellation could even prevent usage; whatever the reason, production and consumption are not simultaneous.

Notwithstanding these exceptions, most services are purchased, produced, and consumed simultaneously. What potential difficulties does this pose for service marketers? Simply stated, the necessity of producing services virtually "on demand" places a great strain on the capacity of many service firms. Fluctuations in demand may make it extremely difficult to estimate production needs. While operating at minimum or less than peak capacity can cause the service firm to forfeit much potential business, gearing production to peak anticipated demand may also cause severe problems with cost-effectiveness. In an effort to minimize the potentially disruptive and damaging effects of demand fluctuation, many service businesses use part-time employees during peak-demand periods. Many firms have also introduced reservation systems, in which a certain amount of time is set aside with a service provider for each client. A service firm may thus be able to deflect demand from

---

EXHIBIT 3–3 Options for Service Prospects

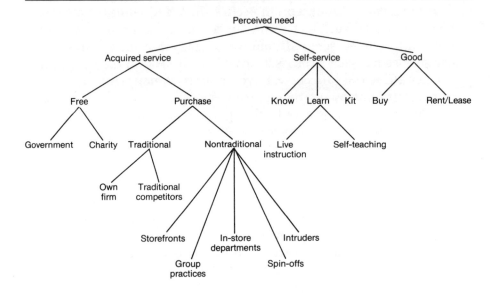

overload periods to lesser-used time slots, making its employment needs more evenly distributed. Another tactic used by some service firms is to make waiting more pleasant for clients. Restaurants have bars or lounge areas; doctors' waiting rooms are stocked with various books and magazines, and generally feature soothing music.

Options for Service Prospects

Potential service buyers are often confronted with a variety of options when attempting to determine the best way to satisfy a perceived need or desire. Exhibit 3–3 demonstrates these options open to consumers. These options are a result of the various forms of competition discussed in Chapter 2—competition from goods, traditional retailers and manufacturers, do-it-yourself products, government agencies, and other providers of the same service. Of course, not all of these options may be available for all types of services and, in other instances, several options may be combined. In the first case, for example, self-service options may not be feasible for various medical services; in the second case, a skill may be learned and a service performed by a consumer with the help of a book that was purchased or equipment that was rented. Service marketers must be alert to these competitive options when making strategic decisions.

In Exhibit 3–3 we see that a consumer with a perceived need or desire may seek out a physical product, or good, that will provide adequate satisfaction. The advent of disposable diapers marked the demise of the diaper service business. Why? The new product not only accomplished the same purpose, but also added the features of convenience and lower cost. While disposable diapers are products that must, by their very nature, be purchased, other products may be purchased or rented, and rentals may be on a short-term or long-term basis. (As we have seen, rental of services is impossible due to their intangible nature.) Telephone answering devices, for example, have replaced answering services in many instances; the necessary equipment may either be purchased or rented. Similarly, corporations may either hire their own attorneys or retain outside counsel on a long-term or short-term basis.

The second option for potential service buyers is the do-it-yourself approach. Examples of do-it-yourself services are lawn care, home permanents, and auto repair. Consumers selecting this option must be capable of performing the service, through a combination of prior and/or acquired knowledge; they must also have the time and desire to do so. The self-service alternative, of course, is not available in some areas, where performance may be limited to practitioners with a certain degree of formal training and/or experience (for example, medical services). In many other areas, however, self-service may be an attractive option. In fact, purchased services are often much more susceptible to competition from do-it-yourself activities than are goods, since many more consumers consider themselves capable of performing a service (or learning how to do so) than building a good. In order to reduce the competition that may come from self-service options, service marketers should attempt to emphasize the competence and professionalism of the company and its employees as well as features such as convenience and efficiency, and any other potential benefits of entrusting the performance of the service to an outside firm.

The third class of options for potential service buyers is acquisition from an outside provider. Some services, especially those designed to satisfy basic health-related needs, may be provided free of charge by government agencies or independent charities. Marketers involved in these services must make the public aware of their availability and of the criteria for their usage. Care must be taken to announce these services in a positive manner that will be acceptable to the intended audience. While many who may avail themselves of these services may not be able to satisfy their needs through alternative sources, the concept of "hand-outs" or charity may have a negative connotation. In order to ensure proper usage by those for whom the service was intended, marketers must emphasize both the purpose of the service and the benefits provided for users.

Not all acquired services are provided free of charge. Most, in fact, are rendered in exchange for an agreed upon sum of money or for a good or service of comparable value. A relatively new example of this latter concept is actually a reinstatement of one of the oldest forms of exchange known—barter. Providers of all types of services—artisans and professionals—make their services available to members of an exchange group. In return, they receive credit that entitles them to use the services of others in the group. This system, which has become increasingly popular during the last few years, should continue to attract those with a variety of skills who enjoy the opportunity to use their talents while acquiring the right to a variety of services for which financial compensation would otherwise be required.

When money is the method of exchange for the acquisition of various services, the beneficiary generally combines the roles of decider, buyer, and user. The provider may be a traditional or nontraditional source. Traditional sources include those firms that specialize in providing a particular type of service in an accustomed way. Examples include a law firm, a physician's private practice, and a commercial bank. Service marketers must remember that they are in competition with any number of other traditional firms that provide the same basic service. Since the latter are engaged in offering one special class of service, they may be well-established, and they may be perceived by clients and potential clients as a source of continuity, trustworthiness, predictability, and professionalism. In several critical areas, there is often great reluctance on the part of clients to change providers once a satisfactory relationship has been established. It is thus of critical importance that service marketers distinguish their firms from those of competitors to give their businesses a competitive edge.

Increasingly, however, traditional service firms have begun to encounter competition from nontraditional sources. Inventive, enterprising individuals or corporations may sense growth opportunities in fields previously unknown to them. These alternate sources include storefront and group practices, in-store departments, spin-offs, and intruders. They may offer attractive additional benefits to prospective buyers: lower cost, more timely delivery, greater range of expertise, easier accessibility, tested programs, and higher yields.

Traditional law firms, for example, operate out of one, or perhaps two, offices. Large overhead costs often lead to higher charges for clients. Legal clinics, on the other hand, have been established to provide low-cost services to clients through a host of *storefront* offices. While the range of services offered by such firms is generally restricted to more routine legal matters, these clinics have enjoyed increasing patronage in recent years. Similarly, tax-return preparation offices, such as H & R Block, have sprung up throughout the United States.

Group practices have been formed by teams of physicians or other health care professionals. Examples include a practice composed of a dentist, an orthodontist, and an oral surgeon, or a practice composed of a general practitioner, a surgeon, and a heart specialist. Benefits to both the practitioners and their clients may be improved by such arrangements, since they provide greater convenience and a wider range of available services, generally at a lower cost than traditional private physicians.

Department stores, which once confined their operations to selling apparel or appliances, have also begun to add a variety of services to their mix of offerings. These include hair care salons, appliance repair services, eye care centers, insurance offices, financial service centers, and ticket outlets.

Spin-offs are services initially developed by manufacturers to satisfy internal needs, which later become profit centers in their own right when these capabilities are made available to others outside of the firm. Xerox, for example, sells its Professional Selling Skills program to other firms, and GE provides subscribers with its economic forecasts. General Electric Credit Corp., originally established to provide consumer financing for

GE appliances, is now one of the largest consumer finance companies in the United States.

Intruders are best seen in the banking industry, where money market funds and other nonbank financial service firms have deflected enormous funds from traditional depository institutions. For example, Merrill Lynch's move to expand into various financial services has been fueled by the introduction of cash management accounts (CMAs).

The range of options available to potential service buyers, then, is really quite extensive. Competition for a prospect's business comes from all sides, and should not be taken lightly. Service marketers must attempt to learn about the various forms of competition particular to their industry, and then counter these competing elements through an organized system of information and/or promotion. Potential buyers should be made aware of the availability of a service and its provider. The range of features and benefits that will accrue to users and the convenience of the service should also be stressed, as well as the professionalism and competence of the firm.

SERVICE NEEDS AND BUYING MOTIVES

With a wide range of options available, service buyers select one supplier over others according to their needs and buying motives. Maslow's hierarchy, a simple but powerful and widely used framework for categorizing needs, postulates that all human needs are organized according to their priority status. Higher-level needs do not serve as stimuli for behavior until lower-level needs are largely satisfied. The hierarchy, outlined in Exhibit 3–4, demonstrates that the first, and hence the most basic, category of needs is physiological in nature—including, for example, the needs for food, clothing, and shelter. Once this primary group has become sufficiently satisfied, safety or security needs become dominant; these include the need for physical, financial, and professional (job) security. Taken together, these first two groups constitute the lower-level needs. The higher-order needs begin with the third level, social needs, which include the desire for acceptance, affection, and interpersonal harmony. These are followed by the esteem needs, the ego-oriented needs that include self-respect and the desire for prestige in the eyes of others. The fifth and highest level encompasses the need

EXHIBIT 3–4 Maslow's Hierarchy of Needs

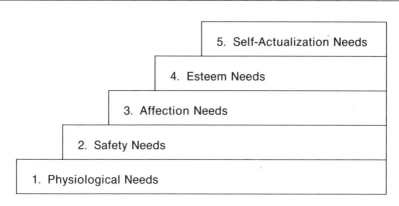

5. Self-Actualization Needs

4. Esteem Needs

3. Affection Needs

2. Safety Needs

1. Physiological Needs

for self-fulfillment or self-actualization—the desire to achieve one's full potential.

There are a host of services that address themselves to the lower-level needs. The physiological needs for food and water require tangible satisfaction but may fall into the realm of services in the event of an emergency, when special help may be needed (for example, Red Cross assistance to earthquake victims). Fast-food restaurants could also be classified as services designed to satisfy these needs. The need for shelter may be satisfied through home ownership or rental. The satisfaction of safety needs may involve public protection from the fire department, police department, National Guard, FBI, U.S. Armed Forces, and the like, or they may involve private protection through security services, burglar alarms, bodyguards, lock boxes, bulletproof limousines, and so on. Job security is fostered by seniority, tenure, and long-term employment contracts, while financial stability and independence are sought by means of federally insured savings accounts, investment vehicles, tax shelters, insurance policies, and so forth.

Unquestionably, a rich harvest may be reaped by the imaginative and sensitive service marketer seeking to satisfy these basic needs, and a great deal of ingenuity and innovation has gone into devising new ways to do just that. The real growth opportunities for progressive service marketing, however, are likely to lie in the range of higher-order needs. At a time when traditional family living patterns are breaking down and when nearly a quarter of all households are headed by single persons, the need for acceptance and meaningful relationships deepen. As affluence increases—particularly in single-person and dual-earner households—services become more affordable and leisure time becomes more valuable. In this situation, people tend to purchase a service rather than do it themselves. (How else, for instance, could dog-walking and lawn care services be explained?) The variety of services that can be geared to the esteem and self-actualization needs is legion, including education, entertainment, travel, personal care, clubs, leisure activities, the arts, and volunteer work.

Attitudes and Buying Behavior

Attitudes may be defined as learned ways of reacting to stimuli that are generally consistent over time. The term *learned* implies that attitudes are formed on the basis of both past and present knowledge and/or experience. Since this learning takes place over time, it is generally well entrenched in the minds of actual and potential consumers. Once formed, attitudes are generally extremely difficult to modify. Equally important to service marketers is that attitudes may become grouped together to form an *image,* or set of beliefs, concerning a particular service. It is often difficult for a consumer to distinguish one service provider from another in a particular industry due to the intangibility of services and the other service characteristics described in Chapter 1. Thus, the image of a particular service firm may be the only factor that gives it a unique position in the minds of buyers. (One insurance company, for example, may be "on your side," while another may keep you in "good hands." One airline may use "friendly skies" as its slogan, while another may claim to be the "most experienced.")

Images can be formed very quickly. The behavior of a single employee may cause a prospect to conclude that a particular firm is friendly or unfriendly, competent or incompetent. This image, once formed, may persist over time, thus deciding patronage patterns for years to come. This is especially true in highly competitive industries where several alternatives are available. It is of critical importance, then, that employees in service firms be carefully selected, trained, and motivated so that they will give their best to their jobs. Each employee may well "be" the service firm in the eyes of the customer, who may find it difficult to separate a service from the impression of the people producing it. The success of a company's offering, then, may be determined by how well it manages its employees.

Creating a Differential Advantage

To enhance the image of a particular service, a provider may attempt to create a differential advantage, the "something extra" that makes a company and its services seem unique, or a little better than its competitors. It is due to this perceived advantage that a loyal group of customers will prefer the company's services to those of competitors. No firm, especially a small service firm, can hope to be all things to all people. Instead, finding an existing need and developing methods of satisfying that need may be the optimal solution. A customer in a local beauty salon, for example, noticed that many women inquired about manicure and nail treatments. She opened a small shop in the neighborhood, and soon had a thriving nail care business.

A differential advantage may be the result of any part of the service firm's marketing program—service quality, price, location, personal attention, and so forth. In many instances, the differential advantage results from buyers' perceptions of the personal elements of the service. Many service companies build on buyers' perceptions and try to create or reinforce a differential advantage through the use of promotional activities. Examples are outlined in Exhibit 3–5.

As these examples indicate, a differential advantage does not just happen; it must be built. It is built with the help of effective marketing and promotional programs designed to meet the needs of the service firm's target market.

The Adoption Process

As customers learn about and decide to accept service innovations, they move through a series of stages known as the *adoption process*. This process consists of five steps:

1. *Awareness*. The potential buyer learns about the existence of the new service, generally through advertisements or publicity. Typically, the information absorbed

---

EXHIBIT 3–5   Creating a Differential Advantage

Basis	Example
Service quality	A dry cleaner who carefully boxes and wraps consumers' garments may be far more successful than one who hastily wraps finished garments in plastic.
Price	A ticket broker who charges $5 for each transaction will often have a greater number of patrons than one who charges $10.*
Location	A pizza shop within convenient walking distance of a college dormitory may enjoy greater success than one located several blocks away, where student traffic is lighter.
Personal attention	A financial service institution that has private areas for discussion of personal matters will be more successful than one where consumers must present their problems within earshot of other customers.

---

* The concept of pricing in service industries is quite complex. For many professional services, such as medical and legal services, price may be seen as synonymous with quality, so that a higher price would imply a greater level of quality. In these nonstandardized service industries, then, a lower price would *not* necessarily represent a differential advantage. Some providers in the legal and medical fields, however, have capitalized on price as a key factor in creating a differential advantage. Examples include Jacoby & Meyers, and various medical clinics.

---

by the prospect is sketchy and incomplete, however, since the learning most likely occurred passively during a limited period of exposure. Should the advertisement or publicity evoke interest on the part of the service buyer, the next step will be to gather the information necessary to evaluate the proposed service offering and determine its compatibility with perceived needs.

2. *Search.* In considering the purchase of tangible goods, potential buyers will often turn to objective and independent sources, such as government studies or *Consumer Reports*. Service buyers, however, are generally deprived of this opportunity since few such sources exist for service purchases. Instead, service prospects attempt to obtain useful, objective information from the service firm itself in the form of a descriptive brochure or a prospectus—an extensive legal document required for certain service offerings such as securities or real estate. They try to supplement this information through newspaper articles and

advice from professional third parties such as certified financial planners. Essentially, this phase is aimed at generating objective, factual input.

3. *Evaluation.* Once prospects have gathered as much information about the new service as they can or want to obtain, they face the task of reviewing the information to determine whether they should proceed further. They weigh the pros and cons of the innovation to decide if it is suitable for them as well as attractive. At this stage, they will consult with relevant others, namely family members or friends, to get their input as to what they should do. Support from others reduces the perceived social and financial risks of a prospective purchase.

4. *Trial.* For buyers of new tangible goods, evaluation is followed by a sampling of the innovation on a limited scale. Such trial is, of course, only possible if the product is divisible, that is, capable of being consumed in small quantities (e.g., a new grocery item). Service prospects rarely have this opportunity to examine a new service on a limited scale for the purpose of containing risk before making a full-scale commitment. Services are normally indivisible and thus can only be tested full-scale. In most instances, therefore, trial of a new service occurs after its full-scale purchase.

   Some service providers, however, approximate the trial experience prior to customer commitment. Speed-reading institutes and other self-development firms offer free initial lessons before sign-up. Advertising agencies bidding on a lucrative account often include a proposed campaign in their presentation to management. Other service businesses may offer easy cancellation of subscription-type services as a way to overcome buyer reluctance.

   Basically, the trial stage represents the first serious contact between a prospect who is ready to buy and the service provider. Explanations by a salesperson can go a long way toward relieving buyer anxiety at this point and reducing the likelihood of post-purchase dissonance (dissatisfaction).

5. *Adoption.* Having tried the new service (before or after full-scale purchase) for some time, the buyer now makes a

EXHIBIT 3–6 Adoption of Service Innovations

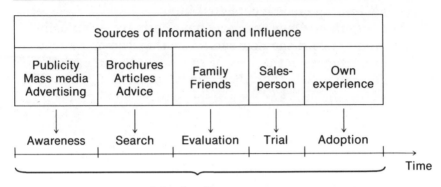

Adoption Process

commitment to continue its use. Due to the intangible nature of services, it is often the absence of unsatisfactory experiences rather than genuine satisfaction that produces this result. In many cases, the buyer develops a personal relationship with a particular service performer. If this individual changes employers or starts an own business, the customer will often follow. Loyalty is then directed not toward the firm but toward the performer who develops a "following." This is a frequent situation in professional or personal services. Successful attorneys joining another firm or health care professionals opening up their own practices will take many of their customers with them.

Exhibit 3–6 shows the stages of the service adoption process and indicates the most influential sources of communication for each of the stages. While any type of information source can have an impact at any point of the process, the pattern shown is typical of new service adoption.

Social Influences on Service Buying

Our society is largely other directed, implying both a desire for acceptance and approval, and the importance of the opinions of significant others on decisions. In such a society, service buyers are guided in their behavior not only by their own motives and attitudes, but also by those of the reference groups to which they relate. Purchasing and consumption patterns for services, then, may well be governed by one's relative position within a social system. Significant others who may influence buyer behavior in service industries belong to one of the following *two types of reference groups:*

1. *Membership groups* are, as the name implies, those groups to which one belongs through some set of common characteristics, such as one's family or friends. Obviously, these groups are of great importance to service marketers because of the substantial degree of influence that they may bring to bear on their constituents. In an attempt to be accepted, supported, and reinforced by family, friends, and associates, service buyers minimize social risk by acting in ways that are likely to be approved by other group members. Membership groups enforce their expectations through a variety of rewards or punishments that serve as powerful controls, keeping individual service buyers in line with group norms and patterns. For example, a member of a fundamentalist church group who is observed leaving an "X-rated" movie might be shunned by the other members of this group.
2. *Aspiration groups* are those to which one eventually hopes to belong. In order to gain acceptance into these groups, service buyers will adopt behavior patterns similar to those of persons who are already group members. People may join a country club, for example, with the hope that membership will gain them acceptance to a specific social group.

A reference group may be exemplified in the minds of actual and prospective customers by an individual reference person— an opinion leader. This person, then, may be the natural focus of a service marketer's strategies and efforts. Celebrity advertising is an example of such a strategy. When all firms within a particular service industry are perceived as essentially equal, a well-known personality serving as a spokesperson for one of these firms may provide a competitive edge for the sponsor and encourage selective patronage. The recent battle for long-distance telephone customers has made use of a host of noted celebrities, each arguing the relative merits of his or her preferred company. In a similar way, banks and savings institutions often feature sports or entertainment personalities in their advertising.

Social class is another powerful determinant of buyer behavior. According to Lloyd Warner, the social class structure in the United States is based on occupation, source of income, and type and location of residence. This results in different status levels and lifestyles. In general, lower-class consumers (blue-collar wage earners with no postsecondary education) are more concrete in their thinking and prefer material possessions to intangible services. They invest discretionary funds in low-risk, low-yield savings accounts and borrow money from loan companies. They use credit cards for necessities, such as furniture and clothing, and pay less than their outstanding balance, thus using their credit line for financing purposes. Upper-class consumers (highly educated, salaried professionals), on the other hand, tend to invest in riskier money market instruments, preferring their significantly higher yields, and borrow from banks or against insurance policies. Their credit purchases emphasize travel and entertainment, and they pay their balances in full, using their credit privileges as a convenience, not as a source of financing.

Cultural values also affect service buying. The American outlook of "buy now, pay later" may contrast with the more conservative European view of credit as something for emergency use, not convenience. The U.S. value system has shifted from relative self-denial to a more positive perspective and even an acceptance of services designed to improve the quality and convenience of life. Different subcultures may constitute prime markets for certain types of services; the elderly, for example, will be most interested in health care, transportation, and travel services. With more and more women joining the labor force, demand has mushroomed for services such as laundry and day care that would find little or no market in less advanced countries.

DIFFICULTY OF EVALUATING SERVICES

Services are, by virtue of their intangible nature and heterogeneous characteristics, *difficult to evaluate*. To many potential customers, services may initially appear to be undifferentiated, giving them little or no reason to prefer one service provider over another. Samples or "trial sizes" are not available; refunds are not possible for dissatisfied customers; ads cannot always effectively demonstrate the nature and importance of a highly intangible service. Potential customers, then, may find it difficult to make a rational decision concerning the quality of competitors' offerings on the basis of objective criteria. Faced with this lack of objective criteria, consumers may react in one of several ways:

1. They may substitute considerations of price for quality, assuming that a higher price is indicative of greater quality. This is especially true for professional services, such as legal or medical services.
2. They may use location and convenience as primary factors, selecting a service provider who is in close proximity to their residence or place of business. This applies to dry cleaners and banks.
3. They may rely on the experience of others, who provide word-of-mouth recommendations. Unfortunately, what is satisfactory to one customer may be unacceptable to another. Nonetheless, it is a common mode for choosing a health care provider.
4. They may consider the entire bundle of benefits received—not just the *core,* or *principal* benefit, but also the *peripheral service*—the configuration of additional benefits provided in conjunction with the core service. The amenities surrounding the service—geographic location, size of facility, layout, decorative style, friendliness and competence of personnel, promptness and courtesy, availability of free parking—all of these may play a role in addition to the core service.

   While the no-frills system may be acceptable in certain instances, service providers must ensure that customers are concerned only with the core service before embarking on this strategy. Likewise, excessive concentration on peripheral elements may dilute the quality of the core service, thus alienating customers. The proper blend of core service and additional peripheral offerings must be carefully planned by the service provider to ensure customer satisfaction while maximizing profit potential.

5. They may postpone the decision until consumption of the service becomes absolutely necessary, and then adopt one of the methods mentioned above.

The decision to purchase or utilize a particular service, then, may be based on far more than conventional considerations of quality, since an objective appraisal may be impossible. Additional considerations—of location, peripheral services (the total service bundle), reputation (word-of-mouth advertising), and convenient hours, to name a few—must be provided far in advance of the service's offering in the marketplace. Failure to do so will cause disastrous results for the unsuspecting service provider.

WHAT THE CLIENT BUYS

What does the client seek when he or she purchases or contracts for a service? While this question may seem elementary, the answer is of critical importance to service marketers. Is the client merely interested in the service itself, without the trimmings (such as no-frills airline flights)? Or, instead, are the peripheral aspects of the total service package the features that determine client patronage (special baggage services, food, newspapers and magazines, and other passenger extras provided by many airlines)? How far will a client go in the search for a service provider? Will proximity and convenience be the dominant factors, or will the client be willing to go out of the way to secure the skills of a particular provider? Once the answers to these questions are known, the true marketing effort can commence.

As mentioned previously, the *core* or *principal service* is the basic service rendered by a provider. Health care, legal advice, a haircut, a completed bank deposit or withdrawal—all are examples of core services. While all providers within a particular industry may provide the same core service, the circumstances surrounding their delivery might be drastically different. One bank, for example, may have a single line for all customers making transactions. Others may have separate lines for senior citizens, for commercial customers, for deposits only, or for cashing payroll checks. Longer banking hours, special services for preferred customers, comfortable rooms for those who use safe deposit boxes, automated teller machines to speed transactions, night deposit and quick deposit services—all are examples of extras offered by banks to their customers.

Often, it is the presence or absence of some of these extra features that causes a client to choose one bank over another. In such an instance, the client would be interested not only in the core service of completing transactions, but the entire bundle of additional benefits or amenities provided—the *peripheral service*. It is only when the service marketer understands the true impact of these additional benefits on the buying decision that any efforts to alter these features should be made. When the airlines introduced no-frills service, they believed that it would be a certain success, appealing to large crowds of travelers. Instead, the plan never really got off the ground, since the little amenities that comprised the peripheral service were more important to many than at first imagined. Now, many airlines are vying for passengers through a series of tactics, one of which is a plan to attract frequent business flyers by emphasizing the special advantages available in business class. Once largely overlooked, airline officials have now come to recognize the potential competitive edge that may be gained through the use of these amenities in advertising campaigns.

The opposite approach, however, may also prove dangerous. The recent demise of Air One, a small ultraplush airline catering to business travelers, demonstrates this point. While business travelers may not wish to give up basic comforts to save a few dollars, they (or their firms!) may also be unwilling to pay extra for what they consider to be unnecessary frills, such as sleeping compartments. It is essential, then, that a balance be struck between what is necessary to ensure comfort and what is merely "fluff."

The amount of time that consumers will spend in selecting a particular service provider is dependent on the relative importance of that service to the consumer. The basic classification scheme used in goods markets can also be applied to services as follows (see Exhibit 3–7):

1. *Convenience service.* Here, the consumer expends very little time and energy in the selection of a service provider. The consumer will generally view the particular service

EXHIBIT 3–7 Consumer Services Classification

	Type of Service		
	Convenience	Shopping	Specialty
Criteria			
Shopping time and effort	Very little	Much	Substantial
Purchase planning	Very little	Some	Considerable
Comparison of price and quality	Little	Much	None
Purchase frequency	Frequent	Infrequent	Rare
Importance to buyer	Little	Significant	Extreme
Examples			
	Car wash, dry cleaning, shoe repair, local telephone service	Hair care, insurance, auto repair, long-distance telephone service	Financial, legal, and medical services
Marketing implications			
	Emphasize convenience	Promote service and price differences	Try to create brand or seller loyalty

class as largely homogeneous, so that one provider would be roughly as good as another. Convenience and proximity are generally the factors that will determine the provider to be selected.

2. *Shopping service.* The consumer will engage in some comparison shopping in an effort to combine quality of performance with such other considerations as convenience, proximity, and price. These services are generally viewed as somewhat heterogeneous, and the peripheral aspects of the service bundle begin to take on more importance.

3. *Specialty service.* This service is considered important to the consumer, who will often exert considerable effort to secure the expertise of a particular provider. Quality of performance and the special amenities provided by a particular person and/or a particular firm are regarded as essential elements of the service. The provider attempts

to create brand or seller loyalty, so that buyers will regard this service as a specialty service.

ROLES OF THE SERVICE MARKETER

The service marketer must perform a variety of critical functions when dealing with clients. These may be outlined as follows:

1. *Information.* It is the responsibility of the service marketer both to introduce the service to potential clients and to keep awareness current among those familiar with the firm's offerings. This is accomplished through a variety of methods, including advertising, promotion, public relations, and community involvement. It is especially necessary that the client or prospect be made aware of the various characteristics of the services being offered and how they relate to the purchase, delivery, and/or use of the service. Failure to do so may result in improper use of the service, or client dissatisfaction and, eventually, client loss.

2. *Client selection.* The primary objective of any service is to deal with as many clients as possible. This attitude must, however, be tempered by the capacity of the firm to provide quality of service. Only those clients whose needs are compatible with the firm's expertise should be accepted by the firm. Otherwise, the firm's inability to satisfy the needs of the consumer will lead to ill will and damaging word-of-mouth complaints from dissatisfied patrons.

3. *Maintaining client relationships.* Maintaining client loyalty is of critical importance to service marketers. While services may be needed only intermittently, it is essential that the firm be kept current in the minds of clients. This may be accomplished through such means as informational mailings, workshops, or seminars.

4. *Monitoring client behavior.* Clients must be aware of the "rules" governing the use of various services. Applicable regulations regarding appointments or reservations, fee schedules—and, of course, available services—must be known by clients to avoid unnecessary confusion, dissatisfaction, and possible ill will.

5. *Internal communication.* No plan, no matter how well conceived, can be successful without the knowledge and cooperation of the firm's personnel. As noted, the provider *is* the firm in the eyes of many clients, and a negative experience with an employee may result in client loss, or at least dissatisfaction. Employees, then, must be aware of the corporate mission, the services offered, the method(s) by which services are delivered, pricing schedules, and other technical aspects—in short, the marketing plan, however informal it may be. In addition, some knowledge of customer relations is essential to ensure proper handling of clients.

BUSINESS SERVICES

Specialized business services range from janitorial services to highly technical business consultation. In addition to these specialized services, industrial buyers also purchase a large proportion of facilitating services, such as transportation, communication, and power. Considerable personal explanation and persuasion are needed to explain the benefits of business services to potential buyers.

One reason why a company purchases a business service is economic. Specialized firms are often able to perform routine business activities more efficiently and effectively than the buyer's firm. Examples of services offered by specialized firms are maintenance, cleaning, and security for office buildings and industrial plants. At the other end of the spectrum, such tasks as locating a new plant, setting up a pension plan for employees, or conducting a marketing research study are often assigned to firms with highly skilled specialists in these areas. Most companies, for example, would find it virtually impossible to duplicate efficiently the services provided by such firms as A. C. Nielsen (marketing research), Dun & Bradstreet (credit ratings), Marsh & McLennan (insurance brokers), and E. F. MacDonald Co. (incentive campaigns).

The purchase of industrial services may involve a limited number of buyers who use systematic purchase procedures that are matters of company policy. An emerging industrial purchasing concept is known as the buying center approach. Here, representatives from those departments that will be affected by the

---

EXHIBIT 3–8 The Selection of an Auto Leasing Company

Participating Department	Role
Finance	Provides input concerning budgeting constraints. Evaluates whether payment schedules are in accordance with corporate policy.
Administration	Monitors day-to-day matters, such as filing accident reports and renewing leases. Also serves as liaison between firm and leasing company.
Sales	Presents its automotive needs for personnel at different levels of the sales organization.
Purchasing	Identifies and screens alternative providers. Leads negotiations between firm and leasing company.

---

ultimate purchase decision are involved in the choice of services and providers. The constructive input received from these departments helps to ensure a closer fit between corporate needs and the best methods of need satisfaction. For example, the selection of an auto leasing company may involve a firm's finance, administration, sales, and purchasing departments. Their respective roles in the process are outlined in Exhibit 3–8. The buying center approach should become increasingly popular as the number and types of available business services increase.

The potential supplier, or marketer of industrial services, then, should be aware of industrial buying characteristics when assembling a marketing plan for purchasers of these services. Flexibility is an essential component of a successful client-provider relationship, due to the constraints that corporate buying procedures may impose. Also essential is a concise and precise presentation of service offerings, so that busy corporate clients will be able to assess the fit between their needs and the supplier's service offerings quickly and easily.

SUMMARY

This chapter has explored the nature of buyer behavior in service industries. The purchasing cycle has been presented, along with an introduction to the differences between purchases of goods and purchases of services. Five roles are played during the course of the purchasing cycle: informer, influencer, decider, buyer, and user. Each of these roles is important to the service marketer.

Potential consumers of services have a variety of options from which to choose when deciding on a way to satisfy their perceived needs. They may select a firm's service, that of a competitor, a do-it-yourself kit, or a competing product. It is important that the service marketer develop and maintain a positive image for the firm's service offerings, since these various alternatives pose the threat of competition.

Attitudes have also been discussed. Since attitudes are long-lasting influences on behavior, it is essential that the service firm's image be positive. Social influences on service buying and the roles played by the service marketer during interactions with customers have also been explored.

Now that the stage has been set, we will turn our attention to the topics of marketing research, marketing planning, and marketing organization, implementation, and control.

SELECTED REFERENCES FOR PART ONE

Albrecht, Karl and Ron Zemke, *Service America!* Homewood, IL: Dow Jones-Irwin, 1985.

Berry, Leonard L. "Services Marketing Is Different." *Business,* May–June 1980, pp. 24–29.

Berry, Leonard L.; G. Lynn Shostack; and Gregory D. Upah, eds. *Emerging Perspectives on Service Marketing.* Chicago: American Marketing Association, 1983.

Bloom, Paul N. "Effective Marketing for Professional Services." *Harvard Business Review,* September–October 1984, pp. 102–10.

Collins, Lora S. "The Service Economy." *Across the Board,* November 1980, pp. 17–22.

Cook, James. "You Mean We've Been Speaking Prose All These Years?" *Forbes,* April 11, 1983, pp. 142–49.

Czepiel, John A.; Michael R. Solomon; and Carol F. Surprenant, eds. *The Service Encounter.* Lexington, Mass.: D.C. Heath, 1985.

"Deregulating America." *Business Week,* November 28, 1983, pp. 80–83, 86, 88–89, 92, 96.

Donnelly, James H., and William R. George, eds. *Marketing of Services.* Chicago: American Marketing Association, 1981.

Eiglier, Pierre; Eric Langeard; Christopher H. Lovelock; John E. G. Bateson; and Robert F. Young. *Marketing Consumer Services: New Insights.* Cambridge, Mass.: Marketing Science Institute, 1977.

Gummesson, Evert. "Toward a Theory of Professional Service Marketing." *Industrial Marketing Management,* April 1978, pp. 89–95.

Hollander, Stanley C. "Is There a Generic Demand for Services?" *MSU Business Topics,* Spring 1979, pp. 41–46.

Kotler, Philip, and Paul N. Bloom. *Marketing Professional Services.* Englewood Cliffs, N.J.: Prentice-Hall, 1984.

Kotler, Philip, and Richard A. Connor, Jr. "Marketing Professional Services." *Journal of Marketing,* January 1977, pp. 71–76.

Levitt, Theodore. "The Industrialization of Service." *Harvard Business Review,* September–October 1976, pp. 63–74.

———. "Marketing Intangible Products and Product Intangibles." *Harvard Business Review,* May–June 1981, pp. 94–102.

Lovelock, Christopher H. "Classifying Services to Gain Strategic Marketing Insights." *Journal of Marketing,* Summer 1983, pp. 9–20.

———. *Services Marketing.* Englewood Cliffs, N.J.: Prentice-Hall, 1984.

Malabre, Alfred L., Jr. "Study Disputes View that Growth of Service Jobs Crimps Productivity." *The Wall Street Journal,* June 19, 1981, p. 27.

Parasuraman, A.; Leonard L. Berry; and Valarie A. Zeithaml. "Service Firms Need Marketing Skills." *Business Horizons,* November–December 1983, pp. 28–31.

Paul, Bill. "Moving It—Freight Transportation Is Being Transformed in Era of Deregulation." *The Wall Street Journal,* October 20, 1983, pp. 1, 18.

Robertson, Thomas S., and Scott Ward. "Management Lessons from Airline Deregulation." *Harvard Business Review,* January–February 1983, pp. 40–42.

Robertson, Thomas S.; Scott Ward; and William M. Caldwell IV. "Deregulation: Surviving the Transition." *Harvard Business Review,* July–August 1982, pp. 20–22.

Robinson, James D. III. "A Full Partnership for Services." *Business Week,* June 29, 1981, p. 15.

————. "The Service Sector's Increasingly Important Role." *American Banker,* May 11, 1982, pp. 22–25.

Shostack, G. Lynn. "Breaking Free from Product Marketing." *Journal of Marketing,* April 1977, pp. 73–80.

————. "Is Service Marketing the Right Way?" *Trusts and Estates,* November 1977, pp. 720–23.

Skipper, Harold, Jr. "The Homogenization of the Financial Services Community." *CLU Journal,* January 1982, pp. 30–40.

Waite, Donald C. III. "Deregulation and the Banking Industry." *The Bankers Magazine,* January–February 1982, pp. 26–35.

Wheatley, Edward W. *Marketing Professional Services.* Englewood Cliffs, N.J.: Prentice-Hall, 1983.

Wilson, Aubrey. *The Marketing of Professional Services.* London: McGraw-Hill, 1972.

Zeithaml, Valarie A.; A. Parasuraman; and Leonard L. Berry. "Problems and Strategies in Services Marketing." *Journal of Marketing,* Spring 1985, pp. 33–46.

PART TWO

SERVICE MARKETING MANAGEMENT

CHAPTER 4

Marketing Research for Service Firms

In order to make meaningful and successful decisions, service marketers need current, relevant information that gives them a good handle on the facts and factors affecting the outcome of their decisions. This kind of substantive information cannot be obtained through casual conversation or curious inquiry. Rather, it requires an organized, sustained effort of collection and analysis. But a mere agglomeration of undigested raw data should not be mistaken for information. *Information* means processed, distilled, and interpreted data.

Thus, generating and using useful marketing information is not an incidental and occasional activity to which a service firm pays little attention and devotes little enthusiasm. Instead, it should be a continuous, systematic activity that is at the very heart of marketing decision making. In fact, it should be emphasized that marketing information is an essential ingredient in the successful application of the marketing concept. Further, it is axiomatic that uninformed decision makers are likely to engage in ill-advised and ill-considered actions since such actions will be based, at best, on hunches. In this day and age, when information means power, if not success, no service business can afford to neglect this vital function.

This chapter presents an overview of the nature, role, and methods of marketing research in service firms. It begins with a discussion of the importance of a comprehensive marketing information system to attune a business to environmental trends, threats, and opportunities and goes on to explore the practice of marketing research as well as its contribution to successful service marketing. As the most action-oriented component of a marketing information system, marketing research addresses a wide range of tasks and offers numerous benefits. Based on experience and insight, its methodology has been steadily refined and enhanced over the years, so that the modern marketing researcher may choose from a host of tools that can be tailored to the task at hand.

MARKETING INFORMATION SYSTEMS FOR SERVICE BUSINESSES

A marketing information system (MIS) is a service firm's carefully orchestrated set of procedures and methods that guarantees an orderly flow of relevant information to marketing decision makers, providing them with an intelligence link to market conditions, trends, and reactions. The larger a service organization becomes, the further removed are the marketing decision makers from the front line of daily customer contact and the more necessary it becomes to bridge the communications gap between service marketers and service buyers. A well-designed, customized marketing information system will provide a service marketer with a number of benefits, including the following:

- Timely, accurate, and complete information that will enable the marketer to control the firm's marketing activities.
- An early warning system that will indicate developing problems.
- Adequate data on unusual challenges that will permit the marketer to take appropriate action.
- Market and economic data the marketer needs to interpret financial results correctly.
- Sufficient information to allow for the optimum utilization of human, financial, and physical resources.

Exhibit 4–1 summarizes what an MIS can and cannot do for a service business.

But how does a marketing information system operate? As Exhibit 4–2 illustrates, the MIS scans and monitors the market-

---

EXHIBIT 4–1   Capabilities and Limitations of a Marketing Information System

---

What an MIS Can Do

1. Track progress toward long-term strategic goals.
2. Aid in day-to-day decision making.
3. Establish a common language between marketing and "back office" operations.
4. Consider the impact of alternative environmental scenarios.
5. Automate many labor-intensive data processing activities, thus effecting cost savings.
6. Serve as an early warning device for portions of a service business that are not on target.
7. Help determine how to allocate resources to achieve marketing goals.
8. Deliver condensed, actionable information in a timely and useful manner.
9. Help service customers.
10. Allow improvement of overall performance through better planning and control.

What an MIS Cannot Do

1. Replace managerial judgment.
2. Provide all the information a manager needs to make an infallible decision.
3. Work successfully without management support.
4. Work successfully without management confidence.
5. Work successfully without being adequately maintained and responsive to management needs.

SOURCE: Adapted from Barbara Howard, "Intelligence: How to Build an Effective Marketing Information System," *Marketing Update,* Issue 20 (New York: Alexander-Norton, Inc., 1977), p. 5.

ing environment for relevant events, developments, and trends, supplementing and complementing this external data input with data gathered internally from different departments. The data are then processed and analyzed so that information can be delivered to marketing decision makers on a regular basis or in response to specific requests. The MIS thus enables service marketers to make informed and accordingly successful decisions.

Exhibit 4–2 makes it evident that the mission of a firm's marketing information system includes the gathering, processing, and analyzing of data from all relevant environments—not just from a service firm's market. This enables service marketers to identify and assess environmental changes early and to

EXHIBIT 4–2 The Role of the Marketing Information System

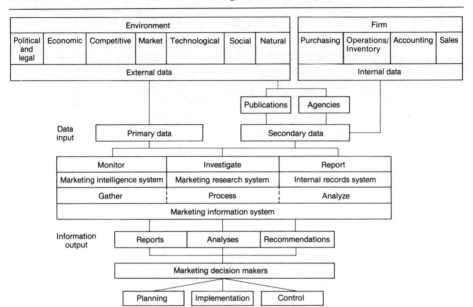

develop appropriate strategic responses. The MIS fulfills its task of environmental assessment by utilizing two types of data: primary and secondary.

Secondary data are data that have been or are being collected for another purpose and thus are often already in existence. This means that the marketing information function has no control over the data collection procedure and the data have to be checked for recency, accuracy, and applicability. Nonetheless, secondary data save time and money and often are readily available from outside or inside sources, rendering primary data gathering unnecessary. The two principal sources of external secondary data are publications (periodicals, reports, and so forth) and marketing research agencies that sell syndicated information services on a subscription basis. Other external sources include trade associations, chambers of commerce, and data banks. Internal sources of secondary data are the record-keeping units in the firm—from purchasing and operations/inventory (for the tangible components) to accounting and sales. All of these units generate, for their own purposes, data and records that may be tapped, coordinated, and integrated for marketing information purposes.

Although some useful information may be provided, secondary data often are insufficient and inadequate, failing to provide a complete and accurate picture of a service firm's marketplace and the forces affecting its success there. This is where *primary data* can come to the rescue. Collected directly at the service firm's own initiative and geared to its specific information needs, primary data help to fill the information gaps left by lacking, outdated, or otherwise inadequate secondary data. Primary data collection and processing generally are placed in the realm of the marketing research subsystem, because they are more project- and action-oriented than the marketing intelligence and internal records subsystems, which are geared more toward monitoring and reporting trends and developments on an ongoing basis.

To summarize, the three major groups of activities carried out by a service firm's marketing information system are *gathering, processing, and analyzing* primary and secondary data, which are then converted into information in the form of reports, analyses, and recommendations. Thus, the MIS can be seen as an internal advisory resource center. With the information provided by the MIS, the service marketer is in a better position to plan, direct, and control the company's marketing efforts.

THE NATURE AND ROLE OF MARKETING RESEARCH

Marketing research can be defined as the systematic collection, processing, and analysis of relevant marketing facts to help management make better decisions and capitalize on marketing opportunities. Because it is a staff function designed to enable service marketers to make more successful decisions, it has to be both timely and cost effective. Data collection, processing, and interpretation, however, do not exhaust the scope of marketing research. It is also called upon to act in an advisory capacity by exploring alternative courses of action, determining their consequences, and offering recommendations as to the most promising strategy.

As part of a service firm's marketing information system, marketing research secures actionable information of a problem- or opportunity-oriented nature on such topics as market structure and trends, geographic, seasonal, and customer sales patterns, new product opportunities, and advertising effectiveness.

With respect to environmental conditions and developments, marketing research has to be the finger on the current pulse and the oracle of future occurrences. The political environment can bring new opportunities, challenges, and restrictions in such forms as deregulation, reregulation, reductions in government health care reimbursement programs, nonbank banks, and free trade in services, or exchange controls on airline ticket sales abroad. The economic environment manifests itself in such ways as credit demand, interest rates, bank failures, health care cost containment, advertising budgets, and taxes. The competitive environment may include entirely new groups of entrants in an industry. Insurance, brokerage, and retailing firms, for example, have entered banking, broadening its definition to financial services. Similarly, ambulatory surgery, birthing, and emergency care centers have entered the health care market. Statewide, regional, or interstate banking, electronic branches, and in-home banking are examples of new forms of competition emerging in service industries whose relevance and impact have to be assessed on an ongoing basis. Insofar as these developments involve delivery systems, they may well intertwine with the technological environment. The latter has also brought such innovations as computer-aided instruction, diagnostic equipment, and fiber optics as well as lasers in telecommunications and medicine.

Innovations like these can simply represent attractive service enhancements or spell revolutionary changes in the ways in which certain services are produced—laser eye surgery, for example. The social, cultural, and demographic environment, finally, is characterized by changing values such as the ones relating to the role of women in society, and population shifts such as the changing age structure and geographic distribution of the population. Such changes can profoundly affect customers' needs, patronage patterns, and trading area composition. Marketing research, therefore, has to keep its ear to the ground to identify significant developments early and guide appropriate responses.

More specifically, though, it has to generate and examine

market data. In a service firm context, traditional sales analysis translates into customer profile studies. The aim is to discover who the patrons of the service establishment are in terms of age, income, education, occupation, and other demographic characteristics. This is done to enable a more efficient and effective design of the marketing effort for the firm's services. Studies testing for awareness of a company's different services often find that customers are only acquainted with a very limited number of them. Commercial bank depositors, for instance, can typically name only about 10 different services in unaided recall out of a total range exceeding 100. Awareness research investigates the effectiveness of a service firm's communications program, since obviously customers cannot buy services of which they are not aware.

Drawing upon a number of internal and external sources and employing techniques adapted from the behavioral sciences, the service marketing researcher studies the needs, attitudes, perceptions, and behavior patterns of the firm's target markets. Whether defined geographically, demographically, by lifestyle, or by buying practices, a service company's identified markets are studied mainly by means of surveys. Among other things, such studies investigate the profitability of specific market segments and service offerings, the reasons for customer discontent and resistance to innovations, the media habits and communications patterns of target audiences, and comparative corporate images.

One of the most important functions of marketing research is to monitor changing marketing opportunities and challenges. This function is of vital importance to service firm managers due to:

- The scarcity of corporate resources available for marketing projects.
- The steadily increasing competitive pressure from other producers of services and goods.
- The growing complexity of marketing decisions.
- The accelerating pace of innovation in the service sector.
- The high price attached to failure in the marketplace.
- The growth of consumerism.
- The legal implications of marketing decisions.

To be useful, the output of the marketing research function of a service business must possess the following characteristics:

- It must be *actionable*. Results of studies should be presented in concise, analyzed form, followed by recommendations that spell out alternative courses of action and their likely consequences.
- It must be *pragmatic*. Research is conducted to help solve a problem. Information is generated on a "need to know" basis. Exotic methodologies and curiosity research are not economically justifiable.
- It must be *reliable*. One of the measures of scientific objectivity is the reproducibility of the results obtained from research. Thus, in all projects, potential bias and error should be minimized so that if a study were to be rerun by somebody else, the findings would be similar.
- It must be *valid*. The research should measure those factors it sets out to measure.
- It must be *timely*. The research program should be completed in time to have an impact on the decision to be made.
- It must be *cost efficient*. The research should be designed to provide the necessary information at an affordable cost.

Tasks and Benefits of Marketing Research in Service Firms

Due to the largely intangible nature of a service firm's offerings, marketing research faces a particularly challenging task in helping to identify the unique needs of its chosen market segments. Professionally executed marketing research will enable a service organization to streamline its strategic decision-making process and utilize the components of its marketing mix to greater advantage. Although marketing research cannot replace entrepreneurial vision and courage, it contributes to an enterprise's success by supplying relevant, concise, up-to-date, and actionable information to key decision makers. More specifically, the marketing research function in a service firm may be assigned responsibility for the following tasks:

Identify and evaluate market segments. Historically, marketing research began as sales analysis, determining key aspects of a company's past sales patterns. To a service marketer, it is of critical importance to know who the firm's customers are and what shares different subgroups contribute to overall sales. Some banks make personal banking services available to major depositors, and airlines make special efforts to woo frequent fliers. To serve the core customer groups well, a service establishment has to investigate their distinctive wants and needs and examine how the latter can be met in such a way as to reinforce customer loyalty and strengthen the company's competitive position. But this task is broader yet: Besides researching the needs of current patrons, marketing research must assist in pinpointing untapped market potential, thus highlighting avenues for future growth.

Describe market segments.   Once a service firm's current and future target markets have been pinpointed, their differentiating characteristics have to be explored, and a thorough review of the competitive situation and of evolving trends in these market segments has to be undertaken. To enhance the service marketer's knowledge of customer needs and wants, their patronage motives and patterns, service consumption characteristics, demographics, and lifestyles should be investigated. To determine how the selected groups may be reached by promotional messages, their media habits have to be studied. Because many service consumers are more affluent and belong to higher social classes, they are more likely to be readers of special interest magazines than to be watchers of popular television programs.

Determine market potential and forecast sales.   Projections of the future state of the economy tend to be less important for service industries than they are for manufacturing because service industries are less subject to the vagaries of the business cycle than goods, expanding less during recoveries and shrinking less during recessions. Thus, the service firm's determination of market size and growth potential is based somewhat less on anticipated swings in the business cycle. Depending on the sales forecasting technique used, marketing research may or may not play a prominent role in the service firm's annual process of projecting sales.

Analyze the firm's image and position.   Due to the largely intangible nature of its offering, a service firm has to rely on its image as a major means of differentiating it from other service firms in the marketplace. Accordingly, image research should be a key concern in any service business. Image research consists of eliciting and measuring consumer attitudes about the firm. Ideally done in a competitive context, image analysis allows comparative profiles to emerge, thereby enabling the firm to take corrective action. A firm may overcome unfavorable public impressions by taking appropriate measures and publicizing the changes. On the other hand, the firm's own strengths and its competitors' weaknesses, as perceived by relevant consumers, may be played up in the firm's promotional efforts, providing impressive persuasive arguments.

Select promising sites. Because their production and consumption occur simultaneously, services have to be distributed directly. This makes location a key element in successful marketing strategy. Of course, the required intensity of market coverage depends on the effort that buyers are willing to expend as well as the criteria by which they select service suppliers. In determining these latter aspects, marketing research can be of considerable assistance. Typically, it will study traffic patterns of target consumers as well as area demographics, site accessibility, competitive presence and patronage, and neighborhood condition. Banks, motels, and fast-food operators are particularly concerned with these factors because their operating results strongly depend on the accuracy of the research done. A facility placed in the wrong location is likely to fail quickly.

Evaluate pricing strategies. Studying the pricing structure of the market for a given service is another important task of marketing research. Price elasticity, competitive pricing policies, and buyer attitudes toward price in relation to the service rendered should be monitored continually for maximum success. Since the advent of deregulation, airlines have aggressively and imaginatively made use of this type of information by varying fares frequently and differentiating them according to the degree of competition, charging less for hotly competitive transcontinental flights than for short hauls. Conversely, in a study of criteria for selecting a marketing research firm, price was only mentioned as 11th in importance. Similarly, a survey of top executives determined that price was far less important in the selection of a CPA firm than its reputation. Only 58 percent considered price "critical" or "very important" while 97 percent indicated that reputation was "critical" or "very important."

Guide promotional programs. A service firm's promotions should be scrutinized carefully to measure their effectiveness. Whether an advertisement actually creates the desired level of awareness, communicates the intended message, and persuades prospects to buy the service should be determined. The efficiency and effectiveness of a chosen set of media in reaching target consumers should also be examined. A host of tools are available to the resourceful marketing researcher intent upon determining the reach of a given media mix as well as its impact on sales and image.

These tasks and benefits of marketing research have been described here in order to highlight the range of issues that can be addressed meaningfully in a service business and the contributions that marketing research can make to a service marketer's decision-making processes. Marketing research can also supply other types of relevant information to marketing decision makers if time and budget allow, such as need gap analysis and studies of overseas marketing opportunities.

Planning and Executing a Marketing Research Project

Once it has been decided that a marketing research project should be undertaken, a series of steps must take place. Each step in the project is characterized by a number of decisions and actions that shape its course as well as its outcome. The kind of questions that have to be addressed as a project unfolds may be gleaned from the following case history:

> The president of a local bank would like to know how to service his retail banking customers better and, in the process, gain a differential advantage over the competition. Accordingly, he initiates a marketing research study. The decisions that researchers have to make at various points in the research process are shown in Exhibit 4–3.

In this particular case, the researchers must take the following steps:

Define the problem. How can the researchers translate

EXHIBIT 4–3   Decision Points in a Marketing Research Project

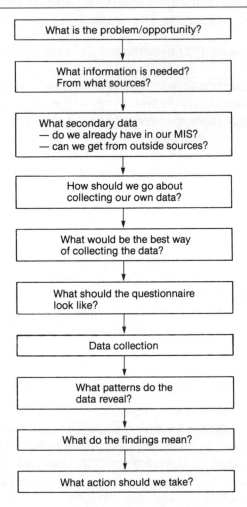

What is the problem/opportunity?
What information is needed? From what sources?
What secondary data — do we already have in our MIS? — can we get from outside sources?
How should we go about collecting our own data?
What would be the best way of collecting the data?
What should the questionnaire look like?
Data collection
What patterns do the data reveal?
What do the findings mean?
What action should we take?

the president's request into a problem that is researchable and that will provide actionable data? Should they define this as a study of the strengths, weaknesses, and overall images of local banks? Or should they define competition more broadly and include other financial institutions? Should the thrust be to identify need gaps and/or bank selection and patronage criteria?

Specify information needs and sources. Precisely what information is required? Some of the information categories that could be covered include demographic and/or lifestyle characteristics of depositors and nondepositors, familiarity with the bank's services and awareness of its promotional activities, and attitudes and opinions of depositors and nondepositors with regard to the bank and its competition.

Searching MIS and other secondary data sources. Is any of the needed information currently available? Past studies conducted by the bank and studies by a local university, the chamber of commerce, newspapers, bankers' associations, and commercial organizations are possible sources.

Plan the primary data collection process. If available data are inadequate, a formal primary data collection process has to be planned carefully. This framework includes formulation of research objectives, identification of primary information sources (consumers, business executives, officials, competitors, officers, etc.), determination of respondent selection method (sampling plan), choice of outside research agency or consultant to aid in the design and execution of the project, budgeting, scheduling, and data processing arrangements.

Choose the data collection method. The bank's marketing research director basically has two choices available: observation and interviewing. Straight observation at the bank's own premises is not likely to reveal any useful information in this case. It is therefore inevitable that researchers interview a select group of people in person, over the phone, or by mail (or a combination of these approaches).

Formulate the questionnaire. What questions shall be included? In what sequence? How should the questions be worded? What instructions are necessary? The research director should be concerned about keeping the questionnaire as simple and short as possible.

Collect the data. Who should collect the data? How should the interviewers be trained and supervised? When and where should the data collection take place?

Process and analyze the data. What categories should be established to code any open-ended responses? What variables should be cross-tabulated? What summary statistics are needed?

Interpret the results. The bank president is not interested in a mountain of undigested data. He does not have time to wade through them, nor is it his job to do so. The research director has to thoroughly review the processed data and interpret their meaning to the bank's business. What the president really wants is a three-page executive summary highlighting key findings of the study.

Recommend appropriate action. The marketing research function does not really serve its responsibility well if it merely acts as a group of glorified number crunchers. Any thorough research director will develop action recommendations that spell out what should be done under the circumstances and what impact can be expected from such measures.

As this example illustrates, complex decisions have to be made at each stage of a research project, and these decisions affect the outcome, cost, and benefits of the project. A closer look at some of the issues involved in designing and implementing a research project in a service firm follows.

Define the problem. Sometimes neglected and often haphazardly managed, problem definition is at the very heart of every research project. Ill-defined problems result in ill-conceived actions. If a symptom is mistaken for the problem, the cure may eliminate the symptom and leave the problem unabated. If, for instance, service quality is the problem and declining sales are a symptom of it, then lowering prices will only make matters worse because, although more people will be attracted to try the service, more people will also be repelled by the poor service.

Accordingly, a research project may easily prove counterproductive unless the utmost care is devoted to the problem formulation phase. Not only is top-management attention required, but prior exploratory research of a qualitative nature would also be beneficial. Ideally, the problem should be formulated as a working hypothesis to be proved or disproved by the subsequent project. Thus, it would be helpful if a discussion of the background that led to the research request were conducted and an outline of the broad marketing areas to be investigated were drawn up.

Specify information needs and data requirements. After the research problem has been carefully defined, a detailed list of the information needed to solve the problem should be made. Only after all the attendant information needs have been spelled out, can researchers determine how each piece of the puzzle should be gathered. For example, some or all of the following types of information may be required in a particular research project:

Sales

By service category
By customer type
By geographic area

Customer Attitudes and Motives

Attitudes toward service, firm,
  competitors
Motives for using service, firm,
  competitors
Dynamics of buying decision (who,
  when, where, how)
Satisfaction and dissatisfaction
  with service

Customer Awareness and Behavior

Service awareness; awareness of
  features, uses
Advertising awareness
Price awareness
Buying behavior; buying intentions

Demographics

Sex, age, marital status, occupation, household size
Education, income, social class,
  dwelling area, dwelling type

Basically, the information checklist should address the who, what, where, when, and how of the service firm's research problem. This information can then be translated into specific data requirements.

Search MIS and other sources of secondary data. A search of the organization's MIS may flush out data gathered for some purpose other than the immediate study at hand that is pertinent to the problem. Secondary data should be examined before embarking on a primary data gathering process since such data may answer the problem immediately and thus alleviate the need for primary data collection. Secondary data are usually less expensive to obtain, save a great deal of time because they are already in existence, help guide and streamline the primary data gathering process, provide supplementary and/or historical information, and assist in interpreting primary research data.

Despite their usefulness, secondary data should be used with caution and conservatism. As mentioned earlier, they have to be examined for recency, accuracy, and applicability. The possibility of changes in market conditions or buyer behavior patterns makes it imperative that only up-to-date information be used. Because the data were generated for another purpose and the researcher did not control their gathering and processing, their reliability has to be investigated. Using available data may be more expedient, but the data must be examined carefully for applicability to the problem at hand.

In spite of these potential shortcomings, the use of secondary data should still be considered. They can be obtained from a variety of sources. The internal components of the firm's own MIS are an obvious source. In addition, a number of outside sources may supply a wealth of secondary data: government sources at the local, state, and federal levels; commercial research organizations that supply syndicated services on a subscription basis; trade associations, universities, and other nonprofit institutions; trade publications; and independent research organizations set up for information retrieval.

If the secondary data obtained by the researcher fully satisfy the information requirements spelled out earlier, the entire primary data collection component can be skipped. The project would then move immediately to the data processing and analysis phase. Needless to say, that is rarely the case. Secondary data are helpful but usually not sufficient. Thus, primary data collection is a reality in virtually all marketing research projects conducted by service firms.

Research plan. At this stage, the service marketing researcher develops a detailed strategy for collecting relevant primary data. The researcher and the sponsoring decision maker within the organization have to make a multitude of decisions. The following are some key elements of the research plan that will determine the structure of the research design:

Study objectives. Is the study intended to be exploratory? That is, will it test service or delivery ideas, concepts, and problem areas in a preliminary, qualitative way to identify growth opportunities? Is the study intended to be descriptive? Will it identify service or client characteristics, relationships, similarities, and differences in a statistically significant, definitive way so that decision making will be enhanced?

Information sources. Relevant information sources could be actual and/or potential buyers of the firm's services:

- *Consumers.* In multiperson households (e.g., families), the roles of service decision maker, buyer, and user may be played by different individuals. Or provider selection decisions may be made jointly. It is essential to determine *who* should be interviewed (e.g., the person in whose name a telephone number is listed).
- *Business executives.* Business decisions to buy services from outside suppliers often involve several employees from different departments (e.g., marketing, purchasing, and finance). Their relative accessibility as well as the dynamics of the decision-making process will determine who should be interviewed (usually the actual user).

Besides these obvious sources, other relevant individuals may be in a position to provide useful insights. Where intermediaries such as agents or franchisees are used in the distribution of services, their opinions and experiences can be most helpful. One airline, for instance, wanted to find out the criteria that determine the selection of a carrier by business-class passengers. In addition to interviewing a sample of business class passengers, it directed a series of telephone interviews to selected travel agents booking a substantial volume of business trips. This two-prong approach added an important dimension to the research project that resulted in a revamping of the company's sales program. Other experts, such as local or trade association officials or company employees in contact with the respective target market (e.g., counter personnel, salespeople, and officers) can report comments and requests received. An industry survey of competitive practices by an outside research organization can enrich the insights gained.

Sampling plan. Since only a limited number of individuals in the defined group can be interviewed within the existing time and budget constraints, a method for selecting interviewees must be determined. Basically, the researcher has a choice between random and nonrandom methods. *Nonrandom techniques* are easier to administer and thus are less expensive but they carry the risk of human bias, which means that the results cannot be projected to the underlying population. *Convenience sampling* is the simplest of these methods, such as when an airline distributes questionnaires to all passengers boarded on a particular flight. Passengers on its other flights have no chance of being included in this sample. *Quota sampling* is a bit more demanding since it requires that relevant characteristics present in the underlying population be reflected in the sample in the same proportions. If an airline with 20 percent women passengers and 60 percent business travelers were to use this approach, it would have to include 40 women and 160 men as well as 120 business travelers and 80 pleasure travelers in a sample of 200. This method quickly becomes difficult to use when too many characteristics have to be met simultaneously, such as women business travelers flying first class to a particular destination. Since the interviewer is at liberty to choose anybody who qualifies, this approach gives rise to personal preferences and biases.

Random methods replace human choice by selection based on statistical methods. Provided that all potential interviewees are known (e.g., an account list), random number tables or other systematic methods can be used to select respondents. Because the likelihood of every element in the population to be selected is known, the results of random sample studies are projectable and thus more reliable than when nonrandom methods are used.

Outside assistance.   No service firm can carry out a marketing research project of any magnitude without outside assistance. It has neither the specialized skills nor the resources to go it alone. A multitude of research suppliers vie for a company's business, ranging from the individual consultant to multinational operations. Many are listed in the "Green Book" issued by the American Marketing Association every year. They can help with any phase of a project (e.g., telephone interviewing) or take on the design and execution of a complete study resulting in a written report with recommendations. If a company does not want to use its internal data processing capability in processing the questionnaires, this phase can be farmed out, too.

Scheduling and budgeting. The following questions must be addressed:

- Will the study involve measurement? At one point in time only, or at regular intervals over time?
- How much time is available for its design and execution?
- How much money can be spent on outside assistance (design, interviewing, and processing) to get the job done?

Each of these decision areas has a strong impact on the scope and content of the research process and its eventual form.

Choice of data collection method. As stated above, marketing researchers can choose between two basic methods of collecting primary data: observation and surveys.

Observation. This method involves watching and/or recording the behavior of people or the results of that behavior. When this is done without the knowledge of the people being observed, the researcher will be able to monitor their behavior under natural and unbiased conditions. Service firms take advantage of this fact by utilizing "mystery shoppers," that is, trained observers posing as regular customers executing normal business transactions. Restaurants, hotels, banks, airlines, and other service businesses thus test their employees' courtesy, competency, friendliness, and efficiency from the crucial customer's perspective, gaining valuable insights as to potential improvements in training, equipment, operations, incentive systems, and the like. Observation can be carried out in two ways:

Personal. A human observer watches the behavior of employees or customers or the results of that behavior and makes a record of the observation. The technique is quite common, at least on an informal basis, for keeping tabs on competitive operations. Marriott's vice president for market development reports that he slept in some 200 competitive rooms while doing research on Marriott's new Courtyard Motels. By tracing customer movement and interaction patterns, personal observation can help improve facilities design and other operating characteristics. Fast-food chains routinely hire college students to record license plates of passing vehicles at prospective outlet sites before selection decisions are made.

Mechanical. A mechanical device records customer behavior for subsequent interpretation. This can range from an air hose–activated traffic counter to sophisticated laboratory equipment used to measure human response to visual stimuli such as advertisements. The latter include eye cameras photographing the degree of pupil dilation and psychogalvanometers that record physical reactions such as heartbeat and perspiration rate.

While these responses are natural and unbiased, observation suffers one severe limitation: It cannot explain *why* people act the way they do since it only records overt behavior and has no means of determining its reasons. This is why surveys are the more versatile of the two basic methods.

Interviewing. Surveys involve interviewing or asking respondents questions about their awareness, attitudes, needs, wants, problems, and personal characteristics. Because the subjects know that they are being investigated, however, their answers may be distorted to please the interviewer or make themselves look good. A marketing researcher therefore has to be forever on guard against the possibility of bias in a project and must attempt to minimize it systematically.

Interviewing can be executed in a number of ways:

1. *Depth interviews.* These are one-on-one personal interviews conducted with a limited sample by a trained psychologist. No formalized questionnaire is used; instead, the psychologist works from a topical outline. The technique used is qualitative and not projectable.
2. *Focus-group interviews.* In these interviews, small groups of relevant customers or prospects are invited to participate in roundtable discussions of topics of interest to the service firm, for example, new service opportunities. While the findings of such interviews are useful, they cannot be generalized and need to be substantiated by a subsequent questionnaire study.
3. *Structured questionnaire interviews.* A formal list of questions, in a rigid format, is administered to a large sample in this type of survey. While depth and focus-group interviews are exploratory in nature, questionnaire studies deliver descriptive, quantitative information.

EXHIBIT 4–4 Comparison of Three Interviewing Approaches

Interview Type	Strengths	Weaknesses
Depth interview	Provides extensive information; can uncover unanticipated and insightful information; is flexible and creative.	Has significant investigator bias; is expensive and time-consuming; gives highly qualitative results.
Focus-group interview	Elicits group reaction; can be adjusted while in progress to probe promising avenues suggested by participants.	Suffers from opinion leader effect; requires highly trained moderators and interpreters.
Structured questionnaire	Controls investigator bias; is easy to administer and process.	Stifles interviewer; is inflexible.

Exhibit 4–4 presents a comparison of the relative strengths and weaknesses of these three interviewing approaches. Structured questionnaire interviews are by far the most frequent approach to primary data collection by service firms as they are relatively easy to employ and result in actionable numbers. Questionnaires can be administered in three ways:

Personal. While costly and time-consuming because of the travel involved, personal interviews are ideal in that they permit simultaneous observation of the respondent and the surroundings. They also enable presentation of visual materials, such as advertisements or promotional brochures.

Telephone. This rapidly growing medium combines efficiency and flexibility with tight control since it is executed from one central facility under close supervision. Service firms increasingly favor telephone interviewing because it gives quick results.

Mail. Widely used in customer-satisfaction surveys, this tool is of limited value to local service firms because they cannot benefit from its potentially wide geographic coverage. Mail interviews are rigid and slow and require powerful incentives to achieve acceptable return rates. One bank not only attached a dollar bill to the cover letter in a survey of doctors, attorneys, and certified public accountants but also promised to donate $3 to the American Cancer Society for every returned questionnaire. The results were twice as high as expected.

Questionnaire design. After the method of data collection has been chosen, the instrument to record the data has to be designed. For personal observation, this would be some kind of recording form with appropriate columns, and for mechanical observation as well as unstructured interviews it is simply film or tape (paper, voice, or video). But the most frequent data collection instrument is a structured questionnaire that must be constructed with the utmost care and skill if it is to yield the desired information. Many potential pitfalls can trap the unwary novice, for example, ambiguous wording ("Do you like to fly?") or improper sequencing (beginning with statistical information).

Ideally, a well-designed questionnaire will consist of the following components (in this sequence):

1. *Introduction.* A brief statement explains the purpose of the survey and encourages the interviewee to cooperate (in a mail survey this statement is contained in the cover letter). This portion also identifies the research organization conducting the survey if the sponsor prefers to remain unknown in order not to bias the answers.

2. *Filter questions.* If the selection process did not determine whether or not the individual to be interviewed qualifies, this determination has to be made now. If the survey deals with the hospitality industry, such a filter question may ask: "Did you stay at a domestic hotel during the last 12 months?" Anybody answering no would be eliminated from further questioning due to lack of recent experience.

3. *Basic information sought.* This is the body of the questionnaire containing the questions aimed at answering the underlying problem. The initial questions should be intriguing in order to pique the respondent's interest and encourage cooperation. Asking somebody in a bank lobby "Do you have an account at this bank?" is definitely not the right way to start an interview. Easy-to-answer questions get an interview off to a good start, for example, "How long have you been a depositor at this bank?" Ques-

tion complexity can start to build then but unnecessary questions, for example, "How many checks do you write per year?" should be avoided.

4. *Classification information.* Answers to a questionnaire are useless unless they can be related to respondent characteristics. Typically, these will be demographic data such as age, sex, income level, occupation, or residence. Only by cross-tabulating answers with these data will the researcher be able to make sense of the answers and develop meaningful segment profiles.

5. *Identification information.* Most sponsors and respondents prefer anonymity to achieve candor. Where appropriate, however (e.g., in customer satisfaction surveys or in attempts at lead generation), names, addresses, and phone numbers can be obtained by the promise of a gift in appreciation for survey participation.

A portion of a sample in-flight airline questionnaire is reproduced in Exhibit 4–5. Questions 1–4 are examples of primary information questions directed to a captive audience where the sponsor is necessarily identified. The results will have to be interpreted with a grain of salt because they will possess more comparative than absolute value. Questions 11–13 are some sample classification questions.

Data collection. After the questionnaire has been designed and tested, interviewers have to be recruited, selected, and trained. To avoid bias, they should not be employees of the sponsoring service firm itself. The trained interviewers, who are duly supervised on a continuing basis, then administer the interviews in the manner prescribed. Upon completion of the fieldwork, the questionnaires are returned for processing.

Data processing and analysis. The responses gathered in the interviews are reviewed and edited—that is, checked for completeness, correctness, and consistency. If they were not precoded, they are given appropriate code numbers. So prepared, the questionnaire results may be entered into the computer and tabulated. Frequency distributions are established and cross-tabulations are run to detect significant patterns and profiles.

Interpretation and presentation of data. Now that the

EXHIBIT 4–5   A Portion of a Sample In-Flight Airline Questionnaire

---

Liberty Airlines

Dear Passenger:

    Welcome aboard! In our continuing effort to provide the best service in the air, we would appreciate your frank opinions of this flight as well as some factual information about you and your needs. Won't you please take a few moments to answer the questions below? For your convenience, when you have finished, your flight attendant will collect your questionnaire. Thank you in advance for your cooperation.

Marketing Research Department

1. What is the main reason for your trip?
   _____ Business visit or meeting
   _____ Attending conference, seminar, convention, trade fair
   _____ Visiting relatives or friends
   _____ Sightseeing or vacationing
   _____ Military
   _____ Other (please specify) _____
   _____

2. How long ago did you make your reservation?
   _____ Days/weeks/months ago (circle applicable period and insert number)
   _____ No reservation

3. What made you choose Liberty Airlines?   (check one or more)
   _____ Satisfaction with earlier flight(s) with Liberty Airlines
   _____ Convenient schedule
   _____ Destination
   _____ Fare
   _____ Recommendation(s) from friend(s)
   _____ Recommendation from travel agent
   _____ Aircraft used by Liberty Airlines
   _____ In-flight extras
   _____ Coupon
   _____ Advertisement
   _____ Other   (please specify) _____
   _____

4. Would you please rate the following aspects of your trip by placing checkmarks on the appropriate lines?

	Excellent	Good	Fair	Poor
Service received from Liberty Airlines personnel:				
Reservation agent	____	____	____	____
Skycap	____	____	____	____
Ticket counterperson	____	____	____	____
Boarding gate personnel	____	____	____	____
Flight attendants	____	____	____	____
Food	____	____	____	____
Drinks	____	____	____	____
Seat comfort	____	____	____	____

EXHIBIT 4–5 *(concluded)*

---

11. What is your total household income before taxes?
    _____ Under $15,000
    _____ $15,000 to $24,999
    _____ $25,000 to $34,999
    _____ $35,000 to $49,999
    _____ $50,000 to $99,999
    _____ $100,000 and over

12. What is your age?
    _____ Under 20 years
    _____ 20 to 29 years
    _____ 30 to 39 years
    _____ 40 to 49 years
    _____ 50 to 59 years
    _____ 60 to 69 years
    _____ 70 years and older

13. What is your sex?
    _____ Male   _____ Female

---

data have been organized and summarized, conclusions may be drawn. It is the researcher's responsibility to recommend to the service marketer an appropriate course of action based on the body of data specifically accumulated to answer the problem at hand. Results, conclusions, and recommendations usually are presented to top decision makers in both written and oral form. The impact of these decisions is then monitored through follow-up marketing research.

SUMMARY

Management intuition is essential in any business, but it is particularly necessary in a service business, where sensitivity and responsiveness to local needs and conditions may be essential to survival and growth. No marketing information system will ever be able to replace managerial judgment—nor is it intended to. Rather, a service firm's MIS provides the factual input without which decision making becomes sheer speculation.

For the enlightened service marketer, the continuous and systematic flow of marketing information is at the very core of the marketing concept. It provides the vital link with the relevant environment and, more specifically, with the company's chosen marketplace, and can mean the difference between success and failure. Well-informed service marketers will have the competitive edge.

CHAPTER 5

Marketing Planning for Services

The service marketing management cycle, presented in Chapter 1, demonstrates the importance of planning service marketing strategies and tactics to achieve desired goals. This cycle—a systematic, integrated approach to the marketing function in service businesses—involves five critical management activities: analysis, planning, organization, implementation, and control. This chapter considers the first two of these elements—analysis and planning—while Chapter 6 continues with a discussion of organization, implementation, and control.

The importance of thorough analysis and planning to service marketing cannot be underestimated. If these steps are not taken, even a service with market potential will surely fail. The U.S. Treasury Department's ill-fated introduction of the Susan B. Anthony dollar illustrates this. Despite the expected cost savings and added efficiencies of the Anthony dollar, and the unusual step of spending over half a million dollars to promote and publicize the new dollar, it failed. Why? The major reason was that the Treasury Department's marketing analysis and planning was faulty. The Anthony dollar was designed poorly (it was too similar in size and appearance to a quarter) and did not meet the needs of businesses and consumers.

As this example suggests, the unique characteristics of services, described in Chapter 1, are important reasons for careful service marketing analysis and planning. Similarly, the uncon-

---

EXHIBIT 5-1   Analysis and the Service Marketing Management Cycle

---

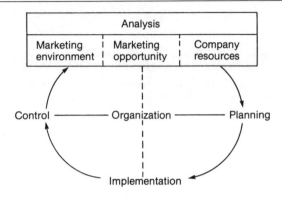

trollable and often unpredictable environmental factors that confront the firm (see Chapter 2) also necessitate planning, as do the buyer behavior issues discussed in Chapter 3. Planning is more than just making "guesstimates" or trusting to luck. It is, instead, an organized system for determining:

- Where the firm is today.
- Where you want the firm to go.
- How to get where you want to go.
- When to get where you want to go.
- How to evaluate the plan's success and how to make modifications when required.

ANALYSIS

The service marketing management process begins with *analysis*. This first step management should take is to answer the fundamental question: "Where is the company now?" Before a service organization's management can begin to plan for marketing, it must first review the firm's current situation by assessing its marketing environment, identifying its marketing opportunity, and appraising its resources. Exhibit 5-1 shows how these essential analysis activities fit into the service marketing management cycle. The marketing intelligence and research techniques described in the previous chapter will assist service marketers in their analysis of the marketing situation.

Marketing Environment

We have already discussed the importance of the marketing environment, that combination of economic, legal, social, competitive, technological, and other external forces that exerts significant influence on the plans and decisions of service marketers but over which they have little, if any, control. Each service firm must examine the relevant changes in these environmental forces and assess their possible impact on the service marketing process.

The legislation that resulted in the All Savers certificate illustrates the critical importance of environmental analysis to service planning. A part of the 1981 tax program, the All Savers certificate represented a lower-cost source of funds for banks and other financial institutions. To adapt to this change in legislation, marketing plans were developed to attract depositors. Some financial institutions paid very high rates of interest in the weeks and months preceding the introduction of the All Savers to attract funds early. Other institutions urged caution, because the exact rate of interest and the income tax ramifications of these policies were unknown at the time. The key point is that each financial institution had to react to a major change in its environment. Those that were most successful understood the All Savers certificate's potential impact on their marketing programs.

Another illustration of the importance of environmental analysis is presented by a professional civil engineering firm located in a small city. This firm is involved with projects that often require zoning changes. Therefore, its principals have become familiar with the city's political process and the views of local politicians and residents toward land use. Having done this, the firm can use public relations, lobbying, and other persuasive techniques to point out the benefits of projects, rather than reacting defensively to political and residential concerns.

As these examples indicate, the importance of a thorough environmental assessment cannot be stressed too much. Further, because service marketers provide intangibles and the firm's reputation is so critical, they must be cognizant of changes in their marketing environment, especially changes in public opinion. Management's failure to anticipate environmental changes will leave the service business vulnerable to outside pressures, and it will be a reactive rather than a proactive marketer.

The plight of Continental Illinois Bank and other financial institutions that have experienced major financial reversals demonstrates how a service firm can suffer from a damaged reputation. Continental lost a significant share of its deposits after it was reported that some of its large loans to risky ventures in the petroleum industry had to be written off. Continental also had a primary lending relationship with International Harvester, another company whose financial problems were widely reported. The difficulties of savings institutions in Ohio and Maryland have also resulted in negative public opinion and consumer actions.

Marketing Opportunity

Changes in the marketing environment often provide service firms with opportunities but, to take advantage of them, the firms must recognize the opportunities when they occur. This is why many production-oriented service businesses have failed. The marketing concept suggests that a service firm must focus its marketing efforts on the needs of its customers, not on what it can produce.

In his classic article, "Marketing Myopia," Theodore Levitt pointed to the shortcomings of those major companies and industries that failed to analyze adequately their marketing opportunities.[1] He noted that the managers of many companies had a limited view of their businesses because they were product-oriented rather than customer oriented. Specifically mentioned as examples were several service industries, including railroads, motion pictures, dry cleaning, and electric utilities. Because of their shortsighted marketing views, these service industries missed marketing opportunities that grew out of the emerging needs of their customers.

More recent examples suggest that this limited view of marketing is still prevalent in some service industries. Individual

---

[1] Theodore Levitt, "Marketing Myopia," *Harvard Business Review,* July–August 1960, pp. 45–56.

optometrists and other vision care professionals may soon lose their market dominance if they do not change their marketing practices. G. D. Searle & Co., a large pharmaceutical manufacturer, now has a chain of vision care centers, and major drug and department store chains offer vision care services as well. Consumers are using these outlets because they are more convenient and offer lower prices than traditional vision care professionals.

The rapid growth of storefront legal clinics and other low-cost providers of legal services has met needs that traditional law firms were either unwilling or unable to satisfy. Likewise, cable television services and independent stations are providing programming to reach target audiences that the networks and their affiliated stations have neglected. An excellent example is Music Television (MTV). MTV's programming of music videos and interviews with rock and roll performers has attracted millions of subscribers, many of whom are in the very attractive 20- to 34-year-old consumer market segment.

Thorough and continuing analysis of marketing opportunities will help service businesses avoid the pitfalls of "marketing myopia." For instance, the recent growth of do-it-yourself automobile repair centers illustrates how the process of marketing opportunity analysis may disclose a potential market. Higher interest rates and rising new car prices have forced many consumers to keep their cars for longer time periods than in the past. These older cars, which often require a greater amount of maintenance than do new cars, present a unique marketing opportunity. This opportunity has been met in some cities by entrepreneurs who provide facilities and tools for automobile maintenance and repair. Consumers may rent lifts or bays and the tools they need to repair their cars in these do-it-yourself automobile service centers.

Another example of successful marketing opportunity analysis is provided by a small bank in California. This bank saw a marketing opportunity in handling bankruptcy deposits since more lenient bankruptcy laws had increased the number of such accounts. While the market was still too small for major banks to pursue, this bank actively solicited bankruptcy trustees and provided them and their clients with special deposit services. This is the type of creative thinking that helps to identify service marketing opportunities.

Company Resources

The third and final step in the analysis process is an assessment of the service firm's resources. Major questions that must be asked include:

- What are our strengths?
- What are our weaknesses?
- What internal resources do we have at our disposal that can help us to service our customers more efficiently and more effectively?
- How will various trends, both within the company and outside, affect our ability to provide our services?

To answer these and similar questions, many service companies are following the lead of successful goods marketers and are beginning to use a marketing audit to assess their marketing functions. Similar to an accounting audit, this is a comprehensive appraisal of all facets of the firm's marketing efforts. It involves a thorough review of the firm's past marketing performance and an evaluation of its marketing objectives, organization, programs, personnel, and practices. This review helps service marketers identify inefficient and/or ineffective components that can be corrected or improved. Service marketing managers also obtain a more realistic picture of what the firm can or cannot do. The marketing audit will be discussed in more detail in the next chapter.

Peter Ueberroth, the new commissioner of baseball and the man credited with organizing and managing the most profitable and successful Olympic Games ever held, has spurred major league baseball owners and executives to examine their marketing efforts.[2] Although the major league teams have lucrative TV contracts, as well as licensing and merchandising arrangements, they have not marketed their sport effectively. Less than half of the available seats at major league ballparks are filled during the season. Ueberroth initiated a survey of fans to find out why they are not coming to games. Individual teams are also examining their marketing efforts closely. For instance, the

---

[2] Kevin Higgins, "Play Ball: Baseball's 'New Breed' Owners Adding Marketing to Pitch of 'National Pastime'," *Marketing News*, April 26, 1985, pp. 1, 8, 10, 11.

marketing director of the Philadelphia Phillies estimates that only 20 percent of the team's fans account for 80 percent of the attendance at Phillies' games. The team plans to place special emphasis on getting infrequent attenders to come to Phillies' games more often.

As this example illustrates, answering the tough questions involved in this portion of the analysis step is not easy. Further, although analysis of the company's resources primarily involves internal issues, some external factors such as the buyer's role in service production should also be considered. This is why major league baseball has quite properly begun its self-analysis with a survey of its fans.

After completing an assessment of their company's resources, service marketers will have a better understanding of their firm's capabilities. They will know which of the marketing opportunities identified earlier should be pursued. This leads them to planning, the next step in the service marketing management cycle.

PLANNING

Simply defined, *planning* is the systematic process of deciding in advance *what* will be done; *who* will do it; *how* it will be done; and *when* and *where* it will be done.

Research has indicated that those service businesses that plan well are most successful—they grow fastest, have the highest return on investment, and so forth. Planning enables service businesses to obtain the maximum return from their resources; to be prepared for future market changes; to respond quickly and effectively to competitive moves; and to coordinate their marketing efforts with other service management activities. In short, good planning is the key to successful service marketing.

The first step in service marketing planning is setting objectives. Next, the firm must identify its target market. Finally, a marketing strategy and a program that will best satisfy the needs of its target market are developed. These three major planning activities are highlighted in Exhibit 5–2.

An annotated outline for developing a service marketing plan is presented in Exhibit 5–3. This time-tested format provides a natural sequence of steps for service marketing planning. The outline and the commentary presented in the remain-

---

EXHIBIT 5–2 Planning and the Service Marketing Management Cycle

---

der of this chapter will enable a service manager to prepare a workable marketing plan. Further, the manager will find that developing and implementing a formal service marketing plan will be an extremely beneficial and eye-opening experience. Profitable service marketing happens by design, not by chance.

Marketing Objectives

After completion of situation analysis and identification of problems and opportunities, the focus of marketing planning shifts to the formulation of marketing objectives. A *marketing objective* is a precise statement that specifies what is to be accomplished by the service firm's marketing efforts.

It is at this point that the assessment of corporate strengths and weaknesses becomes most crucial. What are our best or most positive attributes? Where are we weak? What, if anything, is our differential advantage—our unique selling point that can attract buyers? It is quite easy to see that marketing objectives must coincide with a firm's overall corporate mission and goals. If they do not, marketing personnel may be working against the service firm's basic purpose. If, for example, an airline is pursuing a corporate strategy of placing less emphasis on the northeast region and more on the growing southeast and southwest regions of the country, then an objective to increase

---

EXHIBIT 5–3 An Annotated Service Marketing Planning Outline

I. **Situation Analysis**

A factual report on where your company stands in terms of its services, its competition, and its market, combined with a review of the historic trends that led up to this situation. This section should be kept strictly objective and contain no interpretation. Where possible, show the development over the last five years and let the data speak for themselves.

A. The Market
  1. Description of your firm's service category, its history and significance in its industry.
  2. Sales and market shares of major competitors.
  3. Identification of the industry's stage in the product life cycle.
  4. Determination of the market potential during the planning period.

B. The Buyers
  1. Identification of the persons playing the different roles in the organizational or household buying process: gatekeeper, influencer, decision maker, purchaser, user.
  2. Purchasing motives, considerations, and habits, including time, place, frequency, and quantity of purchases.
  3. Knowledge and attitudes toward your service line versus competitive entries with regard to quality, price, convenience, and so on.
  4. Usage and consumption habits: who, when, where, why, how often, how, how much.

C. The Service
  1. History of your service offering from its beginning to the present.
  2. Current characteristics of your services: quality levels, availability, options, prices, and so on.
  3. Competitive rankings in surveys and other formats.
  4. Ongoing research inside and outside your firm and expected service improvements.

D. Performance Record
  1. Review of your services' sales histories.
  2. Examination of your company's market share evolution over time.
  3. Analysis of structure and trends in operations, personnel, and marketing costs.
  4. Profit history during recent years.

EXHIBIT 5–3 *(continued)*

II. **Identification of Problems and Opportunities**
From the facts presented in the previous section, distill your firm's strengths and weaknesses. By looking at both the marketplace and your company's situation, you can now define challenges that have to be conquered during the planning period as well as emerging opportunities that your company might want to seize on.
A. Marketing Problems
   1. Service problems: shift in buyer preferences with regard to service features and characteristics, performance weaknesses in comparison to competitive offerings, government warnings, or limitations.
   2. Nonservice problems: changes in distribution or buying patterns, intensified price competition, ineffectiveness of promotional approaches, declining profitability.
B. Marketing Opportunities
   1. Expansion of present market through new users, competitive displacement, or stimulation for increased usage of your services.
   2. Entering other geographic markets or opening up new markets by developing new uses for the services.
   3. Improving efficiency of your operations by lowering distribution costs, reducing service demand pressures, or giving profit-oriented bonuses to your sales force.
   4. Modification of your services, streamlining your service mix, addition of new services, diversification into new areas.
III. **Statement of Objectives**
Based on the comprehensive evaluation of your company's situation and of the challenges and opportunities it faces, you are now in a position to develop objectives to guide your marketing effort. For these objectives to be realistic, however, you first have to formulate assumptions and projections about future environmental conditions and trends.
A. Assumptions and Projections about Future Conditions
   1. Economic assumptions: trends of business cycle and industry output, consumer and capital spending, interest rates, inflation, and so on.
   2. Technological assumptions: availability of equipment, cost reductions and obsolescence from technological advances.

EXHIBIT 5–3 *(continued)*

---

3. Sociopolitical assumptions: fate of pending legislation, tax law changes, population shifts, changes in needs and behavior patterns.
  B. Corporate Mission
  1. Statement of company's basic purpose.
  2. Company's objectives and goals.
  C. Marketing Objectives
  1. Sales and/or market share objectives.
  2. Profit or return on investment objectives.
  3. Other marketing objectives: prestige, social responsibility, and so forth.

IV. **Marketing Strategies**
  While objectives serve as targets that your company will strive for during the coming year, strategies are the basic approaches that you employ in pursuing them.
  A. Target Markets
  1. Market segmentation—subdivide market into subsets of buyers.
  2. Identify appropriate segments (target markets) for marketing efforts.
  B. Growth Strategies
  1. Market penetration—selling more to existing customers.
  2. Market development—entering new markets.
  3. Service development—offering new services to existing customers.
  4. Diversification—entering new businesses.
  C. Functional Strategies
  1. Service strategy.
  2. Pricing strategy.
  3. Distribution strategy.
  4. Promotion strategy.

V. **Action Programs**
  Now strategies have to be translated into activities: who, when, where, what, how much. Responsibilities have to be assigned, schedules set, budgets established, milestones identified.
  A. Service Action Program.
  B. Pricing Action Program.
  C. Distribution Action Program.
  D. Promotion Action Program.

EXHIBIT 5–3 *(concluded)*

VI. **Marketing Control**
Having completed the design phase of your marketing plan, you must now decide how you will monitor its execution in order to keep your marketing operation on its preassigned course.
A. Reporting Rules
  1. Feedback mechanism: timing, responsibility, content, form of presentation.
  2. Processing of actual data: schedule, types of analyses, exception reporting.
B. Review Procedures
  1. Review schedule and pattern.
  2. Policy on revisions and corrective actions.

SOURCE: This planning outline has been adapted from E. E. Scheuing, "How To Develop and Implement a Sound Marketing Plan," in *Marketing Update,* Issue 15 (New York: Alexander-Norton, Inc., 1979).

market share on the New York to Cleveland route is inconsistent with its overall strategy.

It thus becomes apparent that there are at least two levels of objectives. First, a service firm must establish its mission and corporate marketing objectives. Then these objectives can be translated into operational objectives for specific services, territories, and other marketing entities. Also, priorities are established so that service marketing personnel know where to concentrate their efforts.

Many service businesses have marketing difficulties because they state their objectives in vague, difficult-to-measure terms. "To provide better service" and "to increase sales" are not good objectives. A much better formulation is the following marketing objective of a major airline: "To increase our market share of the New York to Miami route from 13 percent to 18 percent by the end of the year." This objective provides marketing personnel with a clear, specific direction.

Criteria for Objectives

To avoid the difficulties of unclear marketing objectives, each objective should be a precise statement that specifies what is to be accomplished by the service firm's marketing efforts. Good objectives must be:

- *Simple*—stated in clear, understandable terms that all members of the firm can understand.
- *Concise*—long, complicated statements often lead to confusion, rather than productive action.
- *Precise and quantifiable*—vague, difficult-to-measure objectives present great difficulties for service marketers.
- *Internally consistent*—with overall corporate objectives, and with those of other functional departments.
- *Feasible*—given the firm's available human, physical, and financial resources.

Determining objectives also involves establishing a planning horizon, which is an intended timetable for implementation. Planning should be done with a dual focus in mind—both long-term and short-term objectives should be considered. Long-term objectives provide a framework for the next 5 or 10 years, while short-term objectives narrow the time frame to the forthcoming fiscal year. Short-term objectives are thus designed to provide step-by-step (or year-by-year) assistance in accomplishing the objectives outlined in the long-range plan.

MARKETING STRATEGY

Strategy is the *how* of marketing planning—the overall design for achieving a service firm's marketing objectives. An effective marketing strategy enables a service firm to optimize the use of its resources and realize its marketing opportunities.

Market Segmentation

Marketing strategy begins with the selection of a *target market*. The target market consists of those people or organizations who are most likely to purchase a particular firm's services. Naturally, it is to this portion of the market that the firm wishes to direct its marketing efforts. Selection of a target market can only be successfully accomplished when the firm has a clear understanding of its present resources and intended direction. The process through which a market is studied, broken down into groups, and a target market selected, is known as market analysis and segmentation.

EXHIBIT 5–4 Scope of Market Segmentation

Individual service
for each buyer

Market segmentation
based on:
Demographics
Geography
Psychographics
Volume

Same service for
each buyer

Market segmentation is the process of dividing the market for a service into separate subsets, or segments, of buyers. This enables the service firm to concentrate its marketing efforts on a distinct subset of the market, or to develop different marketing approaches for each market segment. One type of market segmentation divides the market for a service into consumer, industrial, and governmental buyers. A loan is marketed quite differently to these different buyers; the marketing approach will differ depending on whether the loan is sold to a consumer, to a small business, or to a city government.

The scope of market segmentation is shown in Exhibit 5–4. In some ways, service companies have a unique advantage because services may be personalized for individual buyers. However, most service marketers limit the number of market segments to which they appeal.

As shown in Exhibit 5–4, the most frequently used bases for segmenting markets are demographic, geographic, psychographic, and purchase volume characteristics.

Demographic segmentation subdivides a market on the basis of age, sex, occupation, income, education, marital status, or similar variables. Pediatricians, for example, provide their services to patients of a specific age group—children. The introduction of cash management accounts by Merrill Lynch and other financial intermediaries is based on demographic segmentation, because these accounts are designed specifically for people with high incomes.

Geographic segmentation subdivides a market into different locations, such as states, counties, urban versus rural areas, and so on. Utilities organize their marketing efforts around geographic areas.

Psychographic segmentation involves subdividing a market by lifestyle, personality, social class, attitudes, and other behavioral characteristics. Developers who build apartment complexes for young singles are using behavioral characteristics to segment the housing market.

Volume segmentation subdivides a market on the basis of service usage. Heavy, medium, and light users are studied to determine if they have similar characteristics. For example, business travelers use airlines much more frequently than do tourists. While not ignoring pleasure travelers, some airlines, American and United for example, market intensively to the business passenger market segment. In contrast, People Express is trying to attract consumers who have never flown or who have taken few trips by air.

Segmentation Strategies

After studying the market for its services and identifying market segments, a service firm determines an appropriate market segmentation strategy. There are three basic options:

Undifferentiated marketing involves using the same marketing approach for all customers. Because service buyers' needs tend to differ greatly, this approach is unrealistic for most service businesses.

Concentrated marketing directs the firm's services and its marketing efforts toward a single market segment. This is an excellent strategy for a small service firm with limited resources. Some small banks in large cities, for example, have focused their efforts on attracting minority depositors. Because this is a limited market, these small banks may not encounter significant competition from large retail banks. Also, minority banks can base their marketing strategy on an appeal to ethnic pride.

Differentiated marketing is a strategy of developing different services and marketing approaches for separate market segments. Large service firms use this approach. Eastern Air Lines, for instance, has special fares and travel packages for vacation travelers and its air shuttle and automated self-ticketing machines for business travelers.

Whether a service firm chooses a concentrated or differentiated marketing strategy depends on its analysis of the market and its internal resources. A large firm like AT&T Communications has the resources to provide communications services to all components of the consumer and business markets. In fact, AT&T Communications has developed an extensive marketing and distribution strategy to serve the needs of its many market segments. This strategy is based on sales volume considerations. Consumers and small business customers are reached through mass media advertising, direct mail, and telemarketing. Large business customers, in contrast, are served by field sales personnel. For its very large business customers, AT&T Communications has developed sales and service teams headed by national account managers.

Smaller service businesses will need to analyze their market segments just as thoroughly as AT&T Communications does. Suppose, for example, that an entrepreneur wants to open a nightclub in a small city. There are several possible target markets. These might include young adults interested in rock music, mature adults interested in more relaxing music as a background for conversation, people interested in country music, and those interested in a dinner theater and name entertainers. Depending on the target market chosen, the entrepreneur's options range from a large dinner theater featuring plays and name entertainers to a small, intimate club with a single musician providing background entertainment.

In addition to analyzing potential buyers, a small service firm also must realistically consider its ability to meet the needs of its target market. The nightclub entrepreneur would be foolish to open a large dinner theater if he or she could not book good plays and popular entertainers. Another important consideration is the number and type of competitors. If this small city already has an established dinner theater, it is unlikely that a limited market could support another.

Life-Cycle Management

As service firms follow growth strategy options, their managers must be aware of the implications of the life-cycle concept. Studies of service firms and their life cycles have resulted in the identification of a service firm life cycle.[3] This concept, which is similar to the product life cycle, illustrates the growth pattern for a multisite service firm. In fact, the multisite firm's life cycle presents an overall strategy for the service firm that is committed to expansion. At each stage, a service firm will have different objectives and will encounter different problems. The firm's marketing strategy must be adapted to its stage in the life cycle.

The five stages of the multisite service firm life cycle are entrepreneurial, multisite rationalization, growth, maturity, and decline/regeneration.

1. The *entrepreneurial stage* is the introductory step. A service innovator recognizes a need and offers a service at a single location.
2. During *multisite rationalization,* the service innovator begins to add a limited number of other service locations.
3. *Growth* is a period of rapid expansion and often involves franchising. However, the service innovator loses control at this stage of the life cycle.
4. During *maturity,* the service's growth rate levels off because the service concept has lost its uniqueness.
5. When the *decline/regeneration stage* is reached, the service firm must do something (such as develop a new service concept or discover new markets) to avoid its demise).

Deregulation Strategies

The advent of *deregulation* has caused service firms in affected industries to rethink their marketing strategies. Where there had once been relative safety and security, there is now the challenge of competition. Where marketing techniques were once relatively unsophisticated, there are now aggressive, carefully designed marketing strategies for new entries and the old guard alike.

As discussed earlier, service managers must change the way

---

[3] W. Earl Sasser, R. Paul Olsen, and D. Daryl Wyckoff, *Management of Service Operations: Text, Cases, and Readings* (Boston: Allyn & Bacon, 1978), pp. 534–52.

they think to compete in a deregulated environment. They must make the difficult transition from a regulatory mentality to a competitive, market-oriented point of view. Service businesses that have dealt successfully with the new pressures of deregulation have followed one of three approaches—full service, discount, or specialty.

Full-service, or national distribution, companies have decided to continue to serve several target markets with a variety of service offerings and marketing programs. As expected, this strategy can be pursued only by relatively large, financially strong firms. In the communications industry, for example, AT&T Communications has sought to retain its dominant market share by providing a variety of long-distance services and equipment to consumer and corporate clients alike. In addition, innovative communications systems are being developed to meet the changing needs of customers and to prevent erosion of market share by MCI Communications, GTE Sprint, and other new competitors. In the battle for airline passengers, major carriers, such as United and American, have begun to describe themselves as "full-service airlines" to distinguish the services that they provide for their passengers from those of their less expensive, or no-frills, competitors (e.g., People Express and Continental).

In financial services, American Express Company, Prudential, and Citicorp are examples of traditional companies that have pursued a full-service strategy. In contrast, the financial network put together by Sears Roebuck & Co. exemplifies a newcomer's approach to providing a broad array of consumer financial services. These companies, like other service businesses taking this strategic approach, are characterized by a national distribution system, a wide variety of services, and strong, integrated marketing and operations functions.

Discount companies have elected to serve a specific target market—those buyers interested in reduced prices for specific service levels. The no-frills airlines mentioned above, for example, provide transportation between the same points as many larger, full-service airlines. They do it, however, without some of the extra amenities available on full-service flights. While some airlines have enjoyed great success with a low-cost strategy, others that have misinterpreted the target group's concept of "basic necessity" versus "extra amenities" have failed dismally. Vacation travelers, for example, may not regard wider seats and extra leg room as necessities. However, business travelers, who often work during a flight, may find these features essential.

In addition to the discount, no-frills airlines, there are many other examples of discount service marketers. MCI and GTE Sprint were mentioned earlier. Full-service financial service marketers must contend with discount brokers who charge commissions 50 to 70 percent below their full-service competitors. Insurance marketers that sell their services directly through mass media advertising or direct mail are able to offer rates much below those of traditional insurance companies that employ their own sales forces or independent agents to make customer contacts. These and similar discount companies offer a limited number of services, have small staffs, and compete almost entirely by promoting their low prices to price-sensitive market segments.

Specialty firms, as their name implies, are interested in serving a distinct segment of the marketplace. In the financial services industry, for example, investment "boutiques" concentrate on the investment needs of a small, affluent market segment. Such specialization is prevalent among smaller firms within an industry, since it allows for a concentration of resources toward a single, well-defined service target market. These firms usually charge substantial fees for their services since they target their marketing efforts toward nonprice-sensitive market segments.

Regent Air Corporation is trying to find a niche in the airline marketplace by following a specialty strategy. Regent flies once-a-day luxury flights between Newark and Los Angeles. The planes have private compartments that Regent calls "conference rooms in the sky." They have conference tables, air-to-ground telephones, and video screens. Regent also makes in-flight secretaries and copying machines available for its passengers. Also, hairdressers and manicurists are available for passengers who want to take care of their personal grooming needs. As this example illustrates, specialty service firms target their marketing efforts toward customers who are willing to pay for extra attention and service.

The dramatic changes taking place in freight transportation illustrate the impact deregulation can have on an entire industry.[4] On the one hand, a few giant companies are evolving into diversified freight transporters who provide global door-to-door service. These full-service firms use a combination of air, truck, rail, ship, barge, and pipeline transportation modes to distribute goods efficiently. They include CSX Corporation, which was formed from the merger of the Chessie and Seaboard Coast Line railroads and comprises, in addition to the railroads, a trucking company, a natural-gas pipeline, a barge company, and an aircraft services firm; the Denver and Rio Grande Railroad, which has entered the trucking business; United States Line, a large container-shipping company that has also gone into trucking; and two large trucking firms, Consolidated Freightways and Leaseway Transportation, that have started ocean service. At the other extreme are small, independent trucking companies that specialize in the pickup and delivery of less-than-truckload cargoes and consolidate them for shipment. These specialty firms are serving small manufacturers and shippers located in rural areas.

As this and the other examples show, deregulation is creating sweeping changes in the American economy. Consequently, more and more service firms will be forced to evaluate their markets, resources, and corporate mission critically with an eye toward finding the most advantageous strategy to pursue in their industries.

DEMAND FORECASTING AND CAPACITY MANAGEMENT

For service businesses, a critical issue involves demand forecasting and capacity management. Consider the following questions. What is the capacity of a particular service firm? How many clients can reasonably be serviced, given available corporate resources? What would it take to expand capacity? The answers to these questions are of critical importance to service marketers. Indeed, the very success or failure of a service business may depend on the accuracy with which capacity and demand are estimated.

---

[4] Bill Paul, "Moving It: Freight Transportation Is Being Transformed in Era of Deregulation," *The Wall Street Journal*, October 20, 1983, pp. 1, 18.

Services require capacity for performing or producing the service to be in place before marketing can begin. This has been called "capacity in-being." However, construction and start-up costs may be extremely high and, once in place, facilities may be very difficult to expand or contract as new trends affect the marketplace. Consider, for example, the case of a high school in a large metropolitan area. Built when the number of students of secondary school age was at its peak, the school's capacity now far exceeds the demand. Similarly, a hotel may be built with 150 rooms, but changes in traffic patterns have created a demand for twice that many rooms. While the initial cost per room may have approximated $60,000, the cost for redesigning and adding new rooms may easily double after only a few years. Additionally, these new rooms will undoubtedly require additional support facilities (restaurant, laundry, and housekeeping) that, if not properly forecasted and increased to handle the new demand, may spell disaster for the hotel. Finally, what about those airlines that decided that bigger was better, and purchased jumbo jets only to learn that their passengers really wanted greater frequency of flights? Their lack of proper market research left them with costly capital expenditures, but still minus the customer base so necessary for success.

Don't be fooled into believing that such scenarios are confined to large service firms in major industries. What of the small printing firm that accepts business, and then finds itself unable to do the work because of a faulty machine and no backup system? How about the local restaurateur who undertakes a costly renovation project in an attempt to attract patrons, only to find that the real problem was the lack of quick service, not the surroundings? These, too, are the victims of faulty demand/capacity anticipation.

As these examples demonstrate, the pitfalls of poor demand forecasting and capacity management are both numerous and potentially disastrous. Clearly, research is needed to forecast demand and capacity requirements. It is not enough to merely guess; one must attempt to learn as much as possible about the advisability of undertaking a service venture. How can one estimate capacity needs? At best, this is a challenging task. Capacity is not necessarily captured in one figure. A hospital with 300 beds may claim that its capacity is 300. If there is only one operating room, however, can this hospital really accommodate

300 people? Should the hospital's capacity be restated in terms of the operating room's capacity? Obviously, it is essential to seek out a balance between the various aspects of a service operation that constitute capacity. If there is one area that represents a significant bottleneck, it may well dictate what the overall capacity can be.

Research concerning demand and capacity should revolve around the following issues:

- How many firms in the area the service firm wishes to serve now have similar operations?
- What will be the start-up costs for construction and related expenditures?
- What is the potential number of clients the firm hopes to serve?
- At what prices must the firm offer its services to realize a profit? Will customers be responsive to this pricing structure?
- What is the firm's ability to increase or decrease capacity, as the market dictates?

While estimation of demand and capacity requirements is confusing in the manufactured goods sector, it is even more difficult in service businesses, due to the unique characteristics of services mentioned so frequently throughout this book. Simultaneity of production and consumption, intangibility, heterogeneity of output, necessity of customer involvement—each of these factors contributes to the dilemma. What is the service manager to do, especially when faced with fluctuations in demand on a daily, monthly, quarterly, or seasonal cycle? Attempting to alter demand patterns or to control the supply (capacity) involves a clear understanding of the marketplace. Consider these strategies for changing *demand:*

1. Use differential pricing to encourage customers to purchase the service during off-peak periods.
   Example: Charge less expensive telephone rates during evening and weekend hours.
2. Increase volume during nonpeak periods through special incentives. Again, this strategy is often price related.
   Example: Offer discount weekend room rates and free

meals at hotels that serve a large number of business travelers on weekdays.

3. Develop a reservation system that gives each customer a definite time for receiving a service.
   Example: Reservations are used extensively by restaurants, airlines, and physicians.
4. Offer complementary services to deflect attention from "problem" areas.
   Example: Restaurants often have bars for patrons who must wait to be seated for a meal.

The following strategies highlight attempts to modify *supply:*

1. Use part-time employees during periods of peak demand.
   Example: Vacation resorts hire extra employees during peak seasons; banks may use extra tellers to accommodate customers during lunch hours and on Friday evenings.
2. Introduce efficiency routine procedures, so that only essential services are performed during peak-demand periods.
   Example: Hotel employees may concentrate only on essential services during prime check-in or check-out periods.
3. Use paraprofessionals in support of key professionals to perform routine services.
   Example: Specially trained assistants are used extensively in the legal, medical, and dental professions.
4. Cross-train employees to perform more than one task, thus increasing flexibility.
   Example: People Express has trained its employees to perform such varied tasks as passenger check-in, reservations, and in-flight services.
5. Allow consumers to participate more extensively in the service delivery process.
   Example: Restaurants feature "serve-it-yourself" salad bars; health information forms are completed by patients before they visit their physician.
6. Reduce capital expenditures while increasing the service level by joining in cooperative ventures with other service firms with similar equipment needs.

Example: Shared equipment is becoming increasingly prevalent in capital-intensive industries such as health care, where equipment costs may be too extensive for each small hospital or individual health care unit.

These strategies, while alleviating some of the problems caused by the uncertainty of demand in service industries, may also present problems of their own. Special incentives to promote off-peak demand, such as the discount weekend hotel room rates mentioned earlier, may "unfocus" the firm's identity if undertaken too extensively. Increased patronage resulting from these incentives may also prevent the firm from conducting maintenance, training, and other functions generally performed during nonpeak periods. Reservation systems may cause ill-will and dissatisfaction if improper scheduling is consistently practiced. Part-time employees may be unfamiliar with the firm and its overall mission, thus serving as poor representatives to customers. Consumers who are asked to perform "do-it-yourself" functions may resent the need to expend their time and effort in order to receive these "services."

It should thus be evident that planning, rather than merely playing "catch-up," is essential. Forecasting demand, while difficult, will at least provide a framework for constructive action. Examining current capacity—the strong and weak aspects of the firm's resources, the simpler functions that can be performed by customers themselves, and the potential bottle-necks—will enable a firm to develop a sound marketing plan. This plan will help the firm build both revenue and customer patronage while maximizing the efficiency of service operations.

THE MARKETING PROGRAM

Marketing strategies are translated into action plans through the formulation of a marketing program. Called the marketing mix, this blend of service, distribution, promotion, and pricing policies must be carefully coordinated and combined into an integrated program. There are many similarities between the marketing mixes for services and goods, but there are also important differences. Chapters 7 through 12 discuss the various elements of the marketing mix in greater detail.

The Marketing Mix's Focus

As pointed out above, the thrust of a service firm's marketing mix is to create a *differential advantage*. This is the "something extra" that makes a company and its services unique, or a little better than those of its competitors. Consequently, a particular group of customers (hopefully the target market) prefers the company's services.

A differential advantage does not just happen, however; it must be built. And it is built with the help of an effective marketing strategy, through the planning of a marketing program that will meet the needs of the service firm's target market. A firm's differential advantage may be the result of any part of its marketing program—service quality, price, location, psychological benefits created by promotion, and so forth. For many service companies, the differential advantage results from buyers' perceptions of the personal elements of the service.

Many service companies build on buyers' perceptions and try to create a differential advantage through positioning. Positioning involves the creation of a desirable psychological view of the service in buyers' minds. This strategy, which is explained in more detail in Chapter 8, is appropriate especially for intangible consumer services, where perception is so important.

Another important role of the marketing mix for a service involves making the service appear more tangible. As explained in Chapter 1, the intangibility of services makes it more difficult for buyers to evaluate a service prior to purchase. Therefore, marketing techniques should be used to acquaint potential customers with the features and benefits of intangible services.

Perhaps the simplest way to accomplish this task is to make the service more concrete. One approach is to provide a tangible representation of the service, for example, a certificate issued for the successful completion of a prescribed series of courses or a passbook for a savings account. Such tangible items give the customer a physical association with a service, and may strengthen the service's chances of success in the marketplace. Automation may also prove helpful, since it ensures standardization and may provide a concrete record of services rendered (e.g., a receipt, a bank statement, or the like).

AT&T Communications has been searching for ways to provide tangibility to its long-distance communications services.

Most consumers now purchase rather than lease their phones, so the telephone instrument is no longer a major part of the firm's marketing program. The one tangible component that AT&T Communications does have is its calling card, and the company is working to develop a direct billing system for its customers.

After developing the marketing program, a schedule and a budget are prepared. These important planning tools, which contribute to implementation and control, indicate when and how resources will be allocated to various marketing activities.

Schedule

A marketing plan must have a time framework, or a schedule, for achieving stated marketing objectives and identifying priorities. To do this, most marketing planners develop three types of schedules to conform with marketing objectives: Short-range plans cover a time period of one year or less; medium-range plans cover a time period of up to five years; and long-range plans are developed for five years or more. Long-range plans are the most challenging to prepare, since long-range forecasts of rapidly changing markets and environmental conditions are highly speculative.

Budget

Because company resources are limited, a budget for allocating resources to planned marketing activities is required. The budgeted amount for an activity should match its importance in the marketing program. Service firms must be sure to allocate sufficient funds to marketing activities in general. All too often, the marketing budget is not funded adequately by service managers. Also, during periods of economic difficulty, service businesses often cut budgets for advertising, sales training, and other marketing activities at a time when more, not less, money should be spent. Inadequate funds for marketing reflect the lack of a marketing orientation and a shortsighted viewpoint, since a poorly budgeted marketing program will not enable the service firm to achieve its marketing objectives.

SUMMARY

Service marketing management involves a cycle of integrated, interrelated tasks. This chapter has discussed the first two tasks: analysis and planning. Analysis provides the background information and the conceptual framework for planning. This step allows the service marketer to formulate marketing objectives, identify the target market, and develop a marketing strategy and program. The specific elements of the marketing program, known as the marketing mix, will be the subject of the next several chapters, after an examination of organization, implementation, and control in the service marketing management cycle.

CHAPTER 6

Service Marketing Organization, Implementation, and Control

Theory and practice—one should flow smoothly into the other, with relatively few problems or interruptions. The key to the transition from ideas (theory) into action (practice) is effective implementation of marketing plans and strategies. Marketing plans will be successful only if they are carried out properly. In the following chapters we shall describe the marketing mix, that combination of elements through which marketing strategies are implemented. Before doing this, however, it is essential to cover marketing organization, implementation, and control. These are the activities of the service marketing cycle that must be accomplished to successfully implement marketing plans.

ORGANIZATION

As shown in Exhibit 6–1, organization may be viewed as an extension of the planning process. *Organization* is the creation of a structure to achieve a service firm's strategic marketing objectives. Without an effective marketing organization, it is impossible to implement service marketing strategies and plans properly.

Recognition and acceptance of the marketing concept by service businesses have led to the organizational changes that place increased emphasis on identifying and satisfying cus-

EXHIBIT 6-1   The Cycle of Service Marketing Management

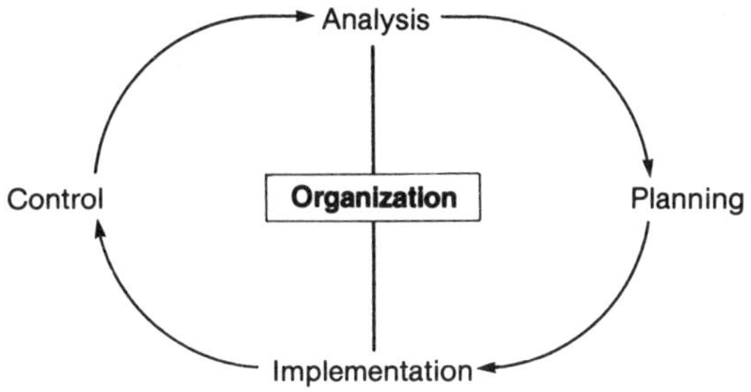

tomers' needs. Many service businesses have used marketing organizations developed by manufacturers. These traditional forms of marketing organization are functional, geographic, customer, and product organization.

Simplified organization charts for these forms of organization are shown in Exhibit 6–2. In addition to the traditional forms, there are special purpose organizations for service marketing, such as project teams and matrix organizations.

Functional Organization

Many service companies' marketing activities are structured around the basic marketing functions such as advertising, marketing research, sales, and customer relations. In this structure, each functional area reports to a top-level marketing executive. Small service businesses may combine two or more of these areas, at least initially, while larger firms might find it necessary to devote full-time personnel to each of these areas. As structure along functional lines develops, it is essential to maintain coordination to ensure that all members of the marketing team are working toward the same goals and objectives. Because of the unique relationship between a service business and its customers, there are some service marketing authorities who feel that a functional organization is not appropriate for all service businesses. This concern will be discussed later in this chapter.

A functional organization is, however, appropriate for small service businesses. These firms have a limited number of services and use direct channels of distribution. For example, as

---

EXHIBIT 6–2 Traditional Forms of Marketing Organization

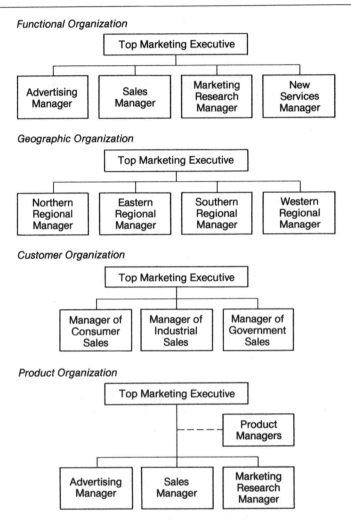

Functional Organization

Top Marketing Executive

- Advertising Manager
- Sales Manager
- Marketing Research Manager
- New Services Manager

Geographic Organization

Top Marketing Executive

- Northern Regional Manager
- Eastern Regional Manager
- Southern Regional Manager
- Western Regional Manager

Customer Organization

Top Marketing Executive

- Manager of Consumer Sales
- Manager of Industrial Sales
- Manager of Government Sales

Product Organization

Top Marketing Executive

- Product Managers

- Advertising Manager
- Sales Manager
- Marketing Research Manager

marketing has begun to emerge in professional service firms, functional responsibility for "business development," as marketing is often called, is assigned to one or a few persons. This may be a junior partner or someone who is hired specifically to perform marketing activities.

Geographic Organization

Geographic organization is another fairly common structure. For instance, large restaurant chains are organized by regions. The major advantage of this marketing structure is that it allows a service firm to adapt its marketing effort to local market conditions. The influence of a geographic organizational structure is evident when a national restaurant chain adds regional food specialties to its menu.

Most banks and savings institutions use a geographic organizational structure to serve their retail customers. Branches are located at appropriate places throughout the financial institution's market area. If there are a large number of branches, there are regional managers who oversee the branch operations and marketing activities in each specific geographical region. This geographic approach enables large financial institutions to adapt their marketing activities to local financial needs and competition.

Customer Organization

Service businesses that accommodate several major types of customers with different characteristics and needs may find a customer, or market, organization is most appropriate. This form of organization permits the firm to concentrate its marketing efforts on the particular needs of each major category of customer. For example, large commercial banks have separate divisions for consumer, corporate, and trust customers.

In recent years, AT&T Communications has made a number of significant organizational changes to streamline its marketing functions and better serve its long-distance customers. After divestiture of the local operating companies, AT&T Communications organized itself into regions that were further structured into separate units to serve business and consumer markets. A particularly significant change was the creation of a national sales force charged with concentrating on AT&T's Communications' most important business customers, the Fortune 1,000 companies with complex communication needs. National account managers, with teams of 30 to 40 specialists, were assigned to coordinate the marketing efforts for major companies such as General Motors and U.S. Steel.

To further strengthen its marketing program, AT&T Communications has also expanded its marketing staff to provide marketing research, market analysis, and other specialized functions to the field sales organization. The intent of these changes is to position AT&T Communications as the leading marketer of communications and information services to industry. These organizational changes reflect the company's shift toward a marketing orientation.

AT&T Communications' marketing organization combines several approaches, although it remains primarily customer-oriented. A similar approach that some service businesses have begun to use is the concept of a *strategic business unit* (SBU). This is a market-centered organizational strategy that clusters services, marketing resources, and activities around common needs or elements. Most often, the focal point for a strategic business unit is a given customer base or target market. For instance, many large banks have developed special banking centers, usually known as "private banks," to serve affluent customers. These centers combine trust, investing, and related services for the wealthy with added personal attention and other amenities such as luxurious offices and refreshments. These special banking centers are headed by a senior officer who is directly responsible to top management.

Product Organization

The product organization structure was pioneered by large consumer packaged goods companies such as Procter & Gamble, Colgate-Palmolive, and General Foods. The product management structure allowed these companies to develop special marketing mixes for different products. The *product manager* (sometimes called a brand manager) is responsible for developing, implementing, and managing the marketing program for a specific product, service, or product line.

There are several advantages to this type of organizational structure. The major advantage is that a single product (or service) manager is concerned with the marketing of an individual product, service, or product line. This places the responsibility for results with one person. Also, since the product/service manager is required to monitor customers' needs and market trends, this form of organization emphasizes staying close to the customer. Finally, many companies have found that product management is an excellent means for developing future top-management talent.

For these reasons, a variety of large service businesses have adopted product management. For example, many major commercial banks and savings institutions have separate product managers for consumer loans, mortgages, savings, and other major service categories. These managers can respond quickly to problems and opportunities such as higher interest rates and regulatory changes. Other major duties of product managers in financial institutions include monitoring competitive products and services, developing and implementing promotion strategies, and sales training.

As the above description of responsibilities suggests, the product manager's role is to be a coordinator for the assigned product or service. Consequently, the product manager has extensive contacts with other departments within a service business. Sometimes, however, product managers encounter resistance from operations personnel. While they are responsible for the sales and profits of their products or services, they do not usually have authority over operations and other functional areas. Therefore, they must not only coordinate marketing activities related to their products, but they must also use their expertise and interpersonal skills to influence others to provide the needed cooperation and assistance. Exhibit 6–3 shows how the product manager in a large bank is linked to various bank departments and operations and to selected outside organizations.

Project Teams

A variation of the product organization is the formation of project teams by service businesses. These teams are created to perform a specific task, such as developing a new service. Usually, they include executives from different functional areas of a service business.

A large commercial bank, for example, used project teams in two different ways. One team was formed to coordinate the closing of a branch that was no longer needed. This team, led by the regional manager, included representatives from advertising, operations, branch administration, and human resources. A similar team was formed to develop a new cash-management

---

EXHIBIT 6-3 A Product/Service Manager's Links in a Bank

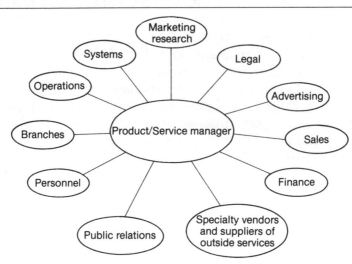

service. Because this team's task was more extensive than closing a branch, an external consultant was employed as the project leader.

Matrix Organization

Another unique form of marketing structure is a matrix organization. This approach also employs a team concept, but a matrix organization is usually permanent while a project team exists for a limited period of time only. A matrix organization exists whenever there is some sort of shared responsibility (and lines of authority) for marketing. For example, AT&T Communications has both service managers responsible for developing and managing services such as "WATS," and segment managers responsible for developing specific markets such as insurance.

Organizational Issues

Some observers of service marketing believe that organization for marketing in a service business should be vastly different from that in a goods-producing company. This is so because the marketing and production of services occur simultaneously;

therefore, almost everyone in a service company has some involvement in service marketing. Christian Gronroos suggests that adapting a traditional goods marketing department to a service firm may not be effective.[1] When such an adaptation is done, other departments may feel that they can give up their marketing responsibilities. This, of course, is the opposite of what should happen.

An extensive study of marketing management at four large service companies highlights service marketing organizational problems.[2] This study emphasizes that marketing is interrelated closely with personnel and operations. The authors describe this mutual dependence of marketing, operations, and personnel as a service management triangle.

It is suggested that an effective way to organize for service marketing is through a facility (site) manager who coordinates the elements of the service business. Examples include a bank branch manager, a hotel manager, and a restaurant manager. The focus of this structure is to assign to a single person the overall responsibility for managing the interactions between customers and the service organization.

The major issue for service marketing is that service businesses require a different organizational structure—one that integrates the simultaneous production and marketing of a service. As Exhibit 6–4 suggests, something other than a traditional marketing structure, which is mostly outside the service production and marketing process, is needed. The orientation of service marketing is on buyer-seller interactions, which Gronroos has described as *interactive marketing*.

IMPLEMENTATION

Marketing plans and programs will work only if they are implemented and managed properly. A marketing plan that remains on the shelf is just as bad as no plan at all. The need to carry out marketing plans points to the importance of implementation as

---

[1] Christian Gronroos, "Designing a Long-Range Marketing Strategy for Services," *Long Range Planning,* April 1980, p. 40.

[2] Christopher H. Lovelock, Eric Langeard, John E. G. Bateson, and Pierre Eiglier, "Some Organizational Problems Facing Marketing in the Service Sector," in *Marketing of Services,* ed. James H. Donnelly and William R. George (Chicago: American Marketing Association, 1981), pp. 168–71.

EXHIBIT 6–4 Traditional versus Interactive Marketing

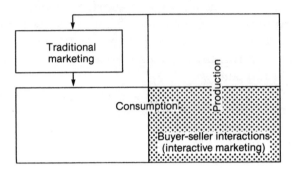

SOURCE: Christian Gronroos, *Strategic Management and Marketing in the Service Sector* (Helsingfors: Swedish School of Economics and Business Administration, 1982), p. 137.

part of the service marketing management cycle. (See Exhibit 6–5.)

In implementing marketing plans, service marketers have become aware of the importance of *internal marketing* within a service organization. All employees who have contacts with customers, and this includes almost everyone in a service business, must be "sold" on providing quality service to customers.

To be more specific, internal marketing is defined as a service firm's efforts to provide all members of the organization with a clear understanding of the corporate mission and objectives and with the training, motivation, and evaluation to achieve the desired objectives. The old adage which states that "it's easier to sell something when you believe in it yourself" is very applicable to service firms. Since each employee is, in effect, a walking advertisement for the firm, the value of a well-informed, committed, and courteous staff cannot be overestimated. Dedication and loyalty will only develop, however, if staff members are knowledgeable and are motivated to transmit their knowledge and enthusiasm to actual and potential clients with whom they come into contact.

Take, for example, a service representative for a utility company. If this person is down on the company and conveys this negative attitude by "bad-mouthing" the company to customers,

EXHIBIT 6–5   The Importance of Implementation

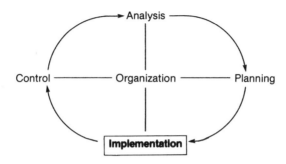

the utility will suffer. On the other hand, a motivated service representative who is enthusiastic about the company will not only perform the required service duties well, but will also project a positive, warm attitude toward the company. As a result, customers will feel good about the utility and will be less likely to complain unnecessarily.

The key to service marketing success is to regard a service firm's employees as its most important customers. This responsibility begins with the chief executive officer—it is not just a marketing responsibility. Implementation, which is the management function for executing internal marketing, involves several important tasks. Service marketers first must communicate marketing plans and programs to the people who will carry them out. They also must coordinate the various programs and activities for which they are responsible. Finally, they must manage their service personnel.

Communication

The first step in implementing service marketing is to transmit objectives, programs, schedules, and budgets to the people who will be carrying them out. These people include company personnel such as salespeople, customer service representatives, and sales and operations managers; and external components of the marketing system such as advertising agency personnel and independent intermediaries.

Proponents of internal marketing emphasize that the communication of marketing plans involves more than just informing people of the plans. Marketing managers also have to sell or persuade people to accept and implement the marketing program. This must be done because many people resist change, even a change that may benefit them. They anticipate that new marketing plans and programs will mean more work for them. Employees of "traditional" service businesses are especially reluctant to accept marketing as an important part of their jobs. Consequently, service marketing managers must convince skeptical members of the service organization that the successful implementation of marketing plans will help them to achieve their personal goals.

An effective technique for introducing new or revised marketing programs to a service firm's employees is to have the chief executive officer personally present the programs in a meeting or series of meetings. This provides the "stamp of approval" and tells the employees that the program is important to them and to the company as a whole. For those service businesses that are too large or too geographically dispersed for personal presentations, a videotaped message from the CEO can serve as an acceptable substitute.

There are a number of other effective techniques for communicating with employees. New product meetings should be held whenever necessary. An internal newsletter or house organ should be used to inform employees about the business. Often overlooked, but very important, are telephone operators, who should be kept informed of pertinent company and product changes. Not only do they need to know changes when dealing with the public, but telephone operators may also be some employees' major contact with the home office.

Coordination

In addition to communicating goals, objectives, and other aspects of the marketing effort, service marketing managers must assign various tasks to service personnel and integrate marketing activities with other aspects of the firm's business. Such coordination is designed to ensure that the systems approach to marketing management is properly implemented.

A trade school in the Northeast learned the need for coordination the hard way. This trade school spent a large amount of money on a direct mail campaign to recruit new students. After the mailing had gone out and calls began to come in, the school's director of admissions realized that she had made a major mistake—the school's telephone operators had not been informed of the campaign. Before this oversight was corrected, the school lost a number of potential recruits.

Three important coordination tasks are required if marketing plans are to be implemented successfully. First, top management must make sure that all members of the organization are working toward the same goals. Next, those managers who are assigned major marketing functions must work closely with managers in operations, finance, personnel, accounting, and other departments to integrate marketing activities with other company functions. Finally, a firm's own marketing activities must be coordinated with the efforts of advertising agencies, financial institutions, intermediaries, and other external organizations that assist in marketing.

Managing Service Personnel

Internal marketing also involves carrying out the important day-to-day personnel management tasks of training, motivation, supervision, and evaluation. A comprehensive personnel management effort will enable a service business to develop and retain qualified employees and to maintain control over the quality of its service output. For example, the Marriott Corporation has developed a series of personnel programs that enables it to maintain a high level of performance and provide the quality of service its customers demand. J. Willard Marriott, the company's founder, has said, "In the service business you can't make happy guests with unhappy employees."

Marriott's observation highlights the significance of personnel, or as it is now often called, human resources management, as a critical aspect of the implementation function in a service business. Human resources management involves the consideration of such key questions as: How can we train service personnel to become more customer-oriented? How can we motivate low-paid, entry-level workers? How can we work with unions to provide more consistent, quality service? These and similar questions have become even more important as deregulation in many service industries changes the relationship between a service business and its employees. For example, since divestiture,

AT&T and the Communications Workers of America have been motivated to work more closely together to adjust to a new competitive environment that demands greater labor efficiency and lower costs.

The success of Marriott, McDonald's, Disney, and other service businesses known for their consistent service quality points out that human resources management begins when new employees enter the service organization and continues throughout their employment with the firm. These successful service firms recognize that it is not enough to provide initial training and then assume that the service employee has been properly indoctrinated. Training prepares service employees to perform their marketing duties and helps to improve their relationships with clients, but training is simply not enough to maintain high performance standards and positive employee morale. The other components of human resources management—motivation, supervision, and evaluation—must also receive suitable attention from service managers.

Training. Preparing service employees to implement marketing plans is a critical marketing activity. Effective training will improve employees' relationships with customers by showing them the right way to serve their customers. Although individual training needs vary, most service employees must be trained to understand fully their company's services, policies, and procedures, and the essentials of customer relations. For specialized service employees with more complex marketing tasks (for example, salespeople or product managers), detailed, more technical training will be required.

Like so many other companies in the highly competitive financial services field, the Prudential Insurance Company is facing new competition and undergoing dramatic changes. One way in which Prudential is preparing its sales agents to cope with these changes is through a training and development program known as the Agent Career Path. This program is a multifaceted guide for agents that teaches them to work with their clients to identify financial needs, to help them establish priorities, and then to propose solutions that are within the client's financial capabilities. The primary purpose of this training and development program is to reorient agents to serve their clients, rather than sell financial products.

Motivation. Motivation is the "how to" of getting people to do their jobs well. Motives are the "whys" of behavior. If service employees are to accept and carry out marketing plans, they must be motivated to do so. This requires the development of incentives to reward those employees who are successful. Some of the incentives used to motivate salespeople, customer service representatives, and other service marketing personnel are financial compensation, sales contests, honors and recognition, and communication. Service marketing managers also motivate their subordinates through effective leadership.

Many service businesses have special motivational problems because the employees who have the greatest number of contacts with customers (e.g., bank tellers, telephone operators, and airline flight attendants) are not well paid or highly esteemed within the organization. This is a mistake! High customer-contact employees must be motivated to serve their customers pleasantly and efficiently.

Although increases in pay and other financial rewards are important to these employees, money is not the only answer to motivational problems. Special recognition, employee contests, and other forms of nonfinancial incentives can be effective. For instance, a large bank had a series of "teller appreciation days" during which small groups of tellers were provided with a morning customer service training program, treated to lunch, and then given the rest of the day off. Another successful motivational technique is to select an employee of the month. This honor might also include a special reward or perks. For example, a large suburban hotel provides a special parking place for its employee of the month.

Supervision. Supervision, a large part of which is leadership, refers to the operational responsibilities of service marketing managers. These responsibilities include issuing necessary orders and directions, maintaining discipline, and guiding subordinate service personnel toward the organization's objectives. Unless a service business has capable marketing supervisors, its plans cannot be implemented properly. For example, a large savings and loan association with many branches spent a substantial amount of money on a sales training program for tellers and new account representatives in an effort to increase sales productivity. The program was unsuccessful, however, because

---

EXHIBIT 6-6   The Control Function

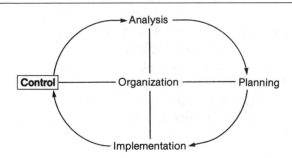

the bank failed to train its branch managers to be sales supervisors.

Evaluation.   The final personnel management task is evaluation. This involves developing programs and techniques for appraising and improving the performance of individual service employees. The key to a successful evaluation program is to focus on personnel development—to find ways to develop a winning team. To do this, the evaluation program must be tailored to the individual service business in which it is to be used. The personnel evaluation program must be realistic, must be positive, and must motivate service employees to improve. Since evaluation of personnel is an integral part of the control function, many of the concepts and principles covered in the next section are applicable to it.

CONTROL

The fifth and final element in the service marketing management cycle is control. It is this element that serves as the pivotal point, since it is through control that results are measured against expectations. As shown in Exhibit 6–6, if these results demonstrate the need for revisions in established marketing plans, the cycle will begin again with a new environmental analysis and a new planning scheme.

The basic control process is shown in Exhibit 6–7. The essential activities are establishing standards, measuring performance, comparing performance with standards, determining

EXHIBIT 6–7   Operation of the Control Process

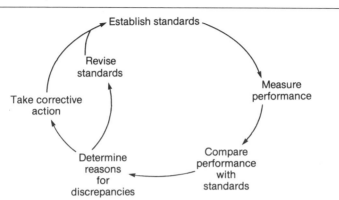

reasons for discrepancies, and initiating corrective action or plan revision.

Establishing Standards

Without criteria against which performance can be judged, the concept of control is virtually meaningless. Standards, which provide quantitative and/or qualitative statements of expected outcomes, enable service marketing managers to establish benchmarks for the measurement of performance within the firm. These standards are closely tied to the firm's overall marketing objectives, which were developed earlier in the service marketing management cycle.

Sales forecasts, schedules, and budgets are frequently used by service companies to establish performance standards. Projections are made for sales volume, market share, marketing costs, profits, and other criteria appropriate for the measurement of marketing efforts. Specific performance goals, known as quotas, are established for services, sales territories, and other relevant marketing units.

Measuring Performance

Once criteria have been established and a program has been set in motion, the service marketing manager must compare actual marketing performance with expected standards. This process allows for an assessment of the strengths and weaknesses of the particular program or activity being managed. The areas in which standards are established—market share, sales volume, marketing costs, profits, and various nonfinancial aspects of the firm's marketing operations—are analyzed both individually and collectively to review the effectiveness of the designated marketing program.

Market share analysis provides an overview of the results of the service firm's marketing efforts compared to those of its competitors. Usually, a declining market share is cause for concern and suggests the need for a more detailed study of other marketing information.

Market share is a critical marketing performance standard for companies in the very competitive car rental industry.[3] Half of all car rentals take place in airports, and Hertz and Avis had dominated this market. In 1975, these two companies held 71 percent of the market. However, 10 years later, Hertz and Avis had dropped to 33 percent and 24 percent, respectively, while National had captured 20 percent of the market and Budget had grown to 18 percent. The growth of National and Budget and fierce competition from smaller car rental companies has caused the major companies to introduce aggressive marketing tactics. These include sales promotion programs that offer reduced airfares and a price war for corporate accounts.

Sales volume analysis concentrates on reviewing dollar and/ or unit sales. Comparisons are made between forecasted and actual sales. However, a manager must go beyond total sales data to analyze detailed information on sales by territories, customer groups, specific services, and so forth. The iceberg principle suggests that total, or surface, information shows only a small part of the picture.

Marketing cost analysis provides service marketing managers with information on operating expenses. Comparisons are made between budgeted amounts and actual expenditures. Again, it is important that the analysis go below the surface and review detailed marketing expenses. Personnel costs are a particular concern in a service business because they are usually a large portion of total costs.

---

[3] "What's Denting Profits at the Car Rental Counters," *Business Week,* May 6, 1985, pp. 122, 126.

Deregulation in the airline industry has caused airlines to carefully assess their personnel costs. Several major airlines, including American, Eastern, and United, have renegotiated union contracts and established a two-tier wage system for current and new employees in an effort to reduce wages and lower long-term personnel costs. One airline, Continental, even used legal bankruptcy proceedings to break its existing union contracts. From these examples, it is clear that deregulation of service industries has increased the need for thorough cost analysis and control.

Profit analysis forces the service manager to determine whether the territory, service, marketing activity, or other relevant factor is making a contribution to the overall profitability of the company. Profits are, of course, the difference between sales dollars brought in and the costs incurred to generate those dollars of income. Traditional service businesses have been forced to become more profit-oriented because they are no longer protected by guaranteed rates of return granted by regulatory agencies.

Nonfinancial control standards can provide managers with meaningful insights into how well service employees are doing their jobs. The numbers of canceled orders, new accounts opened, customer complaints received, and similar information should be reviewed. For instance, an insurance sales manager discovered that a particular agent was not making as many sales presentations as were other agents. After reviewing the situation, the manager learned that this agent had become discouraged and was looking for a new job. Telecommunications companies often tie top managers' bonus systems to customer satisfaction ratings elicited in regular rounds of telephone interviews.

Taking Corrective Action

The analysis of actual performance against expected standards may reveal that the firm's marketing program is operating successfully. In many instances, however, such analysis may bring to light various weaknesses that diminish the effectiveness of marketing efforts. In such instances, one of two actions must be taken. Should the standards prove unrealistic, they must be revised to reflect the true nature of the marketplace. If, on the other hand, the standards appear reasonable but success has not been achieved, it is necessary to probe deeper into the firm's business techniques. It might be that the employees were not adequately trained, or that goals and objectives were not communicated properly, or that any of a multitude of internal or external difficulties exist. Once the true cause of the problem has been uncovered, management can begin to rectify the situation and improve its competitive position.

Applying the Control Process

To illustrate the control process and its application to a service marketing activity, consider the following example. A medium-sized bank with 10 area branches wanted to expand the use of its automated teller machines (ATMs). The bank developed a special marketing program that included a consumer contest and an employee incentive program for branch personnel. The two goals for the special marketing program were to attract new ATM cardholders from the bank's present checking and savings customers and to generate additional usage by existing ATM cardholders.

The bank first established performance standards. Each branch was assigned an ATM user goal of 3 percent of its total checking and savings accounts. The criteria for setting the branch goals were national statistics on ATM usage and the bank's experience with similar promotions. The goals are shown in Exhibit 6–8.

Once the program had been completed, the bank reviewed the results. As Exhibit 6–9 shows, the overall goal was not reached because three of the branches, Benson Street, East Windsor, and State College, missed their goals by wide margins.

The promotion manager's review of the performance at these three branches revealed the reasons for their poor showing. At the State College branch, students were involved in preparing for and taking final examinations and thus did not have time to participate in the bank's promotion. The manager of the East Windsor branch was ill, and the temporary manager did not train and motivate the branch's employees adequately. Finally, the automated teller machine at the Benson Street branch was out of service for two weeks during the promotion period because of an electrical fire in the wiring.

EXHIBIT 6–8   Goals for Bank ATM Promotion

ATM Branches	Total Checking and Savings Accounts	ATM Usage Goal (3 percent)
Avon	1,797	53
Benson Street	3,193	95
Clayton	4,106	123
Crawford Mall	2,148	64
East Windsor	4,650	139
High Street	3,923	117
Marshall Street	3,640	109
Metropolitan	9,588	287
Middletown	2,489	74
State College	6,134	184
Washington Mall	1,919	57
West Redford	3,025	90
Total	46,612	1,392

To correct the situation and make future promotion programs successful, the promotion manager decided to make two major changes in all future ATM promotions: to schedule all future promotions when they would not conflict with college exams and vacations, and to make sure that all branch managers trained their people properly. The electrical fire was considered a unique calamity that was not likely to recur.

THE MARKETING AUDIT

Having described the five major elements of the service marketing management cycle, we conclude our discussion with a tool that can and should be used to assess the total marketing effort in a service business. This is the *marketing audit*. As defined by Philip Kotler:

A marketing audit is a comprehensive, systematic, independent, and periodic examination of a company's—or business unit's—marketing environment, objectives, strategies, and activities with a view to determining problem areas and opportunities and recom-

---

EXHIBIT 6–9 ATM Promotion Results

ATM Branch	Goal*	Actual*	Difference*
Avon	53	62	9
Benson Street	95	41	−54
Clayton	123	125	2
Crawford Mall	64	81	17
East Windsor	139	98	−41
High Street	117	133	16
Marshall Street	109	110	1
Metropolitan	287	297	10
Middletown	74	81	7
State College	184	101	−83
Washington Mall	57	58	1
West Redford	90	92	2
Total	1,392	1,279	−113

* Number of users.

---

mending a plan of action to improve the company's marketing performance.[4]

Kotler's definition indicates the broad scope of the marketing audit. This comprehensive management tool allows service managers to examine their marketing efforts in their entirety—from the earliest stages of planning, through the implementation of marketing plans. Kotler suggests that this comprehensive review of a service company's marketing situation involves six major areas. These areas are listed and described briefly in Exhibit 6–10.

As Exhibit 6–10 indicates, conducting a marketing audit is an extensive, time-consuming process. However, when it is used as a tool for service marketing management, the marketing audit has many benefits. For example, service marketing managers may use an audit to keep up with important environmental changes, to identify marketing problems, to revise unrealistic goals and strategies, and to pinpoint marketing organization weaknesses.

It is more difficult to carry out a total assessment of market-

---

[4] Philip Kotler, *Principles of Marketing,* 2nd ed. (Englewood Cliffs, N.J.: Prentice-Hall, 1983), p. 554.

EXHIBIT 6–10   Service Marketing Audit

---

1. *Marketing environment:* What are the major environmental trends and developments (demographic, economic, competitive, and so forth) that present the service company with marketing opportunities and problems?
2. *Marketing strategy:* What are the service company's mission, marketing objectives, and strategy? Are they appropriate for the company's marketing opportunities?
3. *Marketing organization:* Is the service company's marketing structure appropriate for carrying out its marketing objectives and strategy?
4. *Marketing systems:* Are the company's marketing information, planning, and control systems adequate to support its marketing efforts? Does the company have an effective development system for new services?
5. *Marketing productivity:* What are the sources (services, markets, territories, and so forth) of the service company's profits? Are the company's marketing activities carried out in a cost-effective way?
6. *Marketing functions:* Are the elements of the marketing mix (service, distribution, price, and promotion) managed well?

SOURCE: Adapted from Philip Kotler, *Principles of Marketing,* 2nd Ed. (Englewood Cliffs, N.J.: Prentice-Hall, 1983), pp. 555–58.

ing in a service firm than in a goods business, however. Because marketing and production of most services occur simultaneously, almost everyone in a service business becomes involved in service marketing. Consequently, the marketing audit for a service organization may have to be more comprehensive than the audit for a producer of goods. As a result, few service businesses attempt a complete marketing audit, although many periodically assess individual marketing programs, activities, and personnel as part of their marketing management process.

Several financial institutions have begun to use marketing audits to assess individual elements of their marketing programs. Commercial banks have used the marketing audit as an added element of their credit analysis. The audit identifies trends that are affecting customers and gives loan officers a more realistic view of the marketing environment. Another example is Fidelity Mutual, a Washington, D.C., savings institution, which conducted a marketing audit to learn how its consumer service package compared to those of competitors.

SUMMARY

This chapter completes Part Two by describing the final three steps of the service marketing management cycle—organization, implementation, and control. These are the steps required to implement service marketing plans and to make sure that the service firm's marketing goals are reached. The chapter concludes with the marketing audit—a comprehensive planning and control tool used to examine a service firm's total marketing program. We turn now to the specific elements of the service marketing mix.

SELECTED REFERENCES FOR PART TWO

Carmen, James M., and Eric Langeard. "Growth Strategies of Service Firms." *Strategic Management Journal,* January–March 1980, pp. 7–22.

Chase, Richard B. "Where Does the Customer Fit in a Service Operation?" *Harvard Business Review,* November–December 1978, pp. 137–42.

Connor, Richard A., Jr., and Jeffrey P. Davidson. "Strategic Thinking Should Be the Centerpiece of Professional Services Marketing Programs." *Marketing News,* April 27, 1984, pp. 5–6.

Czepiel, John A. *Managing Customer Satisfaction in Service Businesses.* Report No. 80-109. Cambridge, Mass.: Marketing Science Institute, 1980.

Davidson, David S. "How to Succeed in a Service Industry: Turn the Organization Chart Upside Down." *Management Review,* April 1978, pp. 13–16.

Davis, Duane; Joseph P. Guiltinan; and Wesley H. Jones. "Service Characteristics, Consumer Search, and the Classification of Retail Services." *Journal of Retailing,* Fall 1979, pp. 3–23.

Dearden, John. "Cost Accounting Comes to Service Industries." *Harvard Business Review,* September–October 1978, pp. 132–40.

Denney, Robert W. "How to Develop and Implement a Marketing Plan for Your Firm." *Practical Accountant,* July 1981, pp. 18–29.

Healy, Dennis F. "The Bank Marketing Audit." *Savings Bank Journal,* February 1979, pp. 21–22 ff.; March 1979, pp. 42–43.

Hertzberg, Daniel. "New York's Big Banks Are Seeking Niches in the Wake of Deregulation." *The Wall Street Journal,* November 28, 1984, pp. 33, 44.

Gronroos, Christian. "Designing a Long-Range Marketing Strategy for Services." *Long-Range Planning,* April 1980, pp. 36–42.

————. *Strategic Management and Marketing in the Service Sector.* Helsingfors: Swedish School of Economics and Business Administration, 1982.

Gulledge, Larry G. "Evaluation Services Pay Off in Bigger Bottom Lines." *Marketing News,* October 12, 1984, p. 30.

Knisely, Gary. "Listening to Consumer Is Key to Service Marketing." *Advertising Age,* February 19, 1979, pp. 54–60.

Laurent, C. R. "Marketing's Role in Banking." *The Bankers Magazine,* July–August 1983, pp. 26–30.

Lovelock, Christopher H., and Robert F. Young. "Look to Consumers to Increase Productivity." *Harvard Business Review,* May–June 1979, pp. 168–78.

Pope, N. W. "Mickey Mouse Marketing." *American Banker,* July 25, 1979, pp. 4, 14.

————. "More Mickey Mouse Marketing." *American Banker,* September 12, 1979, pp. 4–5.

Possett, Richard W. "Measuring Productivity Costs in the Service Sector." *Management Accounting,* October 1980, pp. 16–24.

Riggs, Walter E. "Effective Management of Service Organizations: Identifying the Critical Operating Activities." *Southern Business Review,* Spring 1977, pp. 19–24.

Sasser, W. Earl. "Match Supply and Demand in Service Industries." *Harvard Business Review,* November–December 1976, pp. 133–40.

Sasser, W. Earl; R. Paul Olsen; and D. Daryl Wyckoff. *Management of Service Operations: Text, Cases, and Readings.* Boston: Allyn & Bacon, 1978.

Scheuing, Eberhard E., ed. *The Service Economy.* New York: K.C.G. Productions, 1982.

Schneider, Benjamin. "The Service Organization: Climate Is Critical." *Organizational Dynamics,* Autumn 1980, pp. 52–65.

"Service Business Is People Dealing with Other People." *Advertising Age,* May 14, 1979, pp. 57–58.

"Service Industry Researchers Need to Focus on Consumer Expectations." *Marketing News,* June 10, 1983, p. 16.

Storm, Walter K. "Shift Research Focus from Goods to Service Sector; Both Use Same Principles, Techniques." *Marketing News,* May 13, 1983, p. 13.

"Test Marketing Expanding Its Influence." *Advertising Age,* February 28, 1985, p. 17.

Thomas, Dan R. E. "Strategy Is Different in Service Business." *Harvard Business Review,* November–December 1976, pp. 133–40.

Webb, Stan G. *Marketing and Strategic Planning for Professional Service Firms.* New York: AMACOM, 1982.

Wheatley, Edward W. "Auditing Your Marketing Performance." *Journal of Accountancy,* September 1983, pp. 68–75.

PART THREE

THE SERVICE MARKETING MIX

CHAPTER 7

New Service Development and Management

New services are the lifeblood of any service organization. While a firm's current service mix may assure its survival for some time to come, long-term growth requires a steady flow of new services. Prompted and governed by changes in the market-place, new services come about through an elaborate process that begins with initial idea generation and leads to full-scale introduction. While following the step-by-step progression of new product development in the goods sector, the evolution of new services is characterized by a number of unique aspects that will be outlined below.

Once launched in the marketplace, new services can take on a life of their own. Sales progress through a series of stages known as the product life cycle. This concept is adapted from biology where an organism moves from birth to infancy, child-hood, adolescence, maturity, decline, and finally death. Different marketing mixes and strategies are appropriate as a service moves from one life-cycle stage to the next.

REASONS FOR DEVELOPING NEW SERVICES

In a profit-oriented firm, the single most powerful driving force behind new service development is the expectation of higher profits. Well-conceived and well-received new services are money-makers. Mechanics and Farmers Savings Bank of Bridgeport, Connecticut, introduced its "Smart Mortgage" in the mid-1980s, following a concept first developed in Canada. Under this plan, the homeowner makes half the usual monthly payment every two weeks, or 26 payments a year. This minor change cuts the repayment period from 30 to 17½ years and saves the borrower almost $152,000 in interest on a $100,000 mortgage at an interest rate of 13½ percent. This program has been very successful and the bank has earned additional profits by licensing its system to other, less innovative banks.

New services may also be the outgrowth of a desire to capture higher sales or a higher market share. This is the case when a major carrier adds flights or makes arrangements with commuter airlines to feed its long hauls. Technological progress can also trigger new services, even if they are just copycat offerings. Even moderate-sized banks can no longer escape the pressure to offer 24-hour banking through automated teller machines.

New service initiatives can further result from an existing service's movement through the product life cycle. John Hancock Mutual Life Insurance Co. experienced a 30 percent decline in its policyholder base from 1975 to 1985 as buyers switched from its mainstay whole-life policies to less expensive term coverage. Trying to arrest this trend, the company launched a barrage of noninsurance products, such as credit cards, tax shelters, and home mortgages. It also bought a regional brokerage house and several banks so it could offer certificates of deposit and other financial services. But customer and agent response to the new "financial supermarket" concept has been mixed: An investment management account failed with customers, and the individual retirement account finds little favor with agents who earn a mere $20 for selling it.[1]

The rapidly changing forces of competition and/or the impact of deregulation make it imperative to update and innovate services. Today, every major airline has a frequent-flier program to attract, retain, and reward the heavy-user group of business passengers. And even small-town banks are offering credit cards and discount brokerage services.

---

[1] Alex Beam, "Can the Boston Brahmin of Insurance Shake Off the Cobwebs?" *Business Week,* August 26, 1985, p. 51.

Changes in buyers' needs and/or behavior can necessitate new service offerings. Thousands of adults across the country now flock to specialized and flexible certificate or diploma programs of limited duration as opposed to traditional MBA programs.[2] Plastic surgeons report a sharp upturn in their business as consumers become more concerned with their appearance and are able to afford cosmetic operations. As client firms merge and chief financial officers shop aggressively for lower-priced audits, major public accounting firms have had to diversify their service portfolios in order to compensate for lower audit fees. In many instances, management consulting services have helped to cushion the impact.[3]

DEGREES OF NEWNESS IN SERVICE INNOVATION

If new services are a competitive and financial necessity and an essential prerequisite for sustained growth, which courses of action are open to a firm interested in adding new offerings to its service mix? One useful framework distinguishes the following six categories of service innovation: Major innovations, start-up businesses, new products, product-line extensions, product improvements, and style changes.[4]

Major innovations. These innovations create new service categories and thus entirely new markets, starting new product life cycles from ground zero. Federal Express single-handedly created a new industry when it launched nationwide overnight small-package delivery. Such bold ventures are fraught with risk but also carry the huge potential rewards associated with building a new market from scratch and becoming a major force in it.

Start-up businesses. These innovative undertakings address currently served needs in a different way, thus increasing

---

[2] Evelyn C. White, "Older Students See Alternatives to MBA Degree," *The Wall Street Journal,* September 10, 1985, p. 33.

[3] Lee Berton, "Total War: CPA Firms Diversify, Cut Fees, Steal Clients in Battle for Business," *The Wall Street Journal,* September 20, 1985, pp. 1, 24.

[4] Christopher H. Lovelock, "Developing and Implementing New Services," in *Developing New Services,* ed. William R. George and Claudia E. Marshall (Chicago: American Marketing Association, 1984), p. 45 (based on Donald F. Heany, "Degrees of Product Innovation," *Journal of Business Strategy,* Spring 1983, pp. 3–14).

the buyers' array of options. Health maintenance organizations represent such a novel concept in health care in that they emphasize preventive as opposed to acute care. Ambulatory surgery and birthing centers similarly provide alternatives to traditional in-hospital treatment. Merrill Lynch's Cash Management Account, an asset-based account offered by a nonbank institution in combination with a bank (Banc One of Columbus, Ohio) combines brokerage, debit card, and checking services in a single package. It proved so tremendously popular that Merrill Lynch had to keep adding personnel at a rapid pace to keep up with the flood of requests. It also spawned a substantial number of competitive imitations whose corporate parents were rather surprised to find out that Merrill Lynch had obtained one of the few patents ever issued for a service.

New products for the currently served market. This type of innovation involves an expansion of the service mix offered to the present clientele—although the additional service may have been available from other sources for some time. The idea behind this approach is to leverage an existing customer base by cross-selling related services: Credit card issuers attempt to sell their cardholders credit card protection and life insurance; electronic publishers may offer shop-at-home service; a resort hotel may provide sight-seeing tours or exercise classes. See Chapter 9 for a discussion of cross-selling.

Product-line extensions. Extensions offer buyers a more comprehensive menu of choices within existing service lines. This kind of variety is a sign of a maturing business or industry where more carefully defined market segments have to be addressed with more finely tuned offerings. Examples of extension strategies include fast-food chains adding salad bars, airlines flying to new destinations, and life insurance companies offering universal life policies.

Product improvements. Improvements refer to modifications made with regard to features of existing services. They represent refinements and enhancements of these services that are frequently made for competitive reasons in order to either keep up with or gain a temporary advantage over the competition. Often easily accomplished, such changes have the dual advantages of building on the popularity of established services while providing buyers with the excitement of newness. Improvements are generally characterized by moderate growth potential in mature, competitive markets but they also typically carry a very limited amount of risk. They may make the core service faster or more accurate, such as high-speed rail service or computerized laboratory analyses, or they may enhance the peripheral aspects of a service, such as seating comfort in a commercial aircraft or easier-to-use software. Finally, improvements could relate to the service delivery system, for example, extended hours of operation, round-the-clock accessibility, or more outlets.

Style changes. These innovations are cosmetic in nature and alter the appearance of tangible service aspects. This may involve introduction or redesign of uniforms, such as in the ailing Playboy Clubs where most bunny outfits will disappear in favor of a more conventional design. Or it may mean altering the decor of a service facility, such as removal of tellers' cages in banks to create a friendlier impression. A style change also occurs when a creditor (e.g., a bank) moves from "country-club billing" (where a copy of the charge document accompanies the statement) to itemized billing. The latter is common in the credit card business for cost reasons (particularly postage). American Express Company (issuer of a charge card) is among the last holdouts who still subscribe to the country-club mode.

NEW PRODUCT ORGANIZATION

New services do not just come about by happenstance—they require continuous effort and appropriate organizational provisions. Without a focal point for its new service effort, a service firm leaves its future in the hands of chance. Clearly designating a unit within the organization to be responsible for the steady genesis of new services is an absolute necessity if the new service program is to succeed in the long run.

A service firm can structure its new product organization according to a number of alternative organizational formats: product manager, new product department, new product committee, venture team, and/or executive committee.

Product manager. The product manager concept was formulated and first applied by Procter & Gamble in 1928 when it put one person in charge of managing the marketing of Camay soap. The concept, which was described briefly as an organizational strategy in Chapter 6, centers around product marketing specialists in a diversified multiproduct organization who are responsible for every aspect of the marketing effort for their product or product line. Because they are part of lower or middle management, their plans are subject to approval by senior management. They are given substantial responsibility but often limited authority, and they have to compete internally for resources—funding and such services as marketing research, advertising, and sales. What makes this unusual system work is the fact that it attracts young, driven people who become product champions, advocating their cause with great fervor. Since their own careers are directly linked to the success of their products, they have every reason to give their best.

There are four basic types of product managers, who may be responsible for one of the following: established products only, established and new products within a given product line, new products only, and a specific new product only. The first type is used when a product line is mature and represents a substantial portion of a company's business. The product manager's task, then, is maintenance marketing, for example, the careful nurturing of this profitable service with its strong positive cash flow, and its protection against competitive encroachment. The second type is assigned full responsibility for keeping a product line up-to-date. This is done by altering existing products and by recommending additions to and deletions from the product line to maintain its vitality and appropriateness in view of dynamic changes in the marketplace. Occasionally, however, the new product task is considered important enough for one person to devote full time to the creation, development, and introduction of new products—namely the third type of product manager. The final type is utilized when a specific innovation requires considerable attention because of its significance to the firm. This type, also called a project manager, is then exclusively responsible for making this particular new product an operating reality, and typically continues to manage it after takeoff.

Service firms have adopted the product manager concept with great enthusiasm and success. Product managers can be found in insurance companies, banks, airlines, real estate firms, hospitality businesses, health care establishments, and many others. They draw up and administer unique marketing programs for the offerings entrusted to them and contribute greatly to the growth of their firms because of their specialized knowledge and dedication.

New product department. An alternate form of new product organization is the new product department, which is a staff department set up specifically to ensure a steady flow of new services. Fast-food chains forever experiment with new menu items and lodging chains with new hotel/motel concepts to capture additional market segments. Marriott spent three years developing its Courtyard concept, which cuts room size and service in a suburban setting to attract $45–$65-a-night travelers. This effort was spearheaded by Marriott's vice president for market development.[5]

New product committee. A third form of new product organization employs new product committees to screen and analyze new service ideas suggested by and collected from various sources. Since such a committee, composed of members from various units within the company, serves in a reactive rather than in an active capacity, it can only be used meaningfully in combination with an appropriate driving force, such as a new product department.

Venture team. A venture team or task force is a group of people dedicated to a particular new service project, such as establishing or acquiring a discount brokerage service for a commercial bank. It is a temporary coalition of experts from within a service firm who conceptualize and bring into being a significant new service endeavor, then disband and return to their regular jobs within the organization.

Executive committee. An executive committee is a high-level new service decision-making group, usually composed of the president and the senior officers of the different functional

---

[5] Steve Swartz, "How Marriott Changes Hotel Design to Tap Midpriced Market," *The Wall Street Journal,* September 18, 1985, pp. 1, 22.

departments of a firm. While they don't get involved in operational details, the committee members collectively hold the ultimate authority to make go–no go and budget decisions, committing the company to a new direction.

STAGES OF NEW SERVICE EVOLUTION

Service firms used to be criticized for their failure to respond to buyers' needs with innovative, client-centered new service concepts. In some service industries, this was indeed true. Transportation and communication companies, for instance, once enjoyed virtual monopolies due to government regulation and/or extremely high capital requirements for market entry. In other areas, licensing procedures limited access to certain professions. Because these constraints restricted competition, they eliminated the need for innovation. But in a newly competitive environment with increasingly sophisticated and demanding buyers, a do-nothing, business-as-usual approach is a sure prescription for disaster. A year-round effort to create and introduce innovative, market-responsive services as well as update existing components of the service mix is now a competitive necessity for most service enterprises.

The internal genesis of these innovative offerings can be called *new service evolution*. This involves a process consisting of six steps as shown in Exhibit 7–1. Beginning new service evolution with a strategy formulation step, which gives it the proper direction from a long-term business perspective, is only a relatively recent but highly significant occurrence:

> The addition of this step has changed the nature of the beginning of the process. The first three steps—developing a new product strategy, generating ideas and concepts, and screening and evaluating those ideas and concepts [analysis]—are now more closely linked to each other and have become more iterative. The new product strategy development step provides a focus for the idea-generation step in that the ideas and concepts generated are developed to meet strategic objectives. In addition, screening criteria used during the screening and evaluation step are tied to the same strategic objectives.
>
> The purpose of the step to develop new product strategy is to identify the strategic business requirements that new products should satisfy. The requirements, which can be both market and company driven, determine the roles to be played by new products.

EXHIBIT 7–1   Steps in New Service Evolution

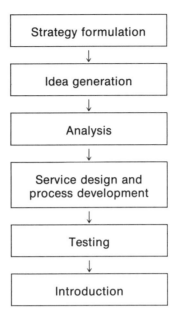

For example, over the last five years, defending a market share position and maintaining position as a product innovator were the two most common new product roles.[6]

With this essential guidance in place, a logical sequence of steps evolves, from the generation of ideas through their analysis and refinement to the ultimate introduction of a new service.

Strategy Formulation

In the past, many service firms engaged in new service development in a haphazard fashion, reacting to emergency conditions, driven by a sense of urgency to "come up with something fast." Such patchwork does not make for a solid foundation for future growth. Well-managed service businesses need to contemplate

---

[6] Booz, Allen & Hamilton Inc., *New Products Management for the 1980s* (New York: Booz, Allen & Hamilton Inc., 1982), pp. 10–11.

EXHIBIT 7–2 Strategic New Service Options

Markets / Offerings	Existing buyers	New buyers
Existing services	Share building	Market extension
New services	Line extension	New business

their corporate mission and make proactive long-term strategic decisions to give clear direction and focus to their efforts. A well-thought-out marketing strategy provides a road map or blueprint for action that prevents stopgap, knee-jerk reactions to current events in the marketplace.

Strategy options for service businesses have been discussed elsewhere in this book. They include market segmentation and careful positioning or image management.[7] In the context of this chapter, however, it is useful to highlight strategic choices by depicting the alternative directions that service firms can take in their new service efforts (see Exhibit 7–2). They can choose to pursue newness either in terms of markets or offerings or a combination of both.[8] There are accordingly four basic avenues available in this framework:

1. Sell more existing services to current buyers—a share-building strategy (also called market penetration).
2. Sell existing services to market segments not previously

---

[7] On the subject of positioning see also Al Ries and Jack Trout, *Positioning: The Battle for Your Mind* (New York: McGraw-Hill, 1981).

[8] This conceptual framework goes back to the early article by Samuel C. Johnson and Conrad Jones, "How to Organize for New Products," in *Product Strategy and Management,* ed. Thomas L. Berg and Abe Shuchman (New York: Holt, Rinehart & Winston, 1963), pp. 360–68. A similar format is used by Philip Kotler and Paul N. Bloom, *Marketing Professional Services* (Englewood Cliffs, N.J.: Prentice-Hall, 1984), p. 56. See also Aubrey Wilson, *The Marketing of Professional Services* (New York: McGraw-Hill, 1972), p. 146.

served—a market-extension strategy (also called market development).

3. Offer new services to current markets—a line-extension strategy (also called product development).
4. Offer new services to market segments not previously served—a new-business strategy (also called diversification).

Share building. Neither the services involved nor the target groups addressed are new in a share-building strategy. What may be different is a newly found aggressiveness in style, for example, a marketing tool used in a new way (e.g., discount pricing), or a marketing tool used for the first time (e.g., frequent flier club). A previously unheard-of aggressiveness in style is certainly present in the "burger battles" being fought between the fast-food giants McDonald's, Burger King, and Wendy's, or in the "accounting wars" taking place between the "big eight" public accounting firms. Discount pricing is used by commercial banks to promote brokerage services. And many professionals, from dentists to podiatrists, are beginning to advertise to attract more patients. This approach is appropriate in growing service markets but can become rather expensive and ultimately futile in mature markets where market shares have stabilized.

Market extension. A market extension strategy reaches out to new groups of buyers with a firm's current service offerings. A health insurer such as Blue Cross/Blue Shield may go beyond group plans offered through employers to individual coverage sold to self-employed persons. Or a company may choose to take its services abroad—common in banking, insurance, and airline operations. Household Finance, however, has found its consumer loan business in Japan tough going and is still struggling to establish itself after several years on the scene.

Line extension. Line extension is indicated in mature service industries where growth is not likely to come from established services. A typical example is the fast-food business where new menu items are being tinkered with on a daily basis. More broadly, the hospitality industry is forever experimenting with new restaurant and hotel designs and formats to obtain

---

EXHIBIT 7–3   Sources of New Service Ideas

Inside Sources	*Outside Sources*
Marketing	Clients
Operations	Intermediaries
New product department	Competitors
Entrepreneur	Suppliers

---

more revenues from existing markets. And credit card issuers attempt to cross-sell a variety of other services to their existing cardholder base.

New business.   The riskiest strategy by far is entry into new businesses, because a service firm has to start from scratch and cannot build on an existing clientele or service delivery system. Aetna insurance company found its venture into satellite business communications (called Satellite Business Systems, a joint venture with IBM) a disappointing experience. And in spite of the alleged synergy between airline, hotel, and car rental operations, a lot of skepticism has accompanied UAL's recent purchase of the Hertz car rental business.

Idea Generation

Ideas for new services can come from a variety of sources whose potential range is only limited by the extent of a service marketer's imagination, ingenuity, and resourcefulness. To ensure an adequate pool of ideas to choose from, it is useful both to collect existing ideas and to generate new ones. Essentially, new ideas can originate either inside or outside a service organization, as shown in Exhibit 7–3.

Inside sources.   A natural source of new service ideas is the marketing function of a service firm. It has constant front-line exposure to both competitors and customers and must be sensitive to opportunities to enhance the company's offerings and keep the service mix current. For example, sales personnel are required to file regular reports on customer comments and competitive activity. And the marketing function encompasses, of course, marketing research, which should go beyond reporting study findings to recommending appropriate action.

A second fertile spawning ground for new service ideas is a service firm's operations function (sometimes called the "back office"). To the extent that marketing and operations are indeed separable, the latter is the part that actually performs the service. Its customer contact personnel in particular—tellers in banks, flight attendants in airlines, reservations agents in hotels, maintenance crews in building service companies—interface with customers and are thus exposed to requests, complaints, and comments.

Where a new product department or new product manager has been established, it is within the explicit mission of this organizational unit to ensure a steady flow of new service ideas. These could come from its own insight and creativity or from systematically tapping other inside and outside sources. An excellent source might be the entrepreneur who founded the service enterprise in the first place. This visionary person, who turned an idea into a reality, is likely to be very creative and thus capable of thinking up additional offerings.

Outside sources. In terms of outside sources, the firm's own clients are an ideal starting point. After all, they are ultimately expected to buy any new services. They may either volunteer suggestions, such as a guest who recommends a fitness center at a hotel, or be quizzed through a marketing research study, such as an airline's in-flight questionnaire. Needless to say, the contemplation of new offerings provides an attractive opportunity to reach out to potential buyers and explore their need gaps and desires to find ways to convert them into actual buyers. In response to input received from the nonflying traveling public, for instance, several airlines have instituted fear-of-flying classes as a new service designed to overcome market resistance.

Another useful resource pool exists in the form of intermediaries involved in the distribution of a firm's services. Travel agents, for instance, interface daily with both business and pleasure travelers and are thus intimately familiar with their needs and objectives. They are also well acquainted with competitive offerings and can accordingly be very helpful in conceptualizing new service offerings. Similar circumstances exist for insurance agents and franchisees. One caveat, however: the intermediaries' interests may occasionally be different from those of the service provider or the ultimate buyer. For example, since they are paid on a commission basis, travel agents tend to favor more expensive travel arrangements, just as insurance agents may not shop aggressively for the lowest-priced coverage.

Competitors constitute a free source of new service ideas. They are vying for the same customers, and the market success or failure of their new services represents a free test of these ideas. When Bankers Trust was still in the retail banking business, it pioneered the "Miss-a-Month Loan" that permitted borrowers to skip one monthly payment per year during periods of strained liquidity (interest continued to accrue). This concept proved to be an administrative nightmare and was therefore not copied by any other bank. Conversely, every major airline now offers a frequent-flier plan. While it has been said that imitation is the sincerest form of flattery, that is hardly the motive of any service firm matching competitive programs. Still, imitation is certainly a low-cost way of coming up with new services. And such competitive imitation is not restricted to the domestic scene. International competitors might just as well be copied successfully. Madison Avenue–type advertising can be found not only in Western Europe but also in the USSR. And Master-Card and Visa credit cards are offered by European banks under franchise agreements.

Outside suppliers of services and/or equipment can also be initiators of new service processes. Vendors of computer hardware and/or software may suggest an on-line data base system for credit-reporting agencies that gives subscribers instant electronic access. Consultants or franchisors may propose new service programs that they will help install and operate. Independent real estate brokers may sign up with an organization that provides advertising, a service mark, and access to a nationwide resource pool. In view of current restrictions on the range of services that may be offered by a commercial bank, Citibank has signed an agreement with H & R Block for tax preparation services in its branches.

Resourceful service marketers can employ a number of different techniques to tap this gamut of inside and outside sources. Written means include letters received from customers and intermediaries, reports from the sales force and operations personnel, articles in trade publications, and special studies conducted by outside organizations. Personal visits overseas to observe competitive operations and carry out interviews may be helpful. But by far the most frequently used idea-generation techniques are brainstorming and focus-group interviews.

Brainstorming. Brainstorming is an idea-generating technique that utilizes group dynamics. A group of people—customers, intermediaries, executives, or salespeople—is asked to think of as many ways as possible to solve a problem or improve an existing service. No attempt is made to screen or evaluate ideas at this time in order not to stifle the creative process. Participants are encouraged to freely express any thought that comes to mind without fear of ridicule and to build on each other's suggestions. It is particularly fruitful to bring together people with diverse backgrounds and give them time to develop their thoughts and interactions. Ideally, the group would be taken to a resort hotel for several days where work sessions can be liberally interspersed with periods of fun and play without interruptions or pressures.

Focus group interviews. Focus-group interviews represent a qualitative technique that is used in exploratory marketing research. A small group of actual or potential customers participates in a roundtable discussion led by a trained moderator. With occasional reference to a checklist of areas to be explored, the moderator guides a free-flowing discussion with open-ended questions, probing for further details where appropriate. A relaxed, informal setting is provided and the session is videotaped for later review and analysis. In fact, in specially designed facilities, representatives of the sponsoring service firm may observe the session live from an adjoining room with a one-way mirror.

The management of a newly opened hotel located at La Guardia Airport in New York City used focus-group interviews to obtain input from business travelers registered at the hotel. The comments received led to a review of check-in and check-out procedures with a view toward improvement as well as the institution of shuttle bus service to John F. Kennedy Airport.

Other techniques. There are two other idea-generating tools that could prove useful in the service marketer's kit: contests and a suggestion system. A contest is a one-time effort to obtain suggestions in written form from a sizable number of people. This method is most applicable to internal audiences and requires a suitable set of rewards. A suggestion system is an ongoing year-round program that encourages employee proposals for service improvement and new services and offers awards for winning ideas. Since every employee is a potential source of better ideas, thousands of service firms have instituted suggestion systems that include review by a committee.

Analysis

Once an adequate pool of raw and unrefined ideas has been assembled, a review has to take place regarding their respective merits and potential. Although this stage in new service evolution is collectively known as analysis, it actually occurs in three distinct steps:

1. Screening—preliminary review to classify ideas.
2. Concept testing—study of buyer response to specific new service concepts.
3. Business analysis—comprehensive examination of the ramifications of surviving concepts.

Essentially, two major requirements, feasibility and profitability, have to be met for a new service to make a contribution to the firm's success. At the end of this stage, recommendations will have to be made to top management as to which projects to authorize.

Screening. The first step of *screening* is basically a weeding-out process that separates the truly promising from the less attractive ideas. Since this entails a quick and somewhat limited analysis of each idea's feasibility and merit, two types of errors may be committed:

1. The potential of a powerful idea is underestimated and it is accordingly rejected.
2. A poor idea looks deceptively attractive and is thus pursued further, wasting corporate resources.

While there are no absolute safeguards against these two potential mistakes, assigning the screening task to a committee rather than an individual brings several minds to the job instead of just one. Keeping a file of rejected ideas and periodically reviewing it may also help to discover latent potential. And a poor idea should theoretically be caught and eliminated during the later steps of concept testing or business analysis.

To make screening less judgmental and more systematic, a uniform procedure should be applied to all ideas. Beside feasibility and profitability, company and market fit of an idea have to be determined in a preliminary fashion. A checklist of criteria to be used in evaluating the merits of an idea is necessary to introduce some measure of objectivity into the process. It is a good idea to rate each idea on a simple scale with regard to each criterion. If appropriate, an overall desirability score might be computed. But care must be taken not to spend an excessive amount of time on screening. To do so would defeat the purpose of screening since it is supposed to be a quick, preliminary analysis and a comprehensive examination is to be reserved only for those ideas that survive the screening process. Typically, about a quarter of the ideas originally proposed and collected will be deemed worthy of further investigation. The overwhelming majority of ideas do not satisfy the dual requirements of feasibility and profitability and are thus eliminated from further consideration.

Concept testing. Those ideas that pass this first hurdle are exploded into full-fledged concepts for the purpose of concept testing. In contrast to a raw idea, which may have been tossed off without much further thought when the creative spark hit, a service concept is a description of a potential new service product. To be converted into a concept, an idea needs to be fleshed out operationally so that it constitutes a genuine possibility worth investigating.

Concept testing represents the presentation of new service concepts to a select sample of potential buyers for the purpose of ascertaining their reactions to them. Typically, focus-group sessions are used to carry out this kind of exploratory work. Where alternative concepts are being considered, participants will be asked to indicate their preferred choice (e.g., a checking account with a minimum balance but no fees versus a checking account with no minimum balance but a monthly service fee and check-processing charges). They will also be questioned as to what features they would like to see incorporated into the new service. Since no investment has been made as yet in designing the service and its delivery system, changes are still easy to accommodate. Even the strength of buyer attitudes and intentions can be measured at this point with a question such as the following:

If this service were available today, I would:
_____ Definitely buy it.
_____ Probably buy it.
_____ Perhaps buy it.
_____ Probably not buy it.
_____ Definitely not buy it.

While buyer intentions could, of course, change between the conceptualization and actual availability of a new service, experience has shown that concepts that do not elicit fairly strong positive answers at the concept-testing stage are not likely to succeed and should either be reformulated or abandoned.

Business analysis. After market reaction to a new service concept has thus been gauged in a preliminary fashion and been found to be sufficiently positive, a more comprehensive analysis is undertaken to definitively determine its merits from the company's point of view. What should emerge from this final portion of the analysis stage are solid recommendations to top management as to which concepts to authorize as new service development projects. In essence, the service marketer has to develop impact statements concerning the likely impact that the proposed concept will have on the operations of the firm if and when it is fully implemented and integrated into its service mix. The fixed and variable costs of both designing and delivering the new service have to be projected and related to its anticipated market and profit potential in a break-even analysis. Capacity utilization considerations, so critical in a service business, must enter into the deliberations: Will the new service utilize off-peak idle capacity or further aggravate the peak-load situation? Or will it require totally new and separate capacity? The impact on personnel in sales and operations has to be examined: Will training or new personnel be needed? Capital investment needs have to be outlined and economic payback analysis has to be performed. And, last but not least, the impact of the suggested service innovation on the firm's all-important image should be assessed very carefully. New services should enhance and capitalize on, not dilute or endanger the corporate image.

Service Design and Process Development

The process of new service evolution has now reached a critical juncture. The preceding stages of strategy formulation, idea generation, and analysis could be referred to as mental stages because they involve only the contemplation of new services, not their actual development and introduction. But now a commitment of corporate resources has to be made. Based on the recommendations formulated during business analysis, top management has to decide whether to authorize the development of several new services.

This means that a selected concept has to be turned into an operational entity, debugged and ready for sale in the marketplace. Essentially, this involves two related activities: design of the service itself and development of the supporting service delivery process and/or system.

Service design. Service design resembles the design of goods in that the components and production of a service should be carefully blueprinted and integrated. These components could be the contributions of various operating units or they may be intangible aspects versus tangible elements. The latter would be facilitating goods, such as statements to be sent to the customer or descriptive brochures, while any special support goods used represent part of the delivery mechanism. Service design also concerns itself with spelling out the precise features of the service, for example, eligibility requirements (e.g., minimum deposits for a certificate of deposit or minimum stay for an excursion fare) and price.

Service delivery process/system. Setting up a smoothly functioning process/system that consistently delivers the new service at the specified level of quality is just as important as designing the service itself. Even the most attractive service will suffer significant setbacks if it is not delivered properly and does not live up to the expectations that have been created on its behalf. Developing the delivery system for a new service involves at least four elements:

1. Designing (blueprinting) the delivery process on a step-by-step basis, outlining the contributions of different operational units.
2. Making appropriate organizational provisions to turn the new service into a functioning reality.
3. Purchasing, installing, and starting up the necessary equipment.
4. Training the affected operating personnel in the newly designed operating procedures.

It is always a good idea to go through one or more dry runs to ensure that all bugs have been eliminated and the new service delivery system functions smoothly. Another concern is to make sure that the newly installed service delivery system will be able to accommodate the anticipated initial demand. If the capacity is inadequate, cancellations and other forms of buyer backlash or even regulatory inquiries could result and the competition might have a field day capitalizing on the confusion. Merrill Lynch certainly had trouble keeping up with the demand for its Cash Management Account, which seems to have exceeded all expectations.

In cases where it is difficult to create an appropriate service delivery system in-house within a reasonable time span, it might be possible or even advisable to go outside for an appropriate solution by buying part or all of an existing service business in the new field of endeavor. This is how Bank of America came to buy the Charles Schwab discount brokerage firm. Acquisition of a successful player in an established field can be a shortcut to market entry—although potential disappointments loom large. Even mighty Citibank has not been able to parlay its Diners Club purchase into a charge card powerhouse. And Sears and Prudential have been disappointed with their acquired brokerage subsidiaries, DeanWitter and Bache.

Testing

Once the new service and its delivery system have been duly developed, tested, and refined internally, the crucial question still remains: Will the market that seemed to welcome it truly accept and support it? Thus a service firm will want to conduct additional marketing research prior to full-scale market introduction. This prelaunch testing takes place in two steps:

1. Product testing—an examination of whether the new service as currently configured meets buyer expectations.
2. Test marketing—actual marketing of the new product in a limited service area.

Provident Life and Accident Insurance Company successfully used testing to evaluate a new program.[9] Provident's retired life reserve policy was developed for the corporate market. The new policy contained, among other attractive features, provisions for the continuation of group life insurance coverage past retirement. To test the retired life reserve policy, Provident arranged meetings with selected independent agents who would be responsible for selling the new service. The agents provided valuable input that resulted in technical changes. Also, the testing informed key agents about the new service prior to its introduction, which helped get Provident's new policy off to a fast start.

Product testing. The purpose of product testing is to ascertain performance and preference. This is relatively easy to do in a goods environment. Using the typical blind pair comparison format, a representative sample of consumers is given both the new product and its leading competitor in neutral packages. Panelists are asked to try both products and then report which one they liked better and why. In a service setting, product testing is more difficult to accomplish. For instance, in order to discern consumer reaction to a new gold credit card, a bank could ask a sample representing the target market to compare its price (annual fee and interest rate) and benefit package with those of competing cards. But this approach differs little from concept testing and omits both the experiential and operational aspects of the new service. It could be quite costly and time-consuming, however, to let customers try the actual service because this would require putting the entire delivery mechanism in place full-scale. If a service firm is willing to make this kind of commitment and investment, its management usually perceives little difference between launching the new service full-scale and giving it a dry run on a limited basis, and frequently opts for full-scale introduction instead.

---

[9] John K. Witherspoon, "Testing Insures Success for Provident Life," *Sales & Marketing Management,* March 16, 1981, pp. 74–76.

When a service firm bypasses product testing, "actual market introduction is often the first real test of functionality and market acceptance. By that point, mistakes in design are harder to correct and service modifications needed to improve acceptance or operating efficiency are more laborious to implement. There is simply no substitute for a proper rehearsal."[10] This is precisely what a product test is all about. By gauging market reaction to the new service both in terms of perceived performance characteristics and preference ranking vis-à-vis competitive offerings, a service marketer gains a valuable opportunity to refine either the service or its delivery system before introducing it to the entire service area and putting the firm's reputation on the line.

Product tests are common in the fast-food business where consumers are invited into test kitchens to taste test new menu items. They are asked to indicate their favorite choice from a variety of alternative recipes, and explain the reasons why they selected this product over similar ones. This enables finalization of the ingredient mix (or mixes if several variants are to be offered, such as the alternative sauces with Chicken McNuggets at McDonald's). Other services with less tangible components may actually have to be delivered to a sample group for some time before any meaningful feedback can be obtained. Because salability is not a key consideration at this point, product test participants usually obtain the service for free for the duration of the test. And sometimes a service is simply not amenable to product testing at all. A new insurance policy, for instance, is so abstract that it cannot be product tested (although it can be concept tested and test marketed).

Test marketing. Provided that the readings are good during product testing or appropriate changes have been made, test marketing can then be used to measure the sales response of the market. This involves actually offering the new service for sale in a limited number of locations, such as individual branches/outlets or all of a firm's facilities in a given city. Essentially, test

---

[10] G. Lynn Shostack, "Service Design in the Operating Environment," in *Developing New Services,* ed. William R. George and Claudia E. Marshall, p. 35.

marketing means trying out the new service's marketing mix on a limited scale to contain risk and to make final improvements.

There are two significant dangers associated with test marketing:

1. Test marketing costs time and money—expenses that could be eliminated altogether by skipping this step.
2. If security has been tight, test marketing will now alert the competition to the innovation and enable competitors to jump in, possibly before the original new service has gone full scale, thus reducing lead time in securing market share.

These dangers have encouraged many firms to avoid test marketing and instead roll out the new service full scale.

But beside merely testing market reaction to one marketing mix for a particular new service, test marketing permits the examination of several alternative marketing mixes. Subscription solicitations for new magazines, for instance, are routinely tested in different packages, combining different rates with different incentives, in order to identify the most powerful combination. Credit card solicitations may test different mailing packages or a waiver of first-year fees versus a full-price offer.

To be truly meaningful, however, the sales results from alternative approaches ought to be augmented by buyer interviews in order to obtain awareness levels, attitudes, buying reasons, and intentions. This clearly makes the process considerably more expensive and time-consuming, but it elevates test marketing above the level of a mere sales test. Sales results, taken by themselves, can be quite deceiving because initial enthusiasm can be followed by disillusionment and abandonment.

Again, fast-food companies find it worth their while to test market new menu items in limited market areas before going national. And, time and again, they find that what drew raves in the test kitchen quickly fizzles in the heat of the competitive battle. Promising product test results are a necessary but not sufficient prerequisite for market success. And a new service that dies in test marketing is better buried before it incurs further expenses.

Introduction

The final stage of new service evolution is market introduction. Very few new services make it to this point, passing all prior hurdles and in particular emerging successfully from test marketing. Introduction means roll-out to the entire customer base and service area, be it local, regional, national, or even international. This may require substantial expenditures for advertising and/or other forms of promotion, but a successful new service will mean a substantial contribution to the company's bottom line for some time to come. The marketing mix that proved the winning combination in the test marketing phase is now applied full-scale to realize the sales and profit targets formulated in the analysis stage.

SUMMARY

New services are the fuel of growth for expansion-minded service enterprises. They have to be developed continuously, following a logical, demanding evolutionary process that helps weed out losers and streamline winners. Without a steady flow of new services, a firm facing aggressive competition is not likely to survive over the long run, far less grow. With a healthy progression of service innovations in the pipeline, however, a service business faces a very promising future indeed.

CHAPTER 8

Service Advertising

As a component of a service firm's marketing mix, *promotion* involves the firm's efforts to communicate with its customers and other relevant audiences. These activities are designed to inform actual and potential buyers about the company's offerings and to stimulate demand for them. Because of their significance to the success of many service businesses' marketing efforts, the management and use of a variety of promotional approaches and techniques will be discussed in some detail in this and the following two chapters.

PROMOTION OF SERVICES

In today's competitive environment, promotion is a vital marketing activity for service firms. Because services are largely intangible, buyers often find it quite difficult to fully comprehend the features and benefits of a particular service, evaluate its ability to satisfy their needs, and distinguish it from the offerings of other service providers. The latter is often true even after purchase and/or consumption of a service. For lack of adequate information about alternatives, hotel guests, for instance, will frequently be unable to determine whether they have chosen the hotel best suited to their needs, whether they have received the best room available, and whether they are being charged the best possible rate. Insurance policy holders are often equally uncertain as to whether they have proper coverage at the best possible premium, and home buyers face such a bewildering array of choices that there are now computerized advisory services available that assist them in selecting the mortgage package that is best for their particular situation.

In view of this uncertainty, it is essential that a firm's promotional messages create and maintain a strong, distinctive image of the company as well as emphasize individual service features and benefits. It is, accordingly, a key purpose of promotion to differentiate a service firm's offerings from those of competitors—in other words, create a difference in buyers' minds.

Goals of Service Promotion

The three major goals of promotion are to inform, to persuade, and to remind buyers about a service business and its services.

1. *Information.* As a form of communication, promotion informs potential buyers about a company's services and capabilities. Because of the uncertainty experienced by prospects and the experiential, intangible nature of services that typically prevents prior examination, service buyers' need for information is heightened in comparison to goods purchasers. Disseminating appropriate information throughout a target market is especially important for new services and companies. For example, professionals will place advertisements in local newspapers to introduce themselves when they open a practice in a community. They will also use indirect promotional techniques, such as speaking to civic groups and community organizations, to make the public aware of the availability of their services.

2. *Persuasion.* A prime thrust of promotion is trying to influence a select target group to take an action—purchase a life insurance policy, open a checking account, use the telephone business directory, or attend a word processing training school—that will have beneficial effects for the company. Through persuasion, a service firm is attempting to get a prospect to decide in its favor. For example, The Travelers ran an advertisement emphasizing that more than half a million people have stayed with this

insurance company for more than 25 years, summing up with the slogan, "Fairness is good business."

3. *Reminder.* Promotion is often used to maintain a service's or seller's position in the marketplace. In a competitive environment, this is quite important for established service companies and offerings to protect them against erosion. For example, United Air Lines keeps reminding consumers to "fly the friendly skies of United" and a local bank sponsors a Little League baseball team.

Exhibit 8–1 highlights the three goals of service promotion and their impact on both buyer and seller.

The Promotion Mix

The four major types of promotional tools are advertising, personal selling, sales promotion, and public relations. All of these activities are used by service businesses in their efforts to inform, persuade, and remind buyers about their offerings. The combination of these elements is known as the promotion mix. It is described in more detail in Exhibit 8–2.

A key promotion mix decision for a service business is whether to emphasize advertising or personal selling. The choice depends largely on the service firm's marketing goals, its resources and organization, buyer characteristics, the features of the firm's services, and the nature of the decisions made with regard to the other elements of the marketing mix. However, unlike for many goods, the needs and demands of service buyers typically require that personal contact play an important part in the promotion mix for most services. Two factors that determine the importance of personal selling are the cost of the service and whether it is a consumer, industrial, or professional service. Personal selling is the dominant component of the promotion mix for relatively expensive consumer services such as insurance, housing, and health care. For relatively inexpensive, frequently purchased consumer services, such as telecommunications and electricity, advertising is more important than personal selling.

For industrial and professional services, personal selling is the key element of the promotion mix. Unlike the purchase of many industrial products, the purchase of an industrial or professional service involves extensive personal interaction be-

---

EXHIBIT 8–1 Goals of Promotional Activities

Goal	*Definition*	*Benefits*
To Inform	Provides knowledge of the existence of a particular service and its characteristics.	Introduces new services and/or new providers in a community.
Examples:	1. A physician or a lawyer may announce the opening of a new practice via ads in local newspapers. 2. Fast-food chains introduce new menu items via television and newspaper ads, coupons, and banners.	
To Persuade	Stimulates action or elicits a response, turning potential consumers into active consumers.	Directs action toward a type of service and/or a particular provider.
Examples:	1. With the advent of deregulation in financial services, commercial banks and savings institutions have increased their advertising budgets, expanded their use of consumer premiums, and initiated sales training programs for their employees, who represent the bank to the public. 2. MCI and GTE Sprint are now attempting to persuade consumers to utilize their long-distance telephone services, rather than those offered by AT&T Communications.	
To Remind	Keeps the name of a particular service or provider fresh in the minds of consumers.	Important for infrequently used services or those that may be taken for granted by consumers.
Examples:	1. The local gardener who maintains the area in front of the town hall has increased his business significantly. 2. NYNEX bus poster advertisements in New York stress that their service is "always there when you need it." Ads feature a young boy perched atop a copy of the Yellow Pages so that he can reach the dinner table.	

---

tween seller and customer personnel. An unpleasant or incompetent goods salesperson may be ignored because the only customer contact occurs at the time of the sale and the product can stand on its own merits. In the case of industrial and professional services, however, the service salesperson is also often the performer, requiring the establishment of a strong bond of trust.

As this discussion indicates, one element of the promotion mix will generally be dominant. The other elements can then be

EXHIBIT 8–2   The Promotion Mix

Element	Definition	Purpose	Area of Use	Examples
Advertising	Paid form of nonpersonal presentation and promotion of services and ideas by an identified sponsor.	To create an awareness of the service and its supplier, and to stimulate desire.	Inexpensive, frequently purchased consumer services.	TV and radio commercials, direct mail, billboards, newspaper and magazine advertisements.
Personal selling	Oral presentation, usually face-to-face with a potential buyer, intended to make a sale.	To present services and to secure a commitment from the customer.	Relatively expensive, infrequently purchased consumer services; industrial and professional services.	Presentation by a life insurance agent; account opened by bank officer; ticket sale by airline agent.
Public relations	Activities that create a favorable impression of the service firm, its employees and its services not directly paid for by the sponsor.	To create awareness and a positive image.	Concerts, sporting events, and other forms of entertainment; also reinforces the image gained through advertising, personal selling, and other promotional activities.	Newspaper article about a new service; sponsorship of college scholarship; and tour of the facilities.
Sales promotion	All other efforts designed to stimulate buyers that are not classified as advertising, personal selling, or public relations.	To provide direct incentives for prompt buyer action.	Consumer services of the convenience variety; generally reinforces advertising at point-of-purchase to stimulate direct action.	Premiums, contests, trading stamps, and point-of-purchase displays.

used by the service marketer, as needed, to round out and strengthen the promotional thrust. For example, a campaign to promote the use of various auto maintenance services may be supported by discount coupons for these services by auto dealers. Similarly, personal selling of life insurance has to be reinforced by promotional materials such as brochures or flyers or by public relations activities designed to enhance the company's image. Whatever the situation, it is essential that the promotional tools be used in concert to achieve the firm's marketing goals. The service marketer must have overall responsibility for the company's promotion mix so that the individual elements are governed by the same goals and do not conflict with each other. When salespeople are not properly informed about the company's current advertising theme and approach, for instance, they cannot build on the advertising message in their presentations. Likewise, special sales promotions, such as premiums, contests, and coupons, will not be effective unless they receive adequate support from advertising and personal selling.

The experience of a savings and loan association with a program to increase its savings deposits illustrates the difficulties that occur when a promotion mix is not well coordinated. The savings and loan association's marketing department developed a hard-hitting advertising campaign that featured special financial incentives for customers opening a new savings account or adding to an existing account. Unfortunately, tellers and customer service representatives were not sufficiently informed about the special promotion. When customers tried to take advantage of the offer, they were met with confusion and doubt. The promotion effort failed.

In contrast, Exhibit 8–3 maps out a cohesive promotional program for a savings and loan association. The following aspects should be noted with regard to this exhibit.

1. The corporate mission or goal determines the nature of the promotional message.
2. The primary promotional tool, advertising, is intended to provide an informative and persuasive message to the greatest number of people as efficiently and effectively as possible.
3. Advertising is reinforced by:

EXHIBIT 8–3 Attracting New Depositors to a Savings and Loan
Association

---

1. Corporate mission: Provide consumer financial services; attract and maintain a large number of depositors; increase number and amount of deposits; provide financial services to meet consumer needs.
2. Promotional message: The institution's wide range of financial services will satisfy the consumer's needs more effectively and efficiently than any competitive institution.
3. Determination of primary promotional tool:
   Options: a. *Advertising (brochures, flyers).* Reaches large target audience. Communicates relevant information concerning available financial services.
               b. *Personal selling (customer service representatives meet one-to-one or in small groups with consumers).* Provides information and immediate answers to questions. Reaches smaller consumer base.
               c. *Public relations (sponsorship of local marathon or a neighborhood clean-up).* Since financial services are relatively complex, must rely on public relations activities merely to reinforce other efforts.
               d. *Sales promotion (raffle for new depositors).* Generates interest and excitement but will not, by itself, yield desired consumer response.
   Selection: *Advertising.* Will provide the most effective and cost-efficient manner of reaching the target audience.
4. Reinforcement through secondary promotional tools: Personal selling informs and persuades; public relations informs and reminds; and sales promotion provides that "extra ounce" of persuasion.

---

    a. The efforts of customer service personnel who speak with knowledge and enthusiasm about the program.

    b. Sponsorship of a local marathon or a neighborhood clean-up campaign.

    c. The use of a raffle to generate greater consumer awareness and involvement.

  4. The coordination of all these efforts into a unified program, complete with staff briefings and incentives, combines all the purposes of promotional activities. The program provides information, encourages action, and keeps the institution's name fresh in the minds of consumers.

ADVERTISING FOR SERVICE BUSINESSES

Within the context of the promotion mix, advertising is the primary form of nonpersonal promotion used to inform, persuade, and remind buyers of a service organization and its services. Utilizing mass media to present standardized promotional messages to large audiences, advertising has over the years steadily grown in importance as part of the service marketing and, more specifically, promotion mix.

In principle, the advertising of services is similar to the advertising for goods. The advertising objectives, tools, and media are the same, and like large goods manufacturers, national service firms are among the leading advertisers in the United States. The 15 largest service advertisers spend in excess of $2 billion a year to promote their offerings. In 1984, Edison Electric, the trade association that represents more than 180 electric utilities, launched a $6.5 million advertising campaign to promote the use of electricity.

Advertising Intangibles

The characteristics of services pose some unique challenges to service advertisers. G. Lynn Shostack described the difficulties associated with service intangibility as follows:

> To create a service "reality" that will stay in the consumer's mind, marketers must work against the media's capacity to abstract. Since a service is *already* abstract, marketers must strive to establish tangible representations for it. The worst mistake is to compound abstractions with more abstractions. Advertisements for investment management often exhibit this tendency, through copy emphasis on "sound analysis," "careful monitoring," "strong backup," and other such abstractions. It is a technique that stems directly from product marketing, in which abstractions play a vital role in creating image. For services, an opposite tack must be taken.[1]

As this quote indicates, many goods advertisers turn to abstractions in an effort to attract consumers. Recent commercials for Calvin Klein jeans and Diet Pepsi illustrate this trend. Such

---

[1] G. Lynn Shostack, "Is Service Marketing the Right Way?" *Trusts & Estates,* November 1977, p. 722.

EXHIBIT 8–4 Making Intangible Services More Concrete

Service	Problem Area	"Concretizing" Service Marketing Efforts
Insurance	Technical terms and policies make it difficult for consumers to understand their costs and benefits.	These symbols convey an image of safety or security: Allstate: "Good Hands" Hartford: Stag Travelers: Umbrella Nationwide: Blanket Prudential: "A piece of the rock" Continental: Soldier
Banking transactions through automated teller machines (ATMs)	Many consumers are skeptical of ATMs and afraid of computer error; many also resent lack of personal attention and service	Many banks have "named" their automated system, often with the help of consumers, to convey a more personalized approach to banking. For example, Old Stone Bank in Rhode Island calls its ATM "Ready Freddy," a name derived from the cartoon character Fred Flintstone, which the bank uses as its symbol.
Air transportation	Many different carriers provide the same basic service between two points.	United: "The Friendly Skies" Delta: "Ready when you are" American: "Fly the American Way" Eastern: "We earn our wings every day"
Radio broadcasting	The abundance of competing stations in large metropolitan areas makes it essential that providers differentiate their intangible service offerings.	Station call letters, slogans, or commercials are designed to reinforce the station's image Examples: "Where rock lives," "All news— all the time."

---

commercials are designed to create an appealing mood or image rather than merely proclaiming the specific merits of the good being offered. Service advertisers must employ the opposite approach. Rather than creating an abstraction from a tangible product, they must attempt to make an intangible service appear more concrete so that it will become more "real" to potential buyers. Consider the examples outlined in Exhibit 8–4. As these examples illustrate, service marketers must attempt to create imaginative advertising that relates a service to buyers' needs. For example, borrowers do not really buy loans from a bank or finance company. Rather, they buy the home, the car, the college education, or the vacation that the loan will finance. Consequently, advertisements for consumer loans should feature these benefits of borrowing money.

Differentiating Service Offerings

A key task of service advertising is to create a difference in buyers' minds. This is particularly challenging because to many buyers, all savings accounts, homeowners' policies, and airline flights are indistinguishably alike. Advertising can be a powerful tool in making buyers perceive that a particular firm's services are different from those offered by other providers.

Lacking tangible aspects to distinguish their offerings, an increasing number of service providers have resorted to celebrities as spokespersons to imbue their services with some measure of uniqueness. These celebrities are usually either well-known actors or sports personalities who can give a service a certain distinctiveness due to their own popularity and image. When Bowery Savings Bank of New York conducted a survey to identify the best-liked New Yorker, Joe DiMaggio of baseball fame emerged as the winner. The bank subsequently retained his services as its advertising spokesperson because of his personal likability and credibility—even though he could not claim recognized financial expertise. In a similar vein, their easy recognizability led to the use of Eli Wallach by Emigrant Savings Bank in New York, John Houseman by Smith, Barney, Cliff Robertson by AT&T, and O. J. Simpson by Hertz ("the Superstar in Rent-A-Car").

Occasionally, there is an implied or actual relationship between the use of a particular celebrity and the nature of the service offered. After playing the role of a detective in a popular television series, Karl Malden was featured in advertisements for American Express Company Traveler's Checks to allude to the possibility of loss through theft and reassure buyers that they were protected in such an event. And Marlin Perkins of the long-running television series "Wild Kingdom," sponsored by Mutual of Omaha, advertised its cancer policy after battling the disease himself.

In several instances, rather than choosing well-known personalities from the worlds of sports or entertainment, companies have chosen to feature their own chairpersons in advertisements. Some service firms have also followed this approach. Gravely voiced Tom Carvel, founder of Carvel Ice Cream Stores, has always intoned his chain's radio and television commercials, although he has rarely appeared in them. David Mahoney, then chairman of the parent company Norton Simon, appeared in print advertisements for Avis, Inc. And former astronaut Frank Borman seemed a natural choice to speak for Eastern Air Lines.

In a few cases, fictitious persons or even animals are chosen or created to represent a major service firm. The clown Ronald McDonald, although not a real person, has become a favorite not only in the United States but also overseas, as the following quote indicates:

> Ronald McDonald was used first in Washington, D.C., in 1963. He went national in 1967 and made his first international TV appearance in 1969. Today, Ronald speaks a dozen languages including Chinese, Dutch, French, German, Gaelic, Japanese, Papiemento, Portuguese, and Swedish. A clown seems to be popular everywhere and Ronald may be the best known character since Santa Claus. Ronald not only opens stores but is a goodwill ambassador who visits hospitals and raises funds for children. In Australia, for example, there is a Ronald McDonald House affiliated with the largest children's hospital. Some international changes: in Japan, he is known as "Donald McDonald" to avoid the difficult R sound. In Hong Kong, he is known as McDonlo–Suk Suk or "Uncle McDonald."[2]

In other cases, a service firm may use an already well-known and liked character to represent it. For example, Metropolitan Life features Charlie Brown, Snoopy, and the other "Peanuts" characters in TV and print advertisements to extol the range of its insurance and other financial services.

Positioning: Creating an Identity

As discussed in Chapter 3, a differential advantage is the "something extra" that makes a company and its services unique, or a

---

[2] Vern Terpstra, *International Marketing,* 3rd ed. (Hinsdale, Ill.: Dryden Press, 1983), p. 437.

little better than those of its competitors. In many instances, the differential advantage for a service is an image, or identity, that results from buyers' perceptions of the service and its provider. Many service companies build on buyers' perceptions and try to create or reinforce a differential advantage through the use of promotional activities. This promotional strategy is known as positioning.

As the leading proponents of this approach to marketing communication have described it, "Positioning is what you do to the mind of the prospect."[3] Through advertising and other forms of promotion, a service is presented in such a way that buyers perceive it as unique or different. To put it another way, positioning is the service firm's creation of a clear, carefully formulated identity that conveys to its customers and the general public what that service business is and why it should be supported.

Ries and Trout describe a number of case histories involving positioning of services. To introduce its electronic mail service, known as the Mailgram, Western Union test marketed several promotional strategies. Research findings suggested that a strategy which highlighted the low cost of the Mailgram was the most effective. Therefore, all advertisements for the Mailgram were built around the positioning theme, "Impact of a Telegram at a fraction of the cost." Another example showed how the Long Island Trust Company used marketing research to assess its strengths and weaknesses. This research led to an advertising campaign that positioned Long Island Trust as the "Long Island Bank for Long Islanders."[4]

There have been many other examples of the successful use of advertising to position a service. One of the best known and most successful was the Avis campaign based on the slogan, "We're No. 2, we try harder." This advertising approach made a clear distinction between Hertz, the industry leader, and Avis, the underdog.

As these examples suggest, the best positioning strategy is one that highlights a clear-cut, straightforward distinction be-

---

[3] Al Ries and Jack Trout, *Positioning: The Battle for Your Mind* (New York: McGraw-Hill, 1981), p. 3.

[4] Ibid., pp. 183–98.

tween a service business and its competitors. Two other key guidelines for successful positioning can be noted from these examples. First, marketing research is needed to identify the advertising theme that must be highlighted to position the service. Second, positioning works only if a service business does what it says it does. For instance, if personal attention is emphasized, the service firm's personnel must be trained and motivated to provide the personal attention.

Promoting Nonpeak Demand

Another concern for service advertisers involves the frequent need to encourage demand during nonpeak periods in order to level out the load factor. Labor-intensive service firms and those with high fixed costs pursue dual objectives with such promotions, in order:

- To deflect demand from peak periods so as not to overtax the system.
- To increase usage during low-volume periods.

Promotion of nonpeak demand may stress the introduction of new services, such as breakfast items at fast-food chains or summer attractions (Alpine slides, for example) at traditional ski areas. It may also emphasize price discounts, such as lower telephone rates on weekends or off-season rates at resort hotels. Advertising can be used to inform peak-time buyers about the existence of nonpeak advantages, to persuade them to utilize these services at those times, and to remind them of the more advantageous time periods.

Promoting "Unsought" Services

Some health care, repair, and other emergency services will not be actively sought by consumers, except in times of sickness or trouble. Promoting these services, then, requires a different approach. Two guidelines should prove helpful to the service marketing manager in this situation. First, advertising should stress the in-being nature of these services, that is, the fact that this particular service provider has the capacity and capability in place to respond swiftly and competently to emergency needs, frequently at any hour. For example, commercials for Roto-

Rooter Sewer Service show a uniformed serviceman responding promptly to a nighttime call.

Second, advertising for such services might attempt to persuade prospective buyers to purchase preventive or maintenance care now in order to avoid potentially serious problems later. Oil furnace service contracts provide for annual checkup and cleaning to prevent breakdowns. Health maintenance organizations encourage their members to avail themselves of prepaid periodic consultations in order to enable early detection of emerging health problems and to maintain good health continuously.

Advertising for Professional Services

In 1977, the United States Supreme Court ruled that a state bar association could no longer prohibit advertising by attorneys. This landmark ruling, as well as actions taken by the Federal Trade Commission to remove bans against advertising by physicians and accountants, opened the door for professionals to advertise and promote their services. Although change is slow in coming because of traditional attitudes against soliciting clients, advertising has become an increasingly important marketing activity for attorneys, physicians, dentists, engineers, accountants, and other professionals. Consider the following case histories.

> The San Francisco CPA firm of Siegel, Sugarman, and Seput attributes its phenomenal growth exclusively to advertising. Started in 1977 by three partners with annual billings of $8,000, it grew in four years to 27 employees and annual volume of $1.75 million. Its advertising budget in 1981 was $100,000.[5]

> A civil engineering firm ran full-page advertisements in *Coal Age* and other coal industry publications. Over a five-year period, it was able to attract $5 million in billings from new clients acquired in this fashion.[6]

> Legal clinics rely heavily on advertising to attract clients to

---

[5] Ellen Terry Kesster, "Advertising Accounting Services: How Effective Has It Been?" *Practical Accountant*, July 1981, p. 40.

[6] Bergen F. Newell, "Advertising Strikes a New Vein," *Magazine Age*, December 1982, pp. 60–63.

their storefront offices. Jacoby & Meyers expanded from 7 to 22 offices within one year after the 1977 Supreme Court decision through the use of television commercials. Today, the company has 140 offices in six states, vigorously competing with Hyatt Legal Services (161 offices in 20 states and the District of Columbia).[7]

In another trailblazing decision, the United States Supreme Court ruled in 1985 that a state may not ban nondeceptive advertisements, even when an attorney is soliciting clients with very specific legal problems.

Columbus lawyer Philip Zauderer had been reprimanded by the Ohio Supreme Court for placing a series of modest newspaper ads in 1982 that showed a line drawing of the Dalkon Shield IUD. Zauderer's text said the device was alleged to have caused injuries and other health problems for women and suggested that victims could still sue, even though the device had been off the market for years. Zauderer eventually filed lawsuits for 106 women who read the ads.[8]

According to the American Bar Association, some 14 percent of the nation's 600,000 lawyers have tried advertising. Of these, 82 percent have been pleased with the results of their advertising efforts and plan to continue them.[9]

Nonetheless, as the above examples show, considerable controversy continues to surround advertising by professionals. Common arguments for and against professional service advertising are presented in Exhibit 8–5.

As more professional service firms begin to advertise, they are finding that a tasteful advertising program consistent with the firm's reputation can enhance its image and contribute to increased business volume. As competition among service providers continues to intensify, and as advertising becomes more widely accepted, more and more professional service organizations will turn to advertising to help build and retain a solid client base in uncertain times.

---

[7] *Target Selling,* a brochure distributed by the Television Bureau of Advertising; and Michael S. Serrill, "Less Dignity, More Hustle," *Time,* June 10, 1985, p. 67.

[8] Ibid., p. 66.

[9] "Lawyers Learn the Hard Sell—And Companies Shudder," *Business Week,* June 10, 1985, pp. 70–71.

EXHIBIT 8–5   Some Pros and Cons of Professional Service Advertising

---

Arguments in Favor

1. Strong professional associations and codes of ethics will prevent deceptive advertising.
2. Areas of specialty, professional fees, and other necessary information will be mentioned in the ads, thus simplifying the buyer's decision-making process.
3. Quality levels will have to be maintained to attract and retain clients.
4. Fees may actually be lower where there is advertising. In the legal field in 1982, for example, rates for simple procedures in cities where ads were more freely allowed were 5 percent to eleven percent lower (although it was not necessarily true that these lower costs were provided by the firms that advertised).
5. Television advertising makes people, especially blue-collar workers, feel more comfortable about approaching a firm to represent their case. One Miami legal firm, for example, spent $3 million in advertising annually, and got back eight times that much in resulting fees.

Arguments Against

1. Advertising and other forms of direct promotion violate professional ethics.
2. If not adequately policed, some professional service advertisers could practice deceptive advertising, misleading and misinforming those consumers who can least afford to make a mistake.
3. Costs of advertising will be passed on to consumers in the form of higher fees.
4. If advertising succeeds in attracting too many consumers, the quality of service offered to each will deteriorate.
5. Advertising could cause consumers to buy services that they do not need.

ADVERTISING MANAGEMENT

The creation and management of advertising programs are complex, highly specialized tasks. Service advertisers need to perform the same basic activities that goods advertisers carry out. These activities include organizing for advertising, developing an advertising campaign, selecting media, budgeting, and measuring the effectiveness of advertising.

Organizing for Advertising

Usually, important strategy and budgeting decisions for service advertising are made by top marketing executives. However, the actual creation, placing, and daily managing of advertising are tasks that are commonly assigned to others. Nationwide service companies have advertising departments that plan and coordinate advertising programs. In small retail service firms, such as dry cleaning establishments or automobile repair shops, the owner or a designated employee often handles all aspects of advertising within the firm.

Many service companies hire advertising agencies, which are themselves specialized business service firms, to create and place advertisements in appropriate media, provide marketing research, and supply related services such as sales promotion and public relations. If the budget is large enough, the agency will work largely for a percentage of advertising expenditures— typically 15 percent which it collects from the media in the form of an agency discount. As an example, according to the Television Bureau of Advertising, five leading fast-food chains spent the following amounts (in millions) on television advertising in 1984:

McDonald's	$254
Burger King	129
Wendy's	74
Kentucky Fried Chicken	63
Pizza Hut	58

The selection of an advertising agency is a key service marketing decision. Although the firm's management provides overall direction, the agency will be largely responsible for developing and presenting the firm's image to the target market. Service marketing executives have to decide what they want from an agency and then select one that provides the needed services and expertise. In addition, before choosing an agency, the service marketer should carefully evaluate the agency's personnel because they will work closely with the service company's marketing staff. The talent, experience, and "chemistry" have to be right to permit a viable match.

Developing an Advertising Campaign

A service company's advertising department, or its agency, will develop an advertising campaign to achieve the company's advertising objectives. A campaign is a carefully planned, coordinated sequence of advertisements, designed to present a basic strategy or theme in a select group of media. Each advertisement must present a message that is consistent with the campaign's overall strategy. For example, the unifying theme, "Don't leave home without it," is used in all American Express Card advertisements, both domestically and overseas.

The establishment of advertising objectives is fundamental to the success of an ad campaign. These objectives must be consistent with the firm's marketing goals and must focus on the target market. The more specific the advertising objectives, the more effectively the ad campaign will be able to appeal to the specific needs of the target buyers. In advertising its trust management services, for example, a bank will focus on persons with wealth or high income potential rather than the general public, since it is to these more affluent buyers that the service is targeted. Similarly, an auto transmission repair service may target a campaign to owners of late-model foreign cars, rather than to all car owners.

The difficulties of advertising intangible services have already been discussed. In order for any advertising campaign to be successful, efforts must be made to overcome these problems. Three strategies for accomplishing this goal are to personalize the service, to create a positive image, and to demonstrate real benefits.

1. *Personalize the service.* This strategy uses employees, celebrities, and satisfied consumers to convey the advertising message while also providing the "personal touch" so often desired by service buyers. Rather than being perceived as an abstract entity, the service becomes concrete through its association with people who have had some degree of experience with the service. This strategy is outlined in Exhibit 8–6.
2. *Create a positive image.* We have already explained the use of advertising to achieve a positive image that provides identity and differentiation for a service business. Institutional advertising promotes a concept, idea, im-

---

EXHIBIT 8–6 Overcoming Advertising Difficulties: Personalizing the Service

---

Strategy	Benefits	Examples
Use of employees in ads	1. Portrays the service firm as a warm and friendly institution that provides courteous and efficient service. 2. Increases the employees' sense of belonging with the company, thus encouraging them to maintain the level of service suggested by the ads.	Often used by airlines, banks, and even fast-food chains to reinforce the image of courtesy, friendliness, efficiency, competence, and professionalism.
Celebrity advertising	1. Allows consumers to associate a well-known personality with a service offering, thus increasing the attractiveness of the service. 2. Provides a credible testimonial to the service firm's effectiveness, especially if the celebrity has a natural or perceived connection with the service being offered.	Karl Malden, among others, for American Express, O. J. Simpson for Hertz, Joe DiMaggio for the Bowery Savings Bank.
Reference group advertising— the use of satisfied customers	Increases the desirability of the service offering to new or potential consumers.	1. Satisfied customers may be asked to recommend the service to friends, or to distribute flyers, leaflets, or brochures to these friends. 2. Ad campaigns are targeted toward opinion leaders.

---

pression, or philosophy of a service company. Unlike other forms of advertising, institutional advertising is directed at people who are not necessarily potential customers. Anyone who may have an impact on the advertiser, such as legislators, stockholders, labor leaders, or the general public, may be the target of institutional advertising.

Institutional advertising for such service businesses as banks, airlines, and insurance companies stresses efficiency, progressiveness, friendliness, competence, security, good corporate citizenship, and similar positive qualities. For instance, in the airline industry, American advertises that it is the airline for business travelers; Delta is "ready when you are"; and United flies the "friendly skies." Frequently, a slogan or symbol provides the integrating element for image-creating advertising. For example, insurance buyers may "get a piece of the (Prudential's) rock," put themselves in the "good hands" of Allstate, or be protected by Travelers' umbrella or Nationwide's blanket.

3. *Show real benefits.* Another way to compensate for the abstract nature of services is to demonstrate the benefits of the service purchase to buyers. Someone who buys an insurance policy is really purchasing the peace of mind the policy may provide; those who buy home care services are buying convenience; the purchase of legal services buys professional advice and counsel. The use of these and similar themes in ad campaigns helps to demonstrate real benefits, not abstractions, to potential buyers.

Federal Express has enjoyed great success using this strategy. On its initial night of operation in 1973, it handled eight packages. During the first full year of operation, it handled only 1.1 million packages and lost $1 million a month. By fiscal 1984, sales volume had increased to $1 billion, with a package count of 75 million. The positive image of reliability and good humor created by television ads is only part of the picture. The more significant impact results from a shift in media focus from the system itself to the consumer. Ads stress the real benefits that harried businesspeople and other anxious customers can derive when it "absolutely, positively has to be there overnight"—and it arrives on time. The "how" is relatively unimportant to the buyer. The main focus is on the successful bid, the wonderful idea, or the important document that reaches its intended destination in a timely manner.[10]

---

[10] "Shift to Consumer-Targeted Ads Launched Federal's Profit Flight," *Marketing News,* July 5, 1985, pp. 10, 12.

Comparative advertising is being used with increasing frequency to demonstrate the relative benefits of one service firm's offering over those of its competitors. Airlines may cite the greater number and more convenient times of flights; a savings institution promotes higher interest rates and longer banking hours; and a restaurant announces a more extensive menu and its highly trained chefs.

Message and Media Selection

Once the advertising objectives have been determined, the service advertiser must focus on the development of an appropriate message to be presented through selected media. Careful message formulation is critical if it is to have the intended effect on the target audience. The advertising message must flow smoothly from the advertising objectives.

As noted in Exhibit 8–7, the message identification may be based on interaction with members of the target market, or on brainstorming sessions with company personnel, or both. Messages can utilize either rational, emotional, or ethical appeals.

Advertising media provide the channels or vehicles for carrying the advertising message to the intended audience. Selecting the proper media mix is a crucial advertising decision because poor media selection is costly in terms of money wasted and sales opportunities lost. Service advertisers should try to choose media that reach the largest number of potential customers with the desired frequency and impact at the lowest possible cost per thousand prospects reached.

The media selection process begins with the identification of the target market, or the desired audience for the advertising message. Then the service marketer or the advertising agency selects the type of media to be used. The major types are television and radio, on the one hand, and newspapers and magazines on the other. These are supplemented by direct mail and outdoor displays. Each of these has advantages and disadvantages that the marketer must review before choosing a specific media mix and schedule. Broadcast media have immediacy and require little audience effort, but commercials go out of existence the moment that they are aired. Print media are preferred over broadcast media by many service marketers because:

EXHIBIT 8–7   Message Selection for Service Advertisers

---

1. Identify corporate mission or goals.
2. Identify target market.
3. Identify advertising objectives.
4. Identify advertising message.
   a. Through interaction with members of the target market who express needs and desires.
   b. Through brainstorming sessions with company personnel who wish to convey a particular message through advertising.
   c. Through a combination of interactions with the target market and company personnel.
5. Select type of appeal
   a. Rational: Uses concrete facts to convince consumers of the superiority of one supplier over its competitors; good for use with those services where objective differences distinguish the offering of one provider from that of another.
      Example: A financial service institution publishes a schedule of interest rates, fees, and available services.
   b. Emotional: Relies on consumer feelings to present its appeal; best suited for use with personal or sensitive issues such as educational or church marketing.
      Example: A university distinguishes itself by designating "tradition" as the emotional appeal that separates it from its competitors and encourages alumni to contribute toward its continued viability.
   c. Ethical: Founded upon basic principles of "right" or "proper" behavior; used in support of medical services, social issues, or the like.
      Example: A hospital stresses the quality of patient care and efficiency of service as the factors that distinguish it from other available medical service institutions.

---

1. They can be targeted more carefully and may be more cost-effective.
2. They have more "staying power" or longevity due to their tangibility, their life span usually being governed by their publication rhythm.
3. They often have "pass-along" audiences whose size is inversely related to the frequency of publication.
4. They can deliver coupons, cards, or other inserts to their readerships.

Several examples illustrate the types of advertising media and their uses. Fast-food operators make extensive use of television because of its action orientation and its dual-sense impact (seeing and hearing). Local dental groups or printers use local radio stations. Financial service companies advertise in na-

SERVICE ADVERTISING / **205**

tional newspapers such as the *The Wall Street Journal.* Long-distance carriers promote their services in business magazines such as *Fortune* or *Business Week.* Airlines and hotels use billboards along major highways to promote their travel services or accommodations. Credit card issuers conduct direct mail campaigns to affluent consumers, inviting them to sign up for prestige credit cards. These examples show how advertisers try to zero in on carefully defined target groups through media appropriate for the specific service.

Budgeting

Most service businesses use either some form of arbitrary allocation or a percentage of sales to establish their advertising budgets. *Arbitrary allocation* is the simplest technique. Someone, usually the service advertising manager or the top marketing executive will decide how much is to be spent on advertising during a given time period. With this approach, the advertising budget may also reflect the manager's estimate of competitive advertising spending. This is a poor way to budget for advertising, since there is neither an underlying rationale nor any attempt to equate dollars spent with either the quality or quantity of advertising materials produced.

Percentage of sales is another easy way to establish the advertising budget. The percentage may be based on the previous year's sales, or on expected sales for the coming year. For example, a fast-food chain may devote 5 percent of its sales dollars to advertising, or a bank may establish its advertising budget as 2 percent of deposits. The weakness of basing advertising expenditures on a percentage of sales is that the advertising budget is presumed to be a result, rather than a prime determinant, of sales. Of course, the opposite is true. Consumer awareness and desire, created through advertising, is often the reason for sales growth.

The best way to budget for advertising is the *objective and task method.* This approach starts with the establishment of specific, measurable advertising objectives such as: to increase average monthly sales of a restaurant from $150,000 to $200,000 within the next 12 months; to increase the market share of a national automobile rental firm from 13 to 15 percent by the end of the year; to introduce a new interest-bearing

(NOW) checking account service within a financial institution and to open 300 of these NOW accounts during the next six months.

Once the objectives have been established, the next step is to determine the advertising effort, or tasks, required to achieve these objectives. The advertising budget then will equal the total amount of money needed to accomplish the required tasks. The strength of this budgeting approach is its close relationship to the service firm's advertising objectives.

In addition to establishing a total dollar amount to be budgeted for advertising, it is also essential to allocate these dollars to different market segments, geographic areas, media, or time periods. Different target markets may receive different allocations, depending on their relative importance to the firm. In some geographic areas, for example, intense competition may prompt a service advertiser to spend more advertising dollars than in areas where fewer competitors exist. Finally, the seasonal nature of some services may point to the importance of advertising more heavily at certain times, either to reinforce demand during peak periods or to stimulate demand during nonpeak periods. Exhibit 8–8 provides an example of advertising strategy for a seasonal business.

Evaluating Advertising Effectiveness

John Wanamaker, founder of the large Philadelphia department store chain that bears his name, is reported to have said, "Half of what I spend for advertising is wasted, but I don't know which half." As this comment suggests, measuring the effectiveness of advertising is difficult, even under the best of circumstances. Unfortunately, the unique characteristics of services make it even harder to evaluate service advertising effectiveness. Consequently, most efforts to measure the effect of service advertising concentrate on evaluating the communications impact of advertising. This can be done through copy testing that is conducted in the form of pretesting or post-testing.

1. *Copy pretesting.* Pretesting copy involves presenting materials to potential users before the ad campaign begins in order to determine their reactions to the ads and to select the most effective ones. Three methods are commonly used:

EXHIBIT 8–8   Allocation of Advertising Dollars for a Vermont Ski Resort:
The Objective and Task Method

---

1. *Objective:*   To reach affluent consumers in the Northeast for the following primary reasons:
   a. To inform them of the resort's existence and the excellent quality of its facilities.
   b. To persuade them to frequent the resort during the ski season.
   c. To remind last year's skiers to return this year.
2. *Task:*   To use local print media to advertise the resort during the September through February period.
   Annual Budget: $350,000, allocated as follows:

State	Percent
New York	25
New Jersey	20
Connecticut	15
Massachusetts	25
Other New England	15

   Within each market:

Media	Percent
Lifestyle magazines	50
Major metro area newspapers	15
Local newspapers	10
Flyers/brochures at ski shops, etc.	15
Direct mail to last year's skiers	10

---

    a. Comparative ratings of different versions of an ad.
    b. Recall of information contained in different versions.
    c. Measurement of physiological reactions to various ads, such as heart rate, pupil dilation, and so on (generally used only by larger companies with more extensive budgets).
      On the basis of pretest results, changes in the copy may be made to improve the presentation to consumers.
2. *Copy post-testing.* Post-tests are conducted after advertisements have appeared in the media. Two methods are generally used:
    a. Recognition—readers are shown copies of ads and asked to identify what they have seen or read before.
    b. Recall—more difficult than recognition; readers are asked to state what they have seen, without the visual clues provided in recognition tests. Their ability to re-

call the advertisement may have to be assisted, however, by providing a range of choices (aided recall).

Both recognition and recall tests are based on the assumption that effective advertising is that which is remembered. Insurance companies, financial institutions, and other large national service advertisers use post-tests to assess the impact of their advertising programs.

Many smaller service firms will not be able to devote their dollars to advertising research such as pre- and post-testing of copy. Here, the service marketing manager must rely on common sense when preparing an advertisement. The following guidelines may be useful:

1. State the message clearly and concisely.
2. Capture consumer attention with both the headline and the visual presentation; follow through with the body copy.
3. Use a unifying theme throughout the campaign to reinforce the firm's image in the minds of consumers. A distinctive logo or service mark, if possible, will make this identification even easier.
4. Stress the unique image or benefit provided by the firm.
5. Tailor the message to the target audience.
6. Capitalize on word-of-mouth advertising, and reinforce it with other advertising methods.
7. Speak the consumer's language. If possible, get the consumer involved in the advertising effort.
8. Advertise to the employees of the firm, as well as to the outside consumer. Such internal marketing is essential, since it conveys the advertising message clearly to those who will come into contact with consumers and who serve as representatives of the firm. In addition, it involves the employees and makes them feel an essential part of the firm, thus increasing their commitment and encouraging the type of behavior outlined in the advertising.
9. Use media that fit both the advertising budget and the target consumer's lifestyle.
10. Do not overadvertise, or attempt to draw so many con-

EXHIBIT 8–9   Seven Common Pitfalls of Service Advertising

---

1. Lacking coordination of advertising efforts.
   Example: Marketing department fails to inform sales department of new promotion; sales personnel are unable to deal effectively with customers.
2. Promising what can't be delivered.
   Example: Small caterer takes on a party for 150 people; unable to handle volume with only one assistant.
3. Using professional jargon in ads to consumers.
   Example: Insurance firm writes extensively about terms and conditions of life insurance policy, using phrases unfamiliar to target group.
4. Burying the message.
   Example: Ad for housecleaning services wants to promote quick and efficient service. That message, however, is only found after two paragraphs of unnecessary clutter.
5. Understating your capabilities.
   Example: In attempting to avoid clutter, a lawyer opening a new practice announces his location, without stating that he has won acclaim for his work with wills and estates.
6. Using inappropriate celebrities for testimonials.
   Example: Frank Sinatra for MTV music video.
7. Appealing to the wrong target audience.
   Example: Ad for a laundromat in the *The Wall Street Journal*.

---

sumers that the quality of the service offered to each will be diluted.

11. The best ideas are generally the simplest ideas. Tell the truth. Don't promise what cannot be delivered.

Avoiding Advertising Pitfalls

Unfortunately, advertising is not a foolproof undertaking. There are possibilities for mistake that can dilute the effectiveness of advertising efforts. Exhibit 8–9 provides a list of seven common advertising pitfalls that should be avoided by service advertisers.

SUMMARY

This chapter began the discussion of service promotion. After a brief review of the goals of promotion and the elements of the promotion mix, the first major promotional technique—advertising—was discussed. Although advertising an intangible service is a difficult task, service advertisers and their agencies have used personalities, unifying themes, symbols, and other strategies to effectively create positive service images and to demonstrate the real benefits of services. In the next chapter, the role of personal selling in the service marketing mix will be discussed.

CHAPTER 9

Personal Selling and Sales Management

Personal selling has always been an important part of market-ing for most service businesses. In fact, personal selling is a focal point of service marketing. This is so because service buyers want a direct, continuing personal relationship with a service business. All customer contact employees, and this includes al-most everyone in a service business, are engaged in personal selling.

In general, the selling of services is similar to the selling of goods. The same major sales activities must be performed. These include: identifying and qualifying prospects, preparing and making sales presentations, handling buyers' objections, clos-ing, and follow-up. Managing salespeople in a service business also involves tasks similar to those in a goods business. Sales jobs must be defined; qualified sales personnel must be hired and trained; sales compensation plans must be developed and ad-ministered; and salespeople must be supervised and controlled.

Although the major selling and sales management activities are similar, the ways in which these activities are performed by salespeople and sales managers in a service business are often quite different from those used in the sale of tangible products. In this chapter we shall discuss the role of selling and sales management in a service business. We begin with an overview of the personal contact functions.

EXHIBIT 9–1 Personal Contact Functions

Function	Responsibilities	Examples
Selling	To persuade potential customers to purchase services and/or to increase the use of services by existing customers.	Insurance agent; stockbroker; bank calling officer; real estate salesperson.
Servicing	To inform, assist, and advise customers.	Airline flight attendant; insurance claims adjuster; ticket agent; bank branch manager.
Monitoring	To learn about customers' needs and concerns and report them to management.	Customer service representative; repair person.

SOURCE: Adapted from Philip Kotler, *Marketing for Nonprofit Organizations* (Englewood Cliffs, N.J.: Prentice-Hall, 1985), pp. 213–15.

Personal Contact Functions

Philip Kotler provides a useful framework for analyzing the personal contact functions in a service business.[1] Although this framework was developed for nonprofit organizations, it is appropriate for profit-oriented service businesses as well. The three personal contact roles are selling, servicing, and monitoring. They are described in Exhibit 9–1.

As shown in Exhibit 9–1, personal contacts may enhance or reduce a service customer's satisfaction. Although all personal contacts are important, selling often receives the most emphasis because this form of personal contact is a key part of the promotional mix. However, it is essential that all employees of a service business adopt a customer orientation.

Developing a Sales Orientation

Some service businesses, insurance for example, have a tradition of a strong sales orientation. Unfortunately, many do not, and a major problem for many service businesses has been the

---

[1] Philip Kotler, *Marketing for Nonprofit Organizations* (Englewood Cliffs, N.J.: Prentice-Hall, 1985), pp. 213–15.

lack of a sales orientation among their employees. In fact, many customer contact personnel resist selling. Comments such as "I don't have time to sell," "Selling is not my responsibility," and "I was hired to do something else, not sell" are often heard.

The impact of deregulation on traditional service businesses has been discussed elsewhere in this book. Although many facets of service businesses are impacted by deregulation, customer contact employees are especially affected. No longer protected by measures that limit competition, these employees must turn to selling to retain their company's market share. Banks, airlines, trucking firms, and other traditional service businesses are being forced to develop aggressive sales organizations. Even professional service firms, such as accounting firms, are beginning to realize that they must sell if they are to survive and grow.

One of the most interesting conflicts is emerging in the information management industry between AT&T, the telecommunications giant, and IBM, a firm noted for its well-trained, aggressive sales force. Many authorities doubt whether AT&T can develop the proactive sales orientation it needs to go head-to-head against IBM.

The responsibility for developing a sales orientation rests with a service business's top management. The personal style of senior managers will establish the status of sales in the organization. For example, one utility's CEO, who believes in selling, supports its sales training and incentives, makes outside sales calls, and emphasizes to employees that selling is a crucial activity has provided his firm with the sales leadership needed.

A strong sales management system is also essential to the development of a sales orientation. This means that selling must be identified as a major part of the service employee's job. Sales training must be provided to employees, their sales performance must be evaluated, and appropriate rewards and incentives must be given for sales success. Most importantly, first-level supervisors, such as branch managers, office supervisors, and terminal managers, must be trained and encouraged to be sales managers.

One service organization that has begun to develop its field sales managers is the U.S. Postal Service. Confronted with aggressive competition and the need to introduce new services to discriminating business customers, the Postal Service is pilot testing a custom-made sales management training program. This program is designed to create a more professional environment for selling and servicing the Postal Service's business customers by teaching managers how to select, train, and motivate salespeople. Field sales management activities will be discussed later in this chapter.

PERSONAL SELLING

Sometimes called business development in financial institutions and professional service firms, *personal selling* is an interpersonal process intended to assist and persuade a service organization's customers or prospective customers to buy the service. The two major tasks of personal selling are contained in this definition:

1. *Assist.* As a form of communication, personal selling provides customers with information about a service firm's services and capabilities. Because many services, such as insurance, credit, and medical care, are confusing to customers, two-way communication between an employee and a customer is needed to explain these services and their benefits. Buyers also need other forms of assistance to perform their roles as service customers.
2. *Persuade.* Through personal selling, a service firm's representative will attempt to influence the potential customer to do something beneficial to both the customer and the company—purchase a life insurance policy, open a checking account, join a health club, and so forth.

Through the years, personal selling in the United States has evolved from its origin with the Yankee peddlers of the late 17th century, through the era of high-pressure sales, to the modern view of the salesperson as a creative problem solver. This latter view, which is consistent with the marketing concept's customer focus, suggests that a service firm's sales representative must assume the role of a consultant who helps customers to identify and satisfy their service needs.

Life insurance marketing provides a good illustration of the service salesperson's key role. Because insurance is a confusing, complex subject for the average buyer, the buyer expects the agent to be more than a salesperson. The agent must be a professional financial adviser who develops a close personal relationship with the buyer. Further, this must be a long-term relationship because the buyer's insurance needs will change during his or her life cycle. It is this demand for high-quality, personalized service that requires life insurance companies and other service firms to develop well-trained, highly motivated sales forces. Unfortunately, life insurance companies and some other service businesses have a high rate of turnover in their sales organizations. This makes it difficult to develop the long-term relationships that are required.

Service Features and Selling

The features of services (discussed in Chapter 1) pose some unique problems and opportunities for the service salesperson.

Intangibility. As described earlier, services are largely intangible. This characteristic makes it more difficult to portray services in advertisements and displays. These promotional difficulties increase the reliance on personal selling to explain the key features and benefits of services.

Perishability. Because services are perishable, they cannot be produced ahead of time for periods of peak demand. This will cause problems such as long lines at a bank's teller windows or at an airline's check-in counter. Effective personal selling techniques are needed to help minimize the negative impact of demand fluctuations.

Heterogeneity. Because people are involved in performing most services, the services produced by them are often dissimilar. It is difficult to standardize many services or to assure their consistent delivery. However, this can work to the service firm's advantage if its salespeople are creative in their efforts to adapt services to individual customers' needs. In some cases, for example, professional services such as legal advice, accounting, and computer assistance, this is feasible because the service salesperson is also the service performer.

Customer participation. Customers play an important part in the purchase and creation of many services. They write checks, fill out insurance forms, explain their problems to an attorney, and so forth. If customers are to fulfill their roles satisfactorily, they need personal assistance from the service firm's representatives. In particular, it is essential that professional service firms provide personalized attention to their customers.

Guidelines for Service Selling

The features of services and the special problems of selling intangibles suggest several guidelines for selling in a service business. When put into practice through a coordinated sales program, these guidelines will help service salespeople to better serve their customers.[2]

Adopt a professional attitude. An essential part of every successful service transaction is the customer's confidence in the employee's ability to deliver the desired results. For instance, a bank officer is a customer's financial adviser. He or she must create an impression of competence, honesty, and sincerity. Because customers often lack personal experience with and information about financial services, they expect bank employees to compensate for their own lack of knowledge. For this reason, all bank employees must adopt a professional attitude, and calling officers must strive for close, professional relationships with their customers. The same is true for employees in many other service companies.

Develop personal relationships. Service customers have a strong desire to be treated as individuals with different needs, problems, and feelings. In fact, often it is the personal relationship, rather than the service, that leads to a customer's satisfaction or dissatisfaction with a service firm. Service employees and service sales representatives must never forget that they are in a people business.

Contribute to a positive image. For most customers, the salesperson *is* the company. This is true especially for service

[2] These guidelines are adapted from Eugene M. Johnson, "Selling of Services," in *Handbook of Modern Marketing,* ed. Victor P. Buell (New York: McGraw-Hill, 1970), pp. 12-114–12-120.

businesses. Customers' impressions and attitudes are important in service selection decisions, and successful service marketing demands the creation and maintenance of a favorable public image. More and more, personal selling and customer contacts are becoming the keys to creating and maintaining a favorable public image. It is particularly important that a bond of trust exist between service salespeople and their customers.

Recognize the value of indirect selling. Service firms and their employees sell indirectly by becoming involved in the community. Frequently, a service firm's managers and employees will become acquainted with people who may need their services or who may influence others in the selection of services. A successful attorney, who is active in community organizations and projects, and develops personal contacts with bankers, real estate brokers, local business leaders, and others who may need legal services or who may influence those who do is using indirect selling techniques.

Sell services, not a service. Although a specific customer may contact a service firm for a particular service, he or she has many service needs. By concentrating on solving all of their customers' needs, service salespeople will be able to sell several services, not just a single service. Insurance salespeople who emphasize their financial planning expertise have been more successful than those who limit their sales efforts to life insurance. Likewise, successful telecommunications sales representatives concentrate on solving business customers' communications needs, not just on selling telephone services. The technique of selling several services to a customer has become known as cross-selling in banks and other service businesses. Cross-selling is discussed in more detail later in this chapter.

Sales Tasks

H. Robert Dodge's continuum of sales tasks provides a convenient theoretical framework for explaining the selling activities in a service firm.[3] Based on the tasks they perform, service sales-

---

[3] H. Robert Dodge, "The Role of the Industrial Salesman," *Mid-South Quarterly Business Review,* January 1972, pp. 11–15.

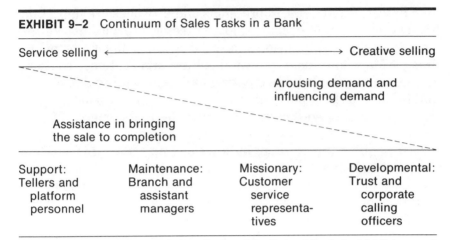

EXHIBIT 9–2 Continuum of Sales Tasks in a Bank

Service selling ← ─────────────────────────── → Creative selling

Arousing demand and
influencing demand

Assistance in bringing
the sale to completion

Support:	Maintenance:	Missionary:	Developmental:
Tellers and	Branch and	Customer	Trust and
platform	assistant	service	corporate
personnel	managers	representa-	calling
		tives	officers

SOURCE: Adapted from H. Robert Dodge, "The Role of the Industrial Salesman," *Mid-South Quarterly Business Review,* January 1972, p. 13.

people may be divided into four categories: support, mainte-nance, missionary, and developmental. To illustrate the applica-tion of Dodge's continuum to a service business, the selling tasks in a commercial bank are described (see Exhibit 9–2).

Support salespeople assist in the selling process, but making sales is not their major function. In a commercial bank, tellers, secretaries, and platform personnel provide selling support. They assist customers, build and maintain goodwill, and some-times help customers purchase additional financial services.

Maintenance salespeople are concerned mainly with increas-ing business from existing customers. They also are responsible for preserving long-lasting, satisfactory relationships with cus-tomers. Branch managers and assistant managers do a lot of maintenance selling. Tellers also are expected to perform main-tenance selling tasks, especially when they are asked to cross-sell services.

Missionary salespeople provide assistance in "pulling" a product through the marketing channel. In recent years, banks have used missionary salespeople to help introduce automated teller machines (ATMs). Customer service representatives are stationed in lobbies to demonstrate the machine's operation to customers. The banks that have had the greatest success in introducing ATMs have been those that have provided specially trained people to help customers learn how to use the machines.

Developmental salespeople have the most difficult task. In fact, Dodge placed people selling new business intangibles at the extreme end of his continuum. These salespeople must sell a bank's services to new customers or sell new services to existing customers. Sometimes branch managers are expected to be creative salespeople, but most developmental selling in commercial banks is done by specialists, usually trust or corporate calling officers. These salespeople sell pension plans, retirement programs, trusts, certificates of deposit, and other specialized services to business, professional, and other knowledgeable buyers.

It is this final form of selling, creative or developmental selling, that is most important to service marketing. Christian Gronroos calls this the "interactive marketing function" of a service organization.[4] As was noted earlier, developmental service salespeople, such as insurance agents or commercial lending officers, must view themselves as consultants who identify customers' needs and adapt their service firms' offerings to those needs. Continuous adaptation of service operations to customers' needs, or managing the buyer-seller interactions, is the interactive marketing function. This vital function requires highly qualified, innovative salespeople. Some of the desired characteristics for service salespeople are outlined in Exhibit 9–3.

THE SELLING PROCESS

The selling process that developmental service salespeople follow includes the primary selling activities that all creative, problem-solving salespeople must perform. These are prospecting, preapproach, presentation, handling objections, closing, and follow-up. As shown in Exhibit 9–4, these activities are all interrelated. They must be adapted to the selling of intangible services.

---

[4] Christian Gronroos, "Designing a Long-Range Marketing Strategy for Services," *Long-Range Planning,* April 1980, p. 38.

EXHIBIT 9–3 Characteristics of Successful Service Salespeople

---

1. Initiative: "self-starter," interested in selling, has strong personal desire for success, able to motivate self, enthusiastic.
2. Intelligence: has problem-solving ability, technical competence, willingness and ability to learn, is well organized.
3. Balance: versatile, flexible, has variety of interests, well-rounded, experienced.
4. Poise: self-confident, able to handle pressure situations, sociable.
5. Communications skills: articulate, persuasive, able to establish rapport with others, has empathy, high verbal skills, effective listener.

SOURCE: Adapted from Albert H. Dunn and Eugene M. Johnson, *Managing Your Sales Team* (Englewood Cliffs, N.J.: Prentice-Hall, 1980), p. 42.

Prospecting

Prospecting involves identifying and qualifying potential customers. Personal observation, advertising, trade shows, phone and direct mail contacts are a few of the techniques used to locate sales leads that might be prospects for a service. The most effective technique, however, is to seek referrals from customers or others who may influence a service buyer. As an earlier discussion indicated, service salespeople can use indirect selling techniques to locate prospects and persons who can refer prospects to them.

Once potential customers have been identified, they must be qualified. That is, the salesperson must make sure that a prospect not only has the need for the service but also has the money to buy and the authority to make a buying decision. For certain types of business services—telecommunications, marketing research, management consulting, and office services, for example—it may be difficult to identify the person in a company who can make the purchase commitment. Thus, qualifying a service prospect is a critical selling activity for these types of complex business services.

Preapproach

Once a prospect has been located and qualified, the service salesperson must plan for the sale. This step, known as preapproach, requires that the salesperson identify the prospect's needs. Some

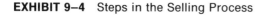

EXHIBIT 9–4 Steps in the Selling Process

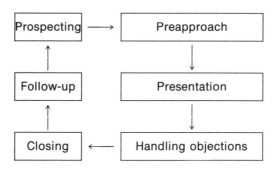

of this can be done prior to a sales call if the salesperson can obtain information about the prospect from other sources. In most cases, however, the salesperson must ask the prospect probing questions to identify needs.

After obtaining the required information about the prospect, the salesperson prepares a sales-call plan. This includes the objective for the sales call, the anticipated sales strategy, and planned selling tactics. For example, a life insurance agent will consider the prospect's age, marital status, number of dependents, income, and other pertinent facts when preparing for a call. This information may be used to formulate a written proposal that serves as the basis for the agent's sales presentation. A written proposal has the additional advantage of presenting the intangible attributes of a service such as life insurance in a tangible format.

Presentation

It is during the sales presentation that the intangibility of services has the greatest impact on the selling process. During the first part of the sales presentation, the salesperson tries to establish rapport with the prospect. More than in any other type of selling situation, service salespeople must sell themselves first. It is essential that the prospect like and trust the service salesperson.

The sales presentation will also require that service salespeople emphasize different selling techniques. In particular, they must rely on appealing to emotional buying motives because there are no tangible product features to demonstrate. Experienced service salespeople are adept at illustrating the emotional benefits of their services. For example, a seasoned travel agent will describe the relaxing feeling one has while enjoying a luxury cruise in the Caribbean.

Another technique used by successful service salespeople to offset the intangibility of services is to show pictures or graphs to illustrate service benefits. For instance, a retirement planner shows a prospect a chart that illustrates the growth of funds invested every year in a retirement account. A similar technique is to give the prospect a small item that signifies the service. For example, transportation salespeople often give their prospects models of trucks or planes used to provide the transportation service.

The key to a successful service sales presentation is getting the prospect to understand the benefits of the service. To do this, the salesperson must "talk the prospect's language." Features of the service must be translated into benefits. A bank customer, for instance, is not interested in how much direct deposit saves the bank in processing costs, but rather in the added security, convenience, and time savings of direct deposit.

Handling Objections

Service salespeople, like all other salespeople, encounter sales resistance. Known as a sales objection, sales resistance is anything a prospect says or does to hinder completion of the sale. Effective salespeople are skilled at anticipating and handling objections raised by prospects.

In many selling situations, an objection is actually a request for more information. When complex services, such as life insurance, investments, and other financial services, are sold, prospects may not understand the unique features and corresponding benefits of the services being presented. To deal with these objections, the service salesperson must make sure that he or she understands the prospect's concerns and answers them in a straightforward manner.

Other objections arise for a variety of reasons. Prospects may want to delay the buying decision, they may feel that the price is too high, or they may lack confidence in the supplier. There are many selling techniques that are used to handle these objections. For the service salesperson, however, the most critical issue is to establish a trusting relationship with the prospect. Once trust has been established, the service salesperson is better able to deal with a prospect's concerns about an intangible service and its provider.

Closing

Closing is the culmination of the sales presentation. This is the point at which the salesperson obtains a commitment to buy. Service salespeople, particularly those in companies and industries that have been slow to develop a sales orientation, have been criticized for their failure to ask for the order. This is often the result of poor sales training and/or the service company's failure to convince its salespeople of the importance of asking for an order.

The intangibility of a service also contributes to closing difficulties. A product demonstration often leads to closing for goods salespeople, but this cannot be done when a service is sold. Service salespeople are forced to rely more heavily on emotional buying appeals during closing.

Sales literature describes many closing techniques that have been used successfully by goods and service salespeople. These techniques must be adapted to the individual sales situation. Most authorities agree, however, that a direct close (i.e., asking for the order in a straightforward manner) is often the most effective approach in service selling.

Follow-Up

Experienced salespeople and managers point to the importance of follow-up after the sale as critical to sales success. Follow-up activities are needed to reassure the customer about the buying decision and to prepare the way for future sales. It is especially critical that service salespeople follow up their sales, since satisfied customers are a major source of future business, in the form of both referrals and repeat sales.

Keep customers informed. There are several specific activities that salespeople should perform to make sure that customers are satisfied with them and their services. First, service salespeople must keep their customers informed of any new services, trends, or information that may be of value to them. To do this, salespeople must make periodic analyses of customers' needs to be certain that requirements are being met. For instance, the growth of business communications needs and rapid technological changes in equipment and services require that telecommunications salespeople keep their customers informed and recommend changes when they are called for.

Handle customer complaints. Another key follow-up activity is handling customers' complaints and problems. The salesperson is usually the first to be informed of customer dissatisfaction and therefore must take quick action to maintain the customer's goodwill. In some cases, the service salesperson can use the prompt resolution of a customer's problem as a means to sell additional services.

Sell additional services. This brings up the third key element of follow-up. By developing and maintaining a satisfying long-term relationship with customers, a service salesperson will find many opportunities to sell additional services. By providing dependable service and sound advice, the salesperson develops a trusting relationship with customers. It is this relationship that leads to more business. A trusted securities salesperson, for example, only needs to call a long-term customer with an investment recommendation to make a sale.

Cross-selling. A final component of effective follow-up is cross-selling. As noted earlier, this is a practice that has become an expected part of the selling duties of salespeople in banking and other service businesses. Simply defined, cross-selling refers to a service salesperson's efforts to sell additional services to current customers. It is one way that service businesses can implement the market penetration and service development growth strategies presented in Chapter 5.

Cross-selling, as it is practiced in service businesses today, has its origins in the time-tested retail selling technique known as suggestion selling. This occurs when a retail salesperson asks a customer to buy additional items before completing the transaction. For example, a man purchasing a new business suit may be shown several ties and shirts that will go with his new suit. Many retail stores stimulate suggestion selling by providing sales personnel with lists of related products.

When a bank's customer service representative recommends that a new checking account customer might also want the convenience of an automated teller machine (ATM) card, this service salesperson is using suggestion selling. However, effective cross-selling in a service business must go beyond basic suggestion selling. Service salespersons must be provided with the knowledge of the firm's services, the insights into buyers' needs and behavior, and the selling skills to cross-sell all of the firm's services. In particular, a service salesperson must learn how services complement each other and which services are used by particular types of customers.

Among service businesses, cross-selling is most prevalent in banking and other financial services. Many banks offer special incentives to employees to stimulate them to cross-sell. For example, a cross-selling program initiated by a major New England bank pays additional commissions to customer service representatives who sell multiple services to their customers. Employees of this bank also receive cash bonuses for recommending prospects who become trust customers of the bank.

Other service businesses can also profit from the benefits of effective cross-selling. When residential customers call a telephone customer service representative of AT&T Communications or another long-distance carrier, they should be informed of other services provided by the carrier. A marketing representative for a data processing firm should be sensitive to other information needs of business customers that the firm can satisfy. An accountant should offer to assist small-business clients with tax and other financial planning assistance in addition to providing routine accounting services.

These examples suggest that service marketers and their customers alike will benefit from cross-selling. Research has shown that the more services a customer has with a service business, the higher the likelihood that the business will retain that customer. In other words, cross-selling is one of the best ways in which a service salesperson can establish a long-term relationship with customers. As stated earlier, this is one of the major desires that service buyers have. Finally, cross-selling is also consistent with the professional, problem-solving approach

---

EXHIBIT 9–5   Sales Management Functions in Service Businesses

---

to service selling advocated throughout this chapter—an approach that concentrates on satisfying customers' needs, not just selling services.

MANAGING THE SELLING EFFORT

Sales management involves the planning, implementation, and control of an organized selling effort. The major functions of sales management in service firms are shown in Exhibit 9–5.

Much has been written about the inadequacy of sales management in service businesses. In their comprehensive study of service marketing practices, George and Barksdale concluded:

> Manufacturing firms gave more attention to sales activities than did the service companies. Manufacturers were more likely to have an overall sales plan. Sales training was less frequent in service firms and, where this activity was carried out, responsibility was more likely to be shared by the marketing department and some other departments.[5]

---

[5] William R. George and Hiram C. Barksdale, "Marketing Activities in the Service Industries," *Journal of Marketing,* October 1974, p. 67.

Additional evidence of service firms' neglect of the sales function is contained in *Sales and Marketing Management's* annual "Survey of Selling Costs." As reported in these surveys, service companies spend much less on sales training and require a shorter training period than do manufactured goods companies. This lesser emphasis on sales training by service firms is in direct conflict with the widely accepted view that intangibles are more difficult to sell. One would expect service salespeople to have more rather than less sales training.

Another important service marketing management activity, which was discussed earlier, is internal marketing, or the efforts of service managers to persuade service employees to maintain service quality and be responsive to customers' needs. As the following discussion will reveal, the functions of sales management and internal marketing are similar. However, internal marketing involves all employees while sales management is concerned specifically with people who sell.

This section will concentrate on the management of those employees in a service business who have direct sales responsibilities. The major sales management functions and their applications to service businesses will be discussed briefly. For more detailed coverage of these functions, the reader should consult a recent sales management book.

Planning and Organizing for Sales

Sales planning involves two activities: (1) the establishment of specific sales goals and selection of the means to accomplish them, and (2) sales personnel planning—determining the number and type of salespeople required. The first task is usually performed by senior management, but service sales managers and department heads also must develop sales goals and strategies. Managers at all levels must plan for the optimum allocation of the resources that have been put at their disposal.

As discussed in Chapter 5, effective sales and marketing planning requires a thorough review of a service firm's strengths and weaknesses, and the environment in which the firm is operating. It is especially important that a firm's salespeople and other key customer contact personnel participate in the sales planning process since they know their customers' needs better than anyone else.

For example, a salesman for a cleaning and maintenance firm learned through his contacts that a large metropolitan bank was planning to build a suburban operations center and move its data processing and other major operations activities out of the city. The salesman recognized that this proposed move would open up two important business opportunities for his firm. First, the new operations center would need cleaning and maintenance services. In addition, the space vacated in the bank's city headquarters building would be leased to new tenants who would also be potential customers for the firm's services. The salesman reported his findings to his sales manager and together they developed a sales plan to obtain the cleaning and maintenance business of both the bank's operations center and the new tenants of the headquarters building. Because of its head start, the firm was successful in obtaining a large share of the new business.

Sales planning, like marketing planning in general, begins with the identification of customers and their needs. In many service businesses, the marketing research or business development department will have information and expertise that will assist the sales planner. With this assistance, the service sales manager or department head can develop sales goals and strategies for specific customers and personnel.

For example, an important source of business for large hotels are business and professional meetings. The national sales manager for a large hotel chain would need information on the size, meeting schedule, key executives, and financial resources of professional and trade associations to develop a sales plan to pursue their meeting and convention business. This information could be more efficiently obtained by a member of the hotel chain's marketing research staff.

The second component of sales planning, sales personnel planning, has both a quantitative and a qualitative dimension. The key planning tool is the service employee's job description. How much of the employee's time should be devoted to selling, and what qualities are necessary in a successful salesperson? By developing a job description that includes adequate time allowances and specifications for selling, a service business has a tool for planning and managing the sales effort. For sales representatives and other employees with major sales responsibilities, the job description should be even more detailed, showing the specific sales functions to be performed and the amount of time, effort, attention, and emphasis that should be placed on each activity. The job description also serves as the basis for selecting, training, supervising, and evaluating the salesperson.

After sales goals have been formulated and job descriptions have been developed, a service manager must determine how many salespeople are needed. Then the sales organization is established—that is, key market segments are identified and the salespeople are assigned to these market segments. For example, a large commercial bank will have both a corporate division, with sales specialists who call on businesses and other large customers, and a community, or retail, division, in which branch managers are responsible for the sales effort.

Colleges and universities have dramatically increased the number of salespeople, or admissions officers, who recruit potential students. As the number of college-age students has declined, the competition for students has escalated. As a result, many colleges and universities have prepared sales and marketing plans and recruited sales professionals to carry out these plans. For example, the University of Pennsylvania has established an admissions office in Los Angeles to handle recruitment of students from the West. Since this office was established, applicants to Penn from this part of the country have soared.

Recruiting and Selection

Some major service businesses, such as insurance companies, employment agencies, and securities brokers, have extensive programs for recruiting and selecting sales representatives. Others, such as banks, savings institutions, and professional services, need to put more emphasis on recruiting people with sales aptitude when hiring professionals, managers, and customer relations people. It is particularly important that the individuals hired possess good human relations skills in addition to the required technical knowledge.

A critical hiring issue for many service businesses is whether to hire people with sales experience or to train those without prior sales experience to sell. There are convincing arguments for both options. Hiring experienced salespeople from outside the service business provides the firm with an "instant" proven sales force. Dime Savings Bank of New York reversed its loss of market share for co-op and home mortgage sales by hiring experienced salespeople, most of whom had previously sold insurance or real estate, and paying them commissions on the loans generated.

Although Dime's experience and that of other service companies has been successful, critics point out that salespeople hired from the outside do not really know the services they are selling and are often not as "professional" as the company's own employees. They argue that a service business that develops its sales force from within by selecting employees who have an interest in, and aptitude for, selling will achieve a more professional sales force that is committed to the long-run interests of the service business.

Regardless of the source of its salespeople, a service business must use proven tools to select the people who are best qualified to sell. In industry, many tools are used to select salespeople. These include application forms, psychological tests, references, physical examinations, and interviews. Although all applicable aids should be used, most service sales managers feel that a personal interview is the best selection tool. How the applicant comes across in an interview often will be a good predictor of how he or she will handle a sales situation.

Training and Development

Sales training is essential for all employees of a service business who have personal contact with customers. New employees should be trained to sell as part of their initial training, and experienced employees should receive periodic refresher training on new services, selling techniques, self-development, and the like.

Most service businesses provide their employees with training to do their jobs, but they neglect the sales and customer relations skills that these employees also need. This is especially true of professional services. They forget that the "bedside manner" of the doctor or other professional service provider may be just as important to the client as professional competence.

One professional sales trainer developed a sales training program for dentists and their employees. This program, which concentrated on needs-oriented selling, has been very successful in expanding the practices of the dentists who have attended.

This example suggests that sales training must be carefully planned to meet the specific needs of a service business, its employees, and its customers. The training program must include service knowledge, institutional policies and procedures, and selling skills. Training techniques that simulate real-world sales situations and that involve the trainees will be most effective. The most frequently used sales training techniques are role playing, group discussions, case studies, and on-the-job training.

For some service salespeople, training programs must prepare them for professional licensing. Insurance salespeople, for example, are encouraged to qualify as Chartered Life Underwriters (CLU) or Chartered Property and Casualty Underwriters (CPCU). These professional designations are granted on the basis of education, experience, and ethics.

Professional service marketers, such as physicians, lawyers, and accountants, are required to continue their training to keep themselves up-to-date professionally. As noted earlier, some professional development programs now also provide sales and management training to participants.

Real estate is another service industry that has professional training requirements. Real estate salespeople must pass state examinations to qualify for licenses. In addition, they are expected to adhere to a code of ethics and to join local and state real estate associations. Industry training programs, such as the Graduate Realtors Institute, have been developed to improve the quality of real estate salespeople.

Leadership and Supervision

Personal supervision of salespeople is a critical sales management activity. To supervise salespeople effectively, a thorough understanding of human behavior, motivation, and alternative types of incentives is needed. Failure to identify the needs of salespeople and to provide effective leadership will result in high turnover and low productivity of the sales force and in unnecessary selling expenses.

In addition to providing personal supervision and leadership, a service business can utilize an assortment of monetary and nonmonetary incentives to stimulate sales. It is essential that these incentives be related to sales goals. For example, the compensation of a bank's calling officers should be based partly on the completion of sales calls and the results obtained. Likewise, a young attorney who is bringing in important new clients to a law firm should be recognized for this achievement.

Many of the sales incentives used by sales managers in manufacturing industries may be applied to the marketing of services. These incentives include sales contests, honors and recognition, special sales meetings, and monetary rewards. The insurance industry has been a leader in the development of incentive programs for salespeople. For instance, a member of the industry's Million Dollar Roundtable is recognized as a top sales achiever.

Evaluation of Sales Performance

All service employees with customer contact responsibilities must be evaluated, at least in part, on the basis of sales performance. Once sales goals have been established, a procedure for reviewing progress toward these goals should be implemented. Also, evaluation is important if compensation is to be related to sales performance.

Formal sales evaluation programs are costly in time, money, and effort, but they are essential to the operation of a sales program. An effective evaluation program provides feedback and assistance to the salesperson. To improve and grow, service salespeople must know in what areas their performance needs improvement. A good evaluation program lets each person know where changes are and are not required in the selling performance.

The development of a sales evaluation program is a difficult task. Each evaluation plan must be tailored to the individual service company in which it is to be used. The starting point for evaluation is a detailed study of the sales job. Next, a job description is prepared. This is the basis for the selection of sales performance criteria.

Most sales evaluation programs use several quantitative and qualitative performance criteria. The specific performance measures are derived from the standards established in the job description. For instance, are sales representatives for an equipment-leasing firm expected to make a certain number of calls in a given time period? If so, the number of calls made should be one performance measure used to evaluate the firm's salespeople.

The final steps in the sales evaluation process are those that put the evaluation plan into operation. These steps include designating the person who will evaluate sales activities, deciding how frequently evaluation should be done, and actually conducting the evaluation follow-up.

Evaluation concludes with the identification of any remedial actions to be taken and the supervisor's check that the remedial plan is being followed. For instance, if a specific equipment-leasing sales representative is not making enough calls, then a time and territory management plan might be suggested as a remedial action.

SUMMARY

Personal contacts are an important part of service marketing. In this chapter, we described the nature of personal contacts and the tasks and activities involved in personal selling. Service businesses need personal selling to assist and persuade customers, and the people who sell must be managed effectively if they are to contribute in a meaningful way to the service firm's promotional efforts. We now turn to the final two forms of promotion—public relations and sales promotion.

CHAPTER 10

Sales Promotion, Public Relations, and Direct Marketing

The two preceding chapters covered advertising and personal selling, the two primary ingredients of the promotional mix for most service firms. In this chapter we turn our attention to sales promotion and public relations, the remaining elements of the promotion mix. In addition, direct marketing, which is a relatively new promotional approach, will be explored briefly.

SALES PROMOTION

Sales promotion for services includes a wide variety of paid promotional activities not classified as advertising or personal selling. These activities encourage the purchase of a service by supplementing and reinforcing the promotional message conveyed by advertising and personal selling. As intermittent nonpersonal selling activities, sales promotion campaigns add "something extra" for the buyer or intermediary in an effort to generate increased sales at a particular point in time.

As shown in Exhibit 10–1, there are two major categories of sales promotion techniques:

1. *Buyer sales promotions* are designed to stimulate prompt action by the service buyer. Their purpose is to "pull" a service through the channel of distribution.

EXHIBIT 10-1   Types of Sales Promotion

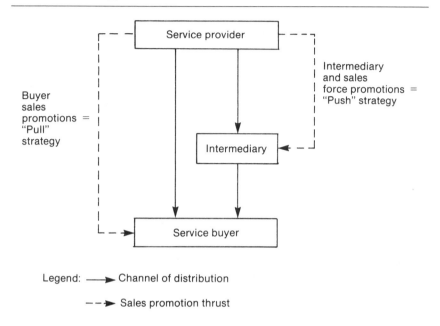

Legend: ———▶ Channel of distribution

— — ▶ Sales promotion thrust

2. *Intermediary (or dealer) and sales force promotions,* on the other hand, are designed to stir intermediaries and/or company salespeople to promote a service. Their purpose is to "push" a service through the channel of distribution.

An important result of deregulation in major service businesses has been the increased use of sales promotion techniques to stimulate sales. For example, after deregulation of the household moving industry in 1980, companies began hiring marketing and sales promotion specialists to develop programs to attract customers. North American Van Lines, the industry leader, has prepared and distributed a 200-item catalog of discounted gifts for customers. Consumers receive discounts on the gifts for obtaining estimates from a North American agent and for using the firm's services.

Sales promotion programs are also being used extensively by credit card companies to attract and retain customers. Known as "enhancements" in the industry, these include card registration, travel and health insurance, travel discounts, and bonus merchandise programs. For example, Citicorp, the largest distributor of credit cards in the United States, issues 20 Citidollars for each $100 charged by a cardholder. These Citidollars can be used to purchase discounted goods and services.

Buyer Promotions

The intangibility of services sometimes makes buyer sales promotion techniques more difficult to use in service businesses than in goods businesses. Sampling and physical displays, for example, may pose particular problems. With imaginative thinking, however, consumer service firms have been successful in their use of point-of-purchase promotions, premiums, coupons, samples, contests and sweepstakes, and demonstrations.

Point-of-purchase promotions include the use of signs, posters, brochures, and other informational activities at the service facility itself. The purpose of these materials is to inform buyers about the nature of the service and to reduce the uncertainty that intangibility may cause. Point-of-purchase materials may spur impulse buying. Such promotion may also reinforce the service firm's advertising by reminding consumers to purchase the service.

There are many examples of point-of-purchase promotion in service retailing. Banks locate racks containing informational brochures where people waiting for a teller can see and peruse the literature. Barber and beauty shops use photos and drawings to demonstrate to their customers what they might look like if they tried a different hairstyle. An orthodontist, a heart specialist, or a gynecologist may provide literature for patients in the waiting room that explains basic procedures and serves to alleviate a patient's fears. Theaters use signs, posters, and previews of coming attractions to stimulate attendance.

Premiums are inducements given for purchasing or, in some cases, trying a service. Some premiums may be provided free of charge; others are offered to consumers at a moderate cost. Commercial banks, savings institutions, and credit unions offer small appliances, luggage, watches, dinnerware, and other gifts to consumers who open new accounts or increase their current savings balances. Soon after divestiture, AT&T Communications introduced its Opportunity Calling program, which provides discounts on leading products for consumers who use the firm's services. This is an attempt to build brand loyalty and stimulate long-distance calling.

Professional baseball teams have used premiums extensively to foster attendance. Many of these premiums, such as bats, balls, batting helmets, and T-shirts, are directed toward children. The idea is to use these giveaways to encourage parents to bring their children to the ballpark for the day. While there, the family will spend money on parking, souvenirs, and food, in addition to the cost of admission. The premiums more than pay for themselves in the form of increased revenues. In addition, children leave the ballpark with a tangible remembrance of the day and thus help to promote attendance among their friends.

In addition to increasing sales, premiums can be used to accomplish other marketing goals. For instance, a dentist in a small Michigan town gives S&H Green Stamps to patients who pay their bills on time. The dentist feels that the use of incentives is more effective than the cash discount policy he had used in the past. Another suggested role for incentives is to use them to encourage patients to be on time for their appointments.

Coupons allow consumers to purchase various services at a reduced cost. As a form of price reduction they offer a modest rebate to customers. Dry cleaners, barber and beauty shops, auto repair centers, and other personal service firms use coupons to attract customers. Fast-food restaurants may include coupons in their ads, or may give coupons to customers who make a purchase.

A variation of couponing, and one of the most interesting recent developments in service marketing, has been the introduction of frequent-flier programs by American, United, Eastern, and other airlines. It has been estimated that three fourths of airline business travelers are enrolled in one or more of these promotional programs. Several airlines have also expanded the scope of their frequent-flier programs to include purchases at participating hotel and rental car companies. Airline marketing executives feel that these programs help them build brand loyalty and bring in incremental business.

The concept of frequent-flier programs has been expanded to other parts of the travel industry. Leading hotel and motel chains, such as Holiday Inn, Ramada, and Marriott, have incentive plans to encourage people to stay in their hotels and to use their facilities. Bonus points are given to promote the opening of a new facility or to encourage people to stay at a resort hotel during the off-season.

Long-distance telephone companies offer another interesting example of couponing to stimulate sale of a service. AT&T Communications and other long-distance carriers are using food and consumer-products coupons to mass-market their services. AT&T Communications will give purchasers of Maxwell House coffee or Tropicana orange juice certificates worth up to $5 in long-distance calls; MCI Communications gives discount coupons worth up to an hour's free calling with the purchase of Cheer detergent; and Sprint offers $5 of free calls to buyers of Shredded Wheat cereal. AT&T Communications also offered long-distance coupons to buyers of GE's small appliances. Like airline and hotel executives, marketing executives of these long-distance carriers are using sales promotion techniques to build brand loyalty.

Contests and sweepstakes are excellent ways to generate publicity and enhance interest in a service. The major difference between these sales promotion techniques is that contests require some sort of skill or knowledge to win while sweepstakes are based on chance alone. Contests and sweepstakes are often tied to a special event such as the World Series, a service facility opening, or the introduction of a new service. Airlines and resorts have used them to stimulate tourist travel. Similarly, major fast-food chains have developed contests and sweepstakes to promote new menu items.

Samples are trial-sized products that allow customers to test a product prior to purchase of the full-sized item. While sampling is used extensively by goods marketers, its usefulness in the service sector is limited by the intangibility of services and by the simultaneity of production and consumption that characterizes service transactions. With a little ingenuity, however, sampling may be used in certain instances. A real estate firm, for example, may attract new customers by offering free home appraisals. A speed-reading service or a stop-smoking clinic may offer a free one-hour session to potential students. A professional sports team may allow fans to view preseason practice and games at a moderate cost or free of charge.

Demonstrations are also difficult for service marketers because there is no product to show. Banks have used demonstrations to introduce automated teller machines to new customers. Beauty salons have probably made the most extensive use of demonstrations by showing new hairstyling techniques and styles to potential customers.

Intermediary (or Dealer) and Sales Force Promotions

Since the channels of distribution for many services are short and direct, dealer and sales force promotions are limited to large service firms that use independent agents, franchised outlets, and/or company salespeople. The most prevalent forms of dealer and sales force promotions for service firms are dealer assistance, cooperative advertising, contests, meetings, trade shows, and conventions.

Dealer assistance programs are used by large service firms to provide promotional and financial aids to intermediaries to encourage sales of their services. For example, airlines, resorts, and other tourist businesses provide travel agents with promotional materials such as posters and brochures. The most extensive dealer assistance is provided to owners of service franchises, such as hotels and motels, car rental agencies, restaurants, and automobile repair shops. Larger service businesses provide their franchise holders with advertising and promotional help, training for employees and managers, accounting procedures, quality control guidelines, and many similar forms of assistance. In fact, most franchise holders must accept these forms of dealer assistance if they are to obtain and retain their franchises.

Cooperative advertising programs are being used with increasing frequency by large service firms as advertising costs become more difficult for intermediaries to afford. In cooperative advertising, a service retailer and a service producer share advertising costs. For example, when a travel agency features an airline's vacation packages in its advertisements, the airline may pay a portion of the advertising costs. This allows the travel agency to purchase more advertising than it might otherwise be able to buy. From the airline's viewpoint, this strategy serves to strengthen and improve its relationship with travel agents, who represent a significant public for the airline. (the concept of "publics" is explained in the section on public relations later in this chapter.)

Contests are used to achieve specific sales objectives—the introduction of a new service, the improvement of service quality, or an increase in sales volume during off-season periods. For example, insurance companies use sales contests to stimulate both company personnel and independent agents to increase sales volume during specified time periods. Likewise, banks and savings institutions use contests to encourage branch personnel to cross-sell services.

Meetings, trade shows, and conventions provide opportunities for service providers, dealers, franchise holders, independent agents, and sometimes potential customers to come together to better understand each other's role in the service delivery process. Participants will have chances to discuss the services being offered, any problems or difficulties that exist, and potential improvements in service quality, delivery, promotion, or pricing. At this time, service businesses may reward those involved in the delivery system for outstanding work on behalf of the firm. New service ideas may be tested also, since most participants will be somewhat familiar with the new service being considered.

Industry trade shows have become effective marketing approaches. For example, computer trade shows bring together equipment manufacturers, software producers, and providers of computer services for the purposes of exchanging information and making contacts in this rapidly changing field. At the consumer level, a home show in a city's civic center provides real estate firms, utilities, insurance companies, financial institutions, and other service businesses with ties to the housing industry with an opportunity to present their services to a large group of potential customers. Insurance companies, airlines, investment companies, and other service industries also use meetings and conventions to provide sales training, motivation, and other forms of sales assistance in a central location at moderate costs.

COORDINATING SALES PROMOTION

Until recently, service businesses did not give much attention to sales promotion management. However, because of the increasing use and the higher cost of sales promotion, this situation is beginning to change. For example, major airlines have begun to take a closer look at their frequent-flier programs. Critics have suggested that these programs may be less effective than they appear to be because free travelers sometimes crowd out paying customers.

A major problem in service companies is their frequent failure to coordinate sales promotion activities with marketing goals and other promotional activities. For example, in their quest for savings, commercial banks and savings institutions may have misused premiums and other sales promotion tools. Critics contend that savers merely switch funds from one financial institution to another in their desire to obtain specific premiums. This switching is costly to the financial institutions involved and to the economy at large.

This criticism of financial institutions' use of premiums points to the limited function of sales promotion. Whereas advertising is intended to provide long-term stimulation, sales promotion's focus is short term. One cannot expect a sales promotion tool, no matter how effective it might be, to be an effective substitute for long-term promotion. At best, sales promotion activities provide a short-term stimulus to achieve a specific sales goal. Advertising and personal selling must be the backbone of a service company's promotion program.

PUBLIC RELATIONS

Public relations includes a variety of communication techniques that are designed to develop and maintain a favorable public image for a service business. Specifically, the major functions of public relations in service firms are to complement the firm's advertising, personal selling, and other marketing communications activities and to help enhance its reputation in the community. Unlike other forms of promotion, which are openly sponsored by a service business, public relations activities involve indirect selling. These indirect promotion efforts try to build credibility for the service business. Further, indirect selling through public relations makes potential buyers more receptive to other promotional efforts.

The public relations industry itself is an example of a thriving service industry. Approximately 125,000 people are employed by public relations firms in the United States. A $2 billion industry, public relations firms provide a wide variety of professional advice and services to companies and nonprofit organizations of all sizes and types. They help an organization assess and monitor public attitudes toward the organization and its activities; plan and develop communications; provide advice on how to avoid negative publicity; and help minimize damage when negative publicity does occur. Many service businesses employ public relations professionals to assist them.

Although public relations activities are intended to help a service business achieve its marketing objectives, there are three major differences between public relations and marketing.

1. Public relations is primarily a communications tool, whereas marketing also includes needs assessment, service development, fee setting, and distribution.
2. Public relations seeks to influence attitudes, whereas marketing tries to elicit specific behaviors, such as buying and providing referrals.
3. Public relations does not define the goals of the organization, whereas marketing is intimately involved in defining the organization's mission, target markets, and services.[1]

Public Relations Management

The modern view of public relations recognizes a business organization's role as part of society. This means that a service business must assess the total impact of its public relations activities on its long-range corporate goals and its relationship with the general public, its employees, stockholders, and others who may influence acceptance of the firm. Most large service companies plan, manage, and coordinate their public relations activities through a director of public relations or director of corporate communications. This executive is responsible for communicating with the service company's various "publics"—customers, stockholders, analysts, employees, vendors, regulatory agencies, and so forth.

A service company's publics include those groups of people and organizations that have some sort of interest in or influence

---

[1] Philip Kotler and Paul N. Bloom, *Marketing Professional Services* (Englewood Cliffs, N.J.: Prentice-Hall, 1984), pp. 228–29.

EXHIBIT 10–2 Major Publics of an Airline

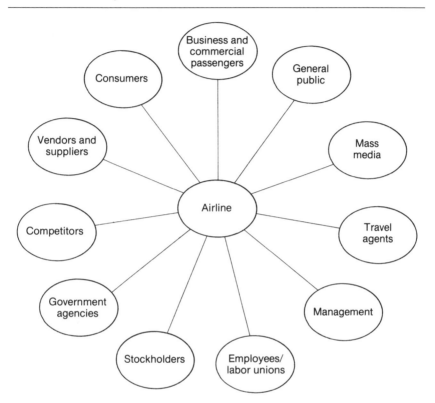

on the company. The major publics of an airline, for example, are shown in Exhibit 10–2.

The primary task of public relations management is to make sure that all of a service firm's contacts with its publics support and reinforce the desired image. To do this well, the form of public relations and the media are adapted to each specific public. For example, the airline shown in Exhibit 10–2 would not want to communicate with government regulatory agencies through news releases.

There are many examples of the use of public relations by service businesses. Entertainment and sports marketers use television, radio, and print media reports of upcoming events to stimulate interest. Banks, utilities, and other regulated service industries prepare press releases to create a favorable impression of the firm and its employees. Many service firms also sponsor community activities and encourage employees to participate in civic and charitable organizations. These and similar public relations efforts lead to contacts with customers and help create a favorable public image for the service business.

Because of the unique features of service businesses, effective public relations is more important to service marketers than to goods marketers. In addition to the normal concern for public credibility and confidence that all businesses have, service firms must deal with two other public relations issues. First, the intangibility of services places additional stress on the service company's need to develop and maintain a favorable public image. Buyers depend more on their perceptions of suppliers when purchasing services than when purchasing goods.

Regulation is a second concern. A service company's public image will affect the actions of legislative bodies and regulatory agencies. Utilities, insurance companies, and other regulated service businesses must work hard to maintain positive relations with regulators and the general public. Consequently, lobbying is an important activity for many service industries.

Robert Ross describes the nature and impact of an effective public relations effort developed by Theodore Vail for the Bell Telephone System in the early 20th century.

> Vail made it clear that the primary goal of the Bell System was to anticipate and satisfy the service requirements of the public. He established the Bell Telephone Laboratories, ensuring the ability progressively to improve and expand telephone service technology. He was responsible for setting up an internal system for measuring and ensuring a quality of service that led to providing telephone service unmatched in most other parts of the world. He was instrumental in the development of a concept of public utility regulation, protecting the public and at the same time being fair and equitable to utilities. This farsighted concept undoubtedly helped protect the Bell System from the governmental takeover that happened to the telephone industry in most other parts of the world many years ago.[2]

Even though the Bell System has now been broken up, public relations continues to be an important marketing activity for

---

[2] Robert D. Ross, *The Management of Public Relations* (New York: John Wiley & Sons, 1977), pp. 4–5.

AT&T and the regional telephone companies created by divestiture. In fact, the confusion and turmoil caused by divestiture has placed even more emphasis on public relations in the telecommunications industry.

Public relations techniques can also be used by small service businesses to create a public identity. For example, a home and office cleaning firm increased its awareness in the marketplace to more than 90 percent through an intensive public relations program. Designed to increase the firm's recognition, the program included weekly press releases, attendance at one or more local groups' meetings each week, use of the company car as a mobile billboard, and weekly mailings of brochures.[3]

Public Relations Techniques

There are a wide variety of proven public relations tools available to service businesses. The major ones are media relations, company publications, exhibits and displays, open houses and tours, and community relations. In addition, a relatively new combination of public relations and sales promotion, known as cause-related marketing, has been widely used by service businesses.

Media relations.   News releases are an efficient way to promote a service because they entail no direct cost for media space or time. Furthermore, news stories have more credibility than advertising, and if the topic is of public interest, a news story may receive greater attention, readership, or viewing than advertising.

Communication in the form of a news story, through mass media such as newspapers, radio, and television, is known as *publicity.* Unlike advertising, publicity represents editorial coverage that is transmitted at no charge by the news medium. However, some critics argue that mass media are more responsive and favorable to businesses that spend heavily on advertising and place their ads in the specific media that feature their news stories.

---

[3] Coleen Milligan and Judith Vindici, "Stressing Existing Services Leads to Growth," *Marketing News,* June 21, 1985, p. 12.

There is much confusion about the relationship between publicity and public relations. Many authorities consider publicity to be a part of public relations. Publicity involves news stories and other relations with the media, whereas public relations involves a more comprehensive communications program and employs a number of tools and media.

Another major distinction is the control exerted over the communications. Public relations include those indirect promotion activities that a service business has under its control. Publicity is what the public media, such as television, radio, and newspapers, do with the information they acquire. As a result, publicity about a service business can be negative. For example, a report of losses by a savings and loan association may result in the withdrawal of funds by depositors. In fact, recent loan write-offs and other financial problems that have been widely publicized by the news media have resulted in "runs" on financial institutions in Ohio, Maryland, and several other states.

The importance of media relations requires that a qualified person be in charge of them. In a large service business, the preparation of news releases and the day-to-day management of relations with the news media are a full-time job usually handled by a member of the public relations staff. In small businesses, the top marketing executive often assumes responsibility for all media relations tasks.

It is especially important that a qualified person coordinate press relations when there is bad news to report. Employee strikes, disasters such as fires and accidents, government investigations, financial reversals, and the like must be reported fairly. Poor press relations will add to the negative impact of bad news. The worst possible situation occurs when the public feels that there is a cover-up or a distortion of the news.

On a more positive note, service businesses prepare news releases to report significant events, such as the opening or remodeling of a service facility, the appointment of a new manager, or the introduction of a new service. The more interesting and newsworthy the topic, the greater is the chance of coverage. For especially important announcements, the service firm may wish to invite media representatives to a press conference, which may involve the preparation of complete press kits for the representatives.

Service firms also prepare news releases for trade publications. These newspapers and magazines serve the needs of readers with specialized interests, and they are an excellent outlet for company news and features. Interviews with key executives, reports of new services and successful management activities, and unique human interest stories are appropriate for trade publications.

Another approach is to submit articles written by a service firm executive or employee to professional and trade publications. For instance, a bank sponsored a state public opinion poll in cooperation with the state university. An article explaining this joint venture was written by the bank's president and a university faculty member. This article was featured in a leading bank trade publication.

Professional service firms find that writing articles and books is a very effective way of gaining credibility for their activities. These publications give professional service providers an opportunity to present their knowledge and expertise. They may also generate inquiries from potential clients. For instance, a management training consultant who writes about a new approach to reduce employee turnover is likely to receive additional publicity and numerous inquiries about the new approach.

Company publications. Unlike news releases, company publications are aimed at readers who already are connected with the service organization, such as employees, stockholders, and key customers. These publications are used to recognize employees' achievements, to inform and persuade readers about company goals and policies, to report earnings and other financial information, and to stimulate sales and improve customer relations. To be effective, these publications must be well written and must contain articles that are interesting to the target readers.

Service businesses use many types of written materials. Airlines, for example, may use annual reports, company newsletters, in-flight magazines, employee training manuals, brochures, and posters to present themselves in a positive light to the various publics outlined in Exhibit 10–2. Two of the most widely used forms of written materials are brochures and newsletters.

Brochures are used by service firms to present an overview of the firm and its services to the general public or to appeal to a specific target reader. For example, a hospital will develop a multipurpose brochure that describes its facilities, professional staff, and services to prospective patients and the community in general. At the same time it will prepare a targeted brochure that identifies major needs for potential donors as part of its fund-raising efforts. As with all promotional activities, it is most important to keep in mind the goals of the communication when preparing brochures.

Many service organizations have begun to use newsletters to communicate regularly with customers, employees, and other desired publics. Newsletters are used to provide useful information to the target readers, to keep readers informed of personnel and other changes within the service firm, and to keep the name of the firm current in the reader's mind. A dentist, for example, sends out a monthly newsletter that highlights dental health tips and staff activities.

The annual report is a special company publication. Publicly held companies are required by law to provide annual financial data to their stockholders. Many service companies view the annual report as an opportunity to provide additional information about the service firm, its activities, and its employees. These reports are sent to the press, financial analysts, major customers, and community leaders as well as to stockholders.

As technology has changed, so also have company publications. In fact, many service organizations are now using audiovisual materials to replace or supplement company publications as public relations tools. A good example is provided by the changes taking place in educational marketing. College recruiters may bring films, videotapes, or slide presentations to college fairs or other gatherings of potential students and their parents.

Regardless of the media used, company publications and other communications materials must be consistent. That is, they must be planned and coordinated to provide a clear-cut, recognizable identity for the service organization. One way to do this is to feature a symbol, or unique logo, on the organization's letterhead, business cards, publications, and other materials. A logo also helps to make the firm appear more real to customers, thus reducing the uncertainty associated with intangibility.

Exhibits and displays. Exhibits and displays range from elaborate exhibits, such as the Eastern Air Lines pavilion at Walt Disney World, to window displays featuring information about local services and employees. The key to effective exhibits and displays is to design them in ways that are both interesting and informative. For large exhibits many service companies hire firms that specialize in designing and constructing exhibits.

Exhibits and displays will attract people to a service facility and stimulate public interest. A bank that features an exhibit on local history, including the bank's role, will be providing a community service and bringing visitors to the bank. Likewise, an energy-saving exhibit sponsored by a utility will stimulate interest in the utility. Other examples of public relations techniques that benefit both sponsor and consumer include health fairs sponsored by hospitals and other health care agencies; financial planning displays sponsored by banks, insurance companies, and stockbrokers; and educational exhibits sponsored by schools and colleges.

Open houses and tours. Open houses and tours provide another opportunity for people to learn more about a service organization. They can be held for the general public or for a specific group of people. An open house and/or tour also may be used to show off a new facility or to celebrate a special event, such as a corporate anniversary.

Banks hold open houses for the general public when they open new branch offices or reopen renovated ones. Special open houses are held for selected customers who have special financial needs, such as realtors, attorneys, and large corporate customers. Usually, at an open house, refreshments are served and small gifts may be given to visitors.

Even if no special occasion exists, tours of a service company's facilities are effective in informing students, politicians, local dignitaries, and other people about the company and its services. For example, a large insurance company sponsors regular tours of its computer facilities for college students enrolled in data processing courses. These students learn how the concepts they are studying are applied in a major business, and the insurance company has a chance to make new friends. Another type of open house that has many benefits is a family night for employees and their families.

Professional sports teams use a variation of an open house to promote themselves. However, instead of inviting the public to come to the business, the professional sports teams send their coaches and players to the public. They stage clinics and appear at charitable functions to promote and stimulate interest in their teams and sports.

Community relations. Having good community relations involves being a good corporate citizen and contributing to a community's welfare. To ensure good community relations, a company must recognize and fulfill its responsibilities to the communities in which it does business. It is especially important that a service business pay close attention to its community responsibilities because service firms are more dependent on local support than are manufacturers. Other major reasons for maintaining good community relations are to attract and retain capable employees, to support the good morale of employees, to maintain a stable customer base, and to obtain cooperation from local government agencies.

A service company's employees are the key to a successful community relations program. Employees must be encouraged to participate in community activities and must be supported, financially and otherwise, in their participation. Appropriate community activities for employees include service on school boards, town councils, and other local government agencies; active involvement in Rotary, Lions, Kiwanis, and other civic clubs; and participation in charity drives. Many service companies, such as major banks and utilities, even go so far as to "loan" executives to charities for fund-raising efforts.

Financial and other forms of direct support for community activities are important, also. Sponsoring youth programs, donating funds to charities, supplying speakers for local clubs and civic organizations, and participating in educational programs are some of the ways service firms can contribute directly to their communities. These efforts, if planned and executed properly, can pay substantial dividends.

The community activities of the First Wisconsin National Bank of Madison provide a good example of the role community relations should play in a service business.[4] The bank's Community Services Division has three major tasks: identifying and supporting community activities, promoting employees' involvement in civic affairs, and developing financial education programs for the public. Each year, the bank's employees contribute more than 21,000 hours to 210 organizations, and the bank gives more than $120,000 to community activities.

Cause-related marketing. An interesting combination of the use of community relations and premiums to stimulate trial and use of a service was developed by American Express Company. In 1983, American Express announced that it would donate a penny to the Statute of Liberty renovation project for each credit card transaction and a dollar for each new card issued. This promotional program, which has become known as "cause-related marketing," resulted in a 30 percent increase in transactions and a 15 percent increase in new cards. As a result of its success, American Express has used this approach to support approximately 50 causes. Other major companies have also used cause-related marketing to promote their products and services.

DIRECT MARKETING

Direct marketing is an emerging form of promotion that combines elements of advertising and personal selling. Although direct mail has been used extensively by insurance companies, credit card marketers, and other service businesses for many years, it has only been a recent event that these and other service marketers have combined direct mail with telemarketing and other promotion tools. Improved telecommunications and computer technology have come together to make direct marketing a powerful, cost-effective way for service businesses to reach specific target markets.

---

[4] "Bank Stresses Involvement in Community Activities," *Marketing News*, June 13, 1980, p. 11

The thrust of successful direct marketing is to use direct mail and telephone contacts in conjunction with each other to supplement and support other sales and promotion activities. This involves a "pull" strategy that, in the words of one service marketing executive, gives service marketers a "one-two punch."

Perhaps the major reason why direct marketing has grown so rapidly is the cost savings provided. As the costs of personal selling have increased, sales and marketing managers have searched for less expensive ways to contact customers. In many service businesses, direct mail and telemarketing have replaced personal selling for the majority of customer contacts. Personal contacts by salespeople are restricted to calling on major customers and to following up qualified sales leads generated by direct marketing. For example, AT&T Communications serves all of its residential and small-business customers through its regional telemarketing sales centers. Field sales calls are made only to those business customers that generate significant long-distance sales volume. An overview of the relative roles of advertising, direct mail, telemarketing, and personal selling is shown in Exhibit 10–3.

Direct Marketing Approaches

The major forms of direct marketing are direct mail and telemarketing. Direct mail, sometimes called direct response marketing, involves contacts with customers through targeted mailings. One of the most successful direct mail businesses in the world is operated by American Express, which is generating sales for hundreds of companies through contacts with its millions of American Express cardholders. Telemarketing, or telephone sales and customer service, has also emerged as a powerful direct marketing tool. As one would expect, AT&T has been a leader in the development of telecommunications procedures and equipment.

There are several ways in which direct marketing techniques can be combined with traditional forms of promotion. One is inbound telemarketing. By including a toll-free 800 number in its advertisements and other promotional materials, a service business encourages interested customers to call for additional information. MCI averages 200,000 calls a month and

EXHIBIT 10–3 The Role of Direct Marketing in the Promotion Mix

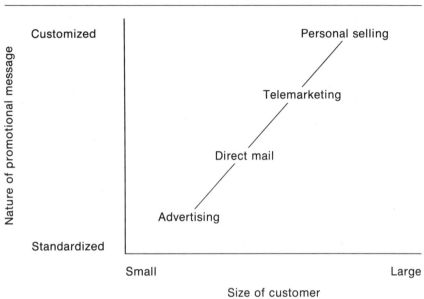

credits its aggressive direct marketing program with helping it grow to over $2 billion in sales.

Another important use of direct marketing techniques is to improve customer service and to cross-sell additional services. A service firm's customers are encouraged to call with requests for information, suggestions, and complaints. By using a toll-free number to prompt customers to call, the service business can respond more quickly to customers' requests and problems. They can also cross-sell other services. For instance, when a customer calls one of AT&T Communications' consumer market sales centers to obtain credit for a wrong number or to correct another problem, the customer service representative will examine the consumer's records and suggest "Reach Out America" or some other service plan that might be appropriate for the customer.

Outbound direct marketing is the third major approach used. This involves contacting customers through a direct-mail appeal or an outbound telephone call. Those service businesses which have had the greatest success with this approach have combined the two forms of communication. A direct mail piece sent prior to a telephone call increases the customer's receptivity to a follow-up phone call and provides a frame of reference for the call.

Many banks have used this approach to reach specific target market segments. Employing service usage, balance levels, demographics, and other relevant variables to segment its customer base, a bank can identify the specific target market for a particular financial service or package of services. Each customer in the target market is then sent a mailing that describes the service and its benefits. Then branch personnel or specially trained telephone sales personnel call the customer to answer questions, emphasize the benefits, and close the sale. Citibank used this approach to sell certificates of deposit to lower-budget consumers. The campaign, which included direct mail, an incoming 800 number, and an outgoing telephone calling program, resulted in 18 percent of the bank's current customers and 6 percent of noncustomers signing up for the certificates of deposit.

Ryder Truck Rental is another service firm that has successfully combined direct mail and telemarketing. Ryder has over 20 direct-mail letters that are used to promote the cost- and time-saving benefits of Ryder's leasing services or to inform customers of special services. These letters are signed by local sales representatives and are targeted to the specific needs of the customer. Specially trained telephone sales representatives follow up the letters with phone calls to qualify prospects and arrange an appointment with a field sales representative. Ryder's marketing executives have been very pleased with this comprehensive direct marketing approach, which they feel has enhanced the productivity of Ryder's sales force.

Managing Direct Marketing Activities

Most direct marketing authorities agree that successful direct marketing requires that a service firm follow three major steps. First, the purpose and objectives of a firm's direct marketing activities must be clearly defined. These may include introducing new services, qualifying sales leads, handling small or geographically distant customers, and servicing customers with special problems or complaints promptly. Specific objectives must be precise and measurable. Perhaps most critical is to specify the desired ratio of sales to cost.

The second major task is to develop a strategy for direct marketing. This involves identifying the activities to be carried out and determining the sequence of these activities. As noted, the most successful direct marketing programs have combined a direct-mail appeal with telephone follow-up.

The third important step is to select and train appropriate people to carry out the direct marketing program. Because direct marketing activities have become so sophisticated, it is wise to hire a consulting firm that specializes in direct marketing. If company personnel are to be involved, they should receive special training in telephone sales techniques and other needed skills.

SUMMARY

This chapter concludes our discussion of service promotion. Sales promotion includes contests, displays, samples, trade shows, and other tools that supplement advertising and personal selling. The key to using sales promotion tools effectively is to coordinate them with the other forms of promotion.

Public relations, another form of promotion, complements other marketing communications activities and enhances the service firm's reputation. The major public relations activities are media relations, company publications, displays and exhibits, open houses and tours, and community relations. A technique that combines public relations and sales promotion is cause-related marketing.

The final segment of Chapter 10 explored the emerging form of promotion known as direct marketing. This approach combines direct mail, telemarketing, and other promotional techniques into a "pull" strategy that can be used to reach specific target markets. In addition to providing an effective promotion tool, direct marketing increases the productivity of a service firm's sales force.

CHAPTER 11

Service Distribution

The third element of the marketing mix, distribution (or "place" within the framework of the four Ps), provides further examples of the similarities and differences between goods marketing and service marketing. Product marketing theory and practice stress the importance of establishing an integrated network, known as a channel of distribution, to transfer a finished product from producer to consumer. In the goods sector, these channels may be numerous and complex, involving a number of intermediaries. While service marketers must also develop channels of distribution, the unique features of services, especially intangibility and perishability, require that the channel of distribution concept be revised when it is applied to service marketing.

In this chapter we shall discuss the distribution component of the service marketing mix. With regard to distribution, the two key concerns for a service business are: (1) making services accessible to customers, and (2) maintaining quality control over the production and marketing of services. This can be accomplished by developing a comprehensive, well-managed service delivery system.

Service Delivery Systems Create Utility

Studies of distribution emphasize that a channel of distribution is a system—a group of interrelated components with the same objectives. Taken together, these components comprise a network, or delivery system, that makes a service available to the customer. The components of the service delivery system are customers, the service producer, intermediaries, and facilitating and regulatory agents. Their distinct roles in service distribution are described in Exhibit 11–1.

More and more, service businesses and their customers are becoming concerned with the accessibility of services. Service buyers want convenience; that is, they want services made available to them in a timely and easily accessible manner. The delivery system for a service must do this by creating time utility and place utility. These utilities, in turn, create the customer satisfaction that is the basic purpose of all service marketing activities.

Time utility means that the service must be available *when* the customer wishes to purchase it; that is, it must be produced on demand. Airline passengers, for example, want flights to take off and arrive at convenient times, and they do not want to spend hours waiting in an airport for connecting flights. Bank depositors may want to do their banking at night or on weekends—this can be accommodated by 24-hour electronic banking.

Place utility refers to making services available *where* buyers want to purchase them. For some services, such as electrical power and telephone, this means distributing the service directly into the consumer's home or place of business. Other services are distributed through retail outlets, but these must be located conveniently in order to maximize the place utility desired by the service buyer. For ultimate convenience, banks are now experimenting with in-house electronic banking.

The creation of time utility and place utility is much more important for a service marketer than for a goods marketer. Intangible services cannot be stored in a central location and transported to markets when demand increases. Service facilities must be in place and large enough to meet demand fluctuations. If a firm's facilities are not adequate, and the service buyer is unable to secure the time utility and place utility desired from that service firm, the buyer will go elsewhere or forgo

---

EXHIBIT 11–1   Roles Played in the Service Delivery System

Role	Function
Primary channel components	
Customer	Purchase and/or consume a service; involved directly in distribution, due to simultaneity of production and consumption.
Producer	Perform or produce a service.
Secondary channel components	
Intermediary	Bring producer and customer together; represent either of the primary channel components.
Facilitating agents	Provide services that assist in the distribution process; includes communication firms, financial institutions, and the like.
Regulatory agencies	Provide a degree of supervision in the distribution process by establishing guidelines and regulations for managing and controlling distribution; includes both private agencies (such as professional and trade associations) and government agencies (such as public utilities commissions).

---

consumption of the service altogether. The critical issue, then, is availability on demand. A restaurant may serve excellent food, but if it is located in an out-of-the-way area, it is unlikely to attract large numbers of customers.

Customer Contacts Are Critical

The concept of a service business as a system has been described by Pierre Eiglier and Eric Langeard.[1] The Eiglier and Langeard system emphasizes the direct contact between a service business and its customers as well as the customers' participation in the

---

[1] Pierre Eiglier and Eric Langeard, "Services as Systems: Marketing Implications," in *Marketing Consumer Services: New Insights,* ed. Pierre Eiglier, Eric Langeard, Christopher H. Lovelock, John E. G. Bateson, and Robert F. Young (Cambridge, Mass: Marketing Science Institute, 1977), pp. 14–15.

production of the service. A service system is based on the interaction between physical support components, contact personnel, and the client.

Physical support includes the tangible materials used to produce and market a service. The instruments necessary for the production of a service to be produced are one major form of physical support. The contact personnel and/or the client will use machines, furniture, and other objects to create or consume a service. For example, in a restaurant, these instruments include stoves, refrigeration equipment, tables, chairs, dishes, and many other tangible materials. The second major form of support is the physical environment, or the location and building where the service is produced.

The service system's contact personnel are those people who are in direct contact with clients. Usually, these people perform a technical or production function, but they also are the most important part of the marketing process. Bank tellers, hotel reception clerks, waiters and waitresses, telephone operators, and airline flight attendants are examples of contact personnel.

Another view of the service business as a system is presented by W. Earl Sasser, R. Paul Olsen, and D. Daryl Wyckoff. They view the distribution of services in terms of a service delivery system.[2] As in the Eiglier and Langeard model, a key part of the service delivery system concept is the buyer's participation. Production and marketing interface when the service is produced and delivered simultaneously. For example, a woman having her hair styled is intimately involved in the production as well as the consumption of that service.

A flowchart can be a useful tool for analyzing a service delivery system.[3] Such a chart should show what activities are performed and how they relate to each other. Of particular importance to distribution is the identification of crucial steps—when the service process interacts with the customer. A flowchart showing the check-in and check-out procedures for renting a car is shown in Exhibit 11–2. There are many points at which the

---

[2] W. Earl Sasser, R. Paul Olsen, and D. Daryl Wyckoff, *Management of Service Operations* (Boston: Allyn & Bacon, 1978), pp. 14–15.

[3] Ibid, pp. 74–81.

EXHIBIT 11-2 Flowchart of Car Rental Check-In/Check-Out Process

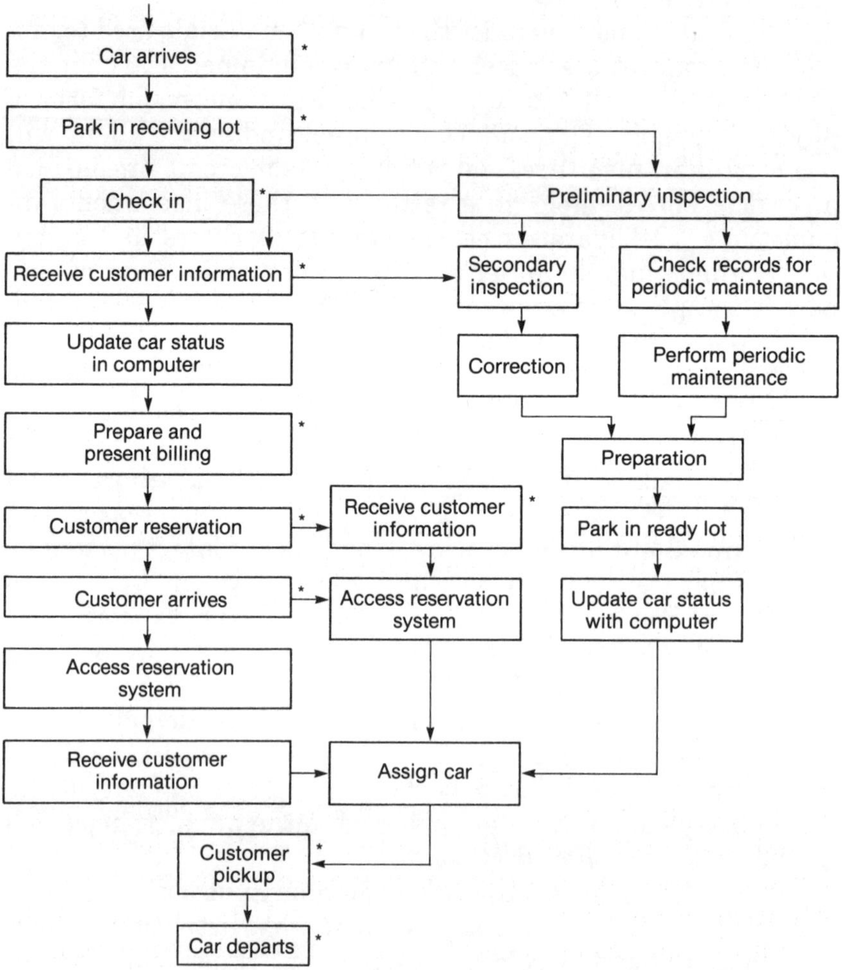

---

* Indicates interaction with customer.

SOURCE: W. Earl Sasser, R. Paul Olsen, and D. Daryl Wyckoff, *Management of Service Operations* (Boston: Allyn & Bacon, 1978), p. 74. Reprinted with permission.

service delivery system and the customer interact. The key concern for the service business, such as a car rental agency, is to make these interactions convenient and smooth for the customer.

SERVICE DISTRIBUTION CHANNELS

As the earlier discussion of utility stressed, the function of *distribution* in the service marketing mix is to make a service available and/or more convenient to the buyer. Unlike goods, services cannot be transported. Consequently, channels of distribution for services must either bring the service to the buyer or bring the buyer to the service facility. For example, a physician delivers medical services directly to a patient, perhaps with the assistance of laboratory technicians who analyze test results; a lawyer works directly with a client; or a teacher works in a classroom directly with students. Insurance may be purchased through an agent; real estate, through a broker; or a loan, through a bank officer. In each case, channels are shorter and more direct than those for most goods.

Why can't services, unlike manufactured goods, be funneled through an extensive number of intermediaries? The unique features of services provide the explanation. Services are intangible, which means that they cannot be stored, inventoried, or transported. Ownership cannot be transferred because services are perishable. The simultaneity of production and consumption requires that consumers become involved in the service delivery system. The personal relationships between service producers and consumers also influence the type of distribution system that may be used.

For all of these reasons, distribution channels for most services are simpler and more direct than those for goods. Conventional intermediaries, such as full-service wholesalers who are key elements in the distribution process for goods, are generally not used to distribute services. An exception are tour wholesalers who buy blocks of seats and rooms from airlines and hotels, package them, then resell them through travel agents. Consequently, service distribution or delivery systems can be classified in two ways: (1) by whether or not the service provider directly or indirectly sells the service to customers, and (2) by the location at which the service is performed.

Services sold directly. Services may be sold and performed on either a direct or an indirect basis. These options are illustrated in Exhibit 11–3. As can be noted, there are two basic *direct sale options* and two *indirect sale options*. The simplest

EXHIBIT 11–3 Channels of Distribution for Services

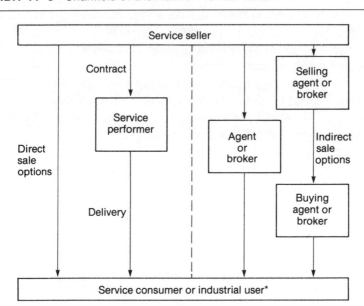

* Includes nonprofit organizations and government agencies.

direct sale channel is from service seller to service consumer. Most professional and business services, such as management consulting, medical and legal services, and industrial laundering services, are delivered in this manner.

The second direct option adds the element of a service performer who is distinct from the service seller. Many home care services, such as gardening and housekeeping, fall into this category, as do temporary-help agencies. This second option may involve contracting for services. Here, a verbal or signed agreement between seller and buyer outlines the terms and conditions under which the service is to be delivered from seller to consumer. Retainers for legal and medical services, and service repair agreements, such as one-year appliance service contracts or automobile repair contracts, are examples of the contractual method of service distribution.

Services sold through intermediaries. Indirect sale options involve the use of *intermediaries,* who act on behalf of the

EXHIBIT 11–4 Multiple Contacts without an Intermediary

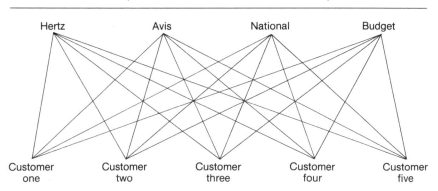

seller, the buyer, or both parties. When such intermediaries are used in the marketing of services, they typically act in the capacity of agents or brokers. They facilitate the delivery of a service by issuing or transferring a tangible representation of the service, such as a ticket, contract, or policy. Familiar examples of service intermediaries include travel agents, securities brokers, real estate brokers, and insurance agents. These intermediaries must be supervised adequately, however, to ensure that they are providing an acceptable level of service. Because of their substantial responsibility in advising clients competently, they are subject to licensing requirements.

The example of travel agents can be used to explain the advantages of using service intermediaries. In many cases, these intermediaries provide added convenience by reducing the number of contacts between service producers and their customers. For example, there are four major national car rental agencies—Hertz, Avis, Budget, and National—plus many smaller regional firms. Suppose there are five customers who wish to obtain information about rates and availability from the four major firms. If there were no intermediaries, there could be up to 20 contacts if each of the five customers went to the four car rental firms directly. (See Exhibit 11–4.)

The number of contacts would be reduced significantly, however, if all customers went to a single travel agent for information and reservations. (See Exhibit 11–5.) By reducing the number of contacts, travel agents and other service intermediaries

---

EXHIBIT 11–5 Reduced Contacts through an Intermediary

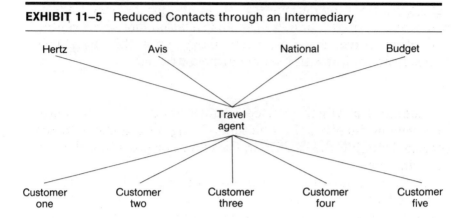

enhance the convenience of customers and increase the efficiency of service distribution.

Deregulation and other changes in traditional service businesses have brought about significant changes in the use of intermediaries. For example, AT&T Communications no longer has a direct link to its customers. The former Bell operating companies, which used to be part of AT&T Communications' vast communication network, now serve as intermediaries for the delivery of its long-distance services. These companies also serve as intermediaries for MCI, Sprint, and other long-distance carriers.

In contrast, deregulation has lessened the importance of intermediaries in other service industries. It has been predicted that the number of independent agents selling auto and homeowner's insurance to consumers and commercial policies to businesses will decline by half over the next 10 years. Direct mail, telemarketing, and direct sales by "captive" company agents are forcing independent agents, who have higher costs, out of business. Travel agents are also concerned about the possible loss of business to automatic ticket machines and direct sales of travel and lodging services to corporate travel departments.

However, as the example described earlier suggested, the fears of travel agents may not be justified. Airline deregulation has also presented opportunities to travel agents. As the number of air carriers has grown and routes and fares have become more and more complex and confusing, many travelers are looking to travel agents for information, guidance, and advice. Travel agents also provide "one-stop shopping" for the busy traveler who wants a single contact for transportation, hotel, car rental, and other travel services, particularly since this assistance comes from an impartial source at no extra cost.

Location at which service is performed. This classification scheme involves three options: bringing the client to the service, bringing the service to the client, or providing the service "in transit."

In the first instance, there are centralized service facilities to which clients must travel to receive desired services. Banks, hospitals, and universities provide examples of this kind of concentrated delivery system. For these service businesses, location of service facilities is a key marketing concern.

Bringing the service to the client is illustrated by in-home visits by insurance agents, physicians, or home service providers such as painters, plumbers, and the like. Some service businesses are attempting to shift service distribution from their facilities to the buyer's home or workplace. For instance, Citibank, Chase Manhattan, and other major banks are heavily promoting home banking. Chemical Bank introduced the first home banking system, known as Pronto, in September 1983. This system provides subscribers with complete, up-to-date account information and enables them to pay their bills and transfer funds from one account to another through their personal computer. However, despite the promoted advantages of home banking, it is estimated that only 10 percent of retail banking customers will use home banking by 1990.

Delivery of services "in transit" is another relatively new concept in which both provider and consumer meet at a specified location and travel together so that educational or other services may be provided. One metropolitan area university, for example, has begun offering courses to certain railroad commuters. These commuters, who are graduate business students, meet in a designated car for 50-minute sessions, then later complete supplementary assignments. In this way, they can earn up to six credit hours per semester during a block of time that had been relatively unproductive. Paramedical services administered to an accident victim en route to a hospital provide another example of "in transit" service delivery.

EXHIBIT 11–6   Service Distribution Policies

Exclusive distribution	Selective distribution	Intensive distribution

One service facility	Several service facilities	Many service facilities

ESTABLISHING A SERVICE DISTRIBUTION POLICY

For many service businesses, a key distribution issue is to establish a policy for the intensity of distribution. This refers to the degree of market coverage. The three possibilities, as shown in Exhibit 11–6, are intensive, selective, and exclusive distribution.

Intensive distribution is a policy designed to obtain maximum market coverage. The primary goal of this policy is to make a service convenient by providing access to it in as many locations as possible. For example, AT&T and the regional phone companies have placed public telephones along highways and in shopping malls, schools, theaters, hotels, and other locations that are frequented by the public. In recent years, banks and savings institutions have also pursued an intensive distribution policy by placing automated teller machines in food and convenience stores, airports, office buildings, and hospitals.

At the other extreme is *exclusive distribution,* which is the most restrictive service distribution policy. Used by many specialty, professional, and business services firms, exclusive distribution means a single service provider or facility in a given market area. Although a service firm with exclusive distribution gives up wide exposure, it gains tighter control over service quality. Since extra effort is required to obtain the service, an exclusive distribution policy may also add to the prestige of the service and its provider.

There are many examples of exclusive distribution in service marketing: professional sports leagues limit the number of available franchises; a professional photographer who caters to affluent, fashionable customers has only one studio in a wealthy suburban city; a leading corporate law firm has its only office in the headquarters building of a large bank. Each of these service providers has restricted access to the services it provides through its policy of exclusive distribution.

Selective distribution represents a midpoint between the extremes of intensive and exclusive distribution. This is a policy of providing more than one but still a limited number of service facilities. Most consumer service businesses have followed a selective distribution policy. In those states in which they are permitted to do so, banks and savings institutions have multiple branches; tickets to sporting events, concerts, plays, and other activities are usually available at a selected number of stores and other outlets; car rental firms will have several outlets for pick-up and delivery in a major metropolitan area.

As buyers' needs and behavior patterns change, service businesses must review and revise their distribution policies. It is significant that many service businesses are moving toward selective and intensive distribution and away from exclusive distribution. These firms recognize their customers' desire for place utility and are providing greater accessibility and added convenience by opening more service locations. As noted elsewhere in this chapter, examples include storefront legal clinics, dentists' offices, and other professional outlets.

FRANCHISING OF SERVICES

For many service firms, financial limitations prohibit their establishing an extensive distribution system with a large number of retail outlets. Therefore, some service businesses have turned to franchising as a way of expanding without having to make a major financial commitment. In addition, the service business has greater control over service quality with franchises than it has with independent agents and brokers.

Franchising is a form of retail distribution that attempts to combine the advantages of centralized management with those of independent local ownership. A franchise is a continuing business relationship in which the owner/operator (known as the franchisee) pays a fee for the right to operate a retail service establishment according to a particular system. The service company granting the right (known as the franchisor) normally receives an entry fee plus continuing royalty fees based on sales.

For its fees, the franchisor provides a name, a service concept, operating procedures, and, possibly, equipment and/or supplies for service operations. In addition, a variety of marketing and management services, such as promotion, personnel training, and management assistance, are provided by the franchisor. The franchisor is primarily concerned with guaranteeing a certain level of service standardization and quality.

The relationship between a franchisor and its franchisees is specified in a contract and other legal documents. These legal agreements outline the responsibilities of each party, performance expectations, financial arrangements, and other appropriate concerns. From the franchisor's perspective the key concern is to obtain an agreement that enables it to control and coordinate the activities of the franchisees.

Over the last 20 years, franchising has become a prevalent form of service distribution. Automobile rental firms, temporary help, hotels and motels, and fast foods are a few of the service industries that have franchised extensively. Examples of franchising are McDonald's, Holiday Inns, Budget Rent-a-Car, and Kampgrounds of America (KOA).

Some service businesses have begun to franchise specific services that they have developed for their customers. For example, Fleet National Bank of Providence, Rhode Island, developed a unique asset management service for the wealthy. Known as the Westminster Account, this service requires a minimum balance of $150,000 in liquid assets. The comprehensive account offers automatic "sweeps" of cash into selected money market funds, a line of credit, checking services, discount brokerage services, an automatic bill-paying service, plus optional tax shelter advice, estate planning, and other financial services. The development costs, especially the computer programs that make the account work, were extensive. Thus, Fleet decided to recoup some of its costs by franchising the service to banks in other parts of the nation. Fleet receives a fee from the franchisees for establishing the program and then will collect monthly fees based on the number of new accounts opened. The bank expects its franchising activities to boost its profit considerably.

Another recent development in service franchising is the trend toward franchising professional services such as selected medical, legal, and accounting services. Proponents claim that franchising makes professional services more available to consumers by lowering fees and making the services more accessible. They claim that the providers of professional services also benefit because franchising relieves service professionals of some of their marketing and management tasks. This allows the service provider to concentrate on the technical aspects of the service. On the other hand, detractors argue that franchised professional service providers do not provide an acceptable level of service, a claim that has not been substantiated.

CHANGING SERVICE DISTRIBUTION STRATEGIES

Distribution strategies for services have changed as the spending for services has increased. In addition to franchising, other significant developments in distribution have been increased offerings of services by traditional retailers, greater automation, improved reservation systems, and greater emphasis on the selection of convenient retail sites.

Major Retailers Provide Many Services

Large retailers now offer many consumer services to their customers, providing tough competition for traditional service marketers. Sears Roebuck & Co., J. C. Penney, and other major retailers have established repair centers, beauty shops, eye care centers, and other consumer service facilities. In addition, Sears, which has been the leader in offering consumer services, has established a network of consumer financial service centers in its larger stores. Even Kroger, the large supermarket chain, is testing hairstyling salons in its stores.

The recent move toward the establishment of eye care centers by retail stores illustrates the changes taking place in service industries. Eye care services are being provided through a variety of "traditional" regional and local retail chains. These outlets attract busy people, who find their central locations and longer hours more convenient than those of conventional optometrists and opticians. It is possible that this trend, along with other factors such as the offering of dental services through Sears, Montgomery Ward & Co., and other retailers, may be an indication of major changes in the delivery of health care services.

Some service businesses lease space in retail outlets. For example, some banks and savings institutions lease out space to firms that provide compatible financial services that they are unable to offer because of legal restrictions. These include insurance, brokerage, travel, and tax preparation services. Conversely, many financial institutions are moving in the other direction. They are leasing space from supermarkets and other retailers for automated teller machines and mini-branches.

One of these retailers is the Southland Corporation, operator of 7-Eleven Convenience Food Stores. Southland plans to install bank automated teller machines in close to half of its 8,000 national convenience stores. The chain hopes that the machines will attract more female and upscale customers to its stores.

Increased Use of Automation

The use of automation by service businesses has three distinct advantages. It helps to decrease personnel costs, which are the major cost element for many services. Automation also reduces service heterogeneity and increases productivity. It can further make a service more accessible to consumers. Most banks and savings institutions, for example, have introduced automated teller machines (ATMs) that enable their customers to withdraw funds and make deposits at any time, rather than being tied to normal banking hours.

For busy travelers, Eastern Air Lines has installed self-ticketing machines in major terminals such as Boston's Logan Airport and New York's LaGuardia. This automated ticketing system offers one-way and round-trip tickets to selected cities. The customer simply inserts a major credit card, selects the destination, and waits for the flight coupon and receipt. Some experts predict that in the near future a traveler may even be able to view flight options on a home computer, make a selection, and arrange payment by punching in a credit card number.

Some financial institutions are moving beyond ATMs in their efforts to cut costs and make banking services more accessible. The industry leader is Banc One of Columbus, Ohio. The first bank to introduce ATMs in 1970, Banc One continues to introduce self-service through the use of automated equipment. Its latest move is the introduction of interactive video systems that provide a customer with basic information, answer simple questions, and prepare an application for the customer's signature. It has been estimated that new technology will be able to perform over 90 percent of the teller's functions.

As noted earlier, other banks and savings institutions are stressing bank-at-home delivery systems. Similarly, other computerized systems now available in various markets allow customers to make purchases from a variety of store catalogs, obtain up-to-the-minute weather reports, buy and sell stocks, prepare for standardized exams, check road maps, and complete a variety of other transactions simply by turning on their home computers.

Another example of service automation is provided by telecommunications. Unless a special service is required, such as a person-to-person call, long-distance calls can be dialed directly. Further, AT&T Communications and other long-distance carriers are introducing new equipment that makes long-distance calling even easier. The new public telephones being installed in airports and other busy locations are examples.

Developing Reservation Systems

Efficient reservation systems offer a way for service businesses to manage demand and serve their customers better. Reservations may be made by mail, by telephone, or in person at conveniently located retail outlets. Computerized reservation systems have been developed to provide up-to-date information, and some even print tickets or reservations on the spot.

There are many examples of reservation systems used to distribute services. Most hotel and motel chains use computerized systems to reserve rooms for travelers. Tickets to sporting and entertainment events may be purchased through Ticketron and other reservation systems. The airlines make extensive use of computerized reservation systems, too, but the problems of "no-shows" and overbookings that they experience point to the difficulties inherent in using these systems. No-shows are a particular problem if there are no financial penalties for the service buyer who fails to honor the reservation. In an effort to compensate for the problems caused by this situation, airlines have adopted a system of reserving more seats than are actually available. This, too, causes serious problems, especially when travelers who believed they were assured of a seat suddenly find that they must wait for the next flight. In addition to the obvious inconvenience, no-shows and overbookings can lead to poor relationships with the airline's various publics.

Selecting Convenient Locations

Since a convenient location is a dominant patronage motive for many service purchasers, retail site selection is a key distribution decision for motels, car rental agencies, and many other service businesses. A related concern is the need to determine the appropriate number of branch locations that will be required.

The simplest solution for a service firm is to operate out of one central location to which consumers must travel or from which service performers are dispatched. While this may be the most economical strategy, it may not suit the particular needs of the service firm or its customers. The geographic area that can be covered from this one location may be severely limited. For this reason, service producers seek to expand the locations from which they can provide services to retail consumers, industrial purchasers, and government users.

Airlines have developed a "hub and spoke" strategy in the design of their route structures. This strategy involves the selection of one or more major cities (e.g., Chicago, Atlanta, Denver, or Kansas City) to serve as the "hub," or focal point for flights. Passengers are flown to the "hub" city from smaller cities and then transfer to other flights to reach their destinations.

Piedmont is an airline that has developed a unique distribution strategy. Rather than compete directly with dominant airlines in major markets, after deregulation Piedmont decided to concentrate instead on serving smaller cities. Piedmont selected Charlotte, North Carolina, as its first "hub" city, and has since moved into Dayton, Ohio, and Baltimore, Maryland. By electing to develop smaller routes, Piedmont was able to establish itself as a factor in the airline industry. However, other airlines have now begun to follow a similar distribution strategy, and Piedmont is being severely challenged.

Another example of how distribution channels are being changed to offer more convenience and greater accessibility to customers is presented by the legal profession. For the most part, consumers' purchases of legal services, for example, wills and uncontested divorces, may be classified as convenience purchases. In several states, storefront clinics have been established to provide consumers with low-cost legal services. These clinics are in accessible locations, rather than being clustered around courthouses. Some, for example, have been located in department stores. Furthermore, the legal clinics offer more convenient hours for working people.

A related development was an agreement between H & R Block, the nation's largest tax preparation firm, and Hyatt Legal Services to open legal clinics throughout the United States. The clinics share facilities with Block's tax preparation offices, and Block provides administrative and marketing assistance. The goal of this endeavor is to make low-cost legal services as accessible as Block's low-cost tax preparation operation.

SERVICE LEVEL AND QUALITY

Since the distribution of services involves direct participation by the buyer, it is imperative that the service seller consider the level and quality of service that will be provided. While individual, one-on-one attention may be the optimum strategy, it simply may not be feasible. The costs may be prohibitive, which the perceived value to the customer may not justify. For this reason, trade-offs may be necessary. Limited hours, fewer employees, and a smaller number of facilities may still provide acceptable service levels at realistic costs.

Such trade-offs must be made carefully, after a thorough consideration of the type of service business, the level of skill needed to provide that service, and the perceived value of the service to the customer. While specialty services may be seen as important enough to warrant some inconvenience such as waiting, convenience services necessitate promptness. Without it, customers may simply seek another provider who is also viewed as being capable of satisfying their needs.

SUMMARY

Distribution, the third element of the service marketing mix, is becoming a more important part of the marketing strategy for service businesses. Traditional concepts of distribution must be modified to account for the unique characteristics of services, such as intangibility, perishability, buyer participation, and simultaneity of production and consumption. Service delivery systems, or channels of distribution, must provide the time and place utilities desired by service customers. Furthermore, service distribution strategies must continually be adapted to the changing needs of customers.

We now turn our attention to the fourth and final element of the service marketing mix—pricing.

CHAPTER 12

Pricing of Services

The pricing of services, like the pricing of goods, is a complex and difficult task. The service marketer must consider demand trends, cost estimates, buyers' perceptions, and competition when establishing pricing goals and strategies. In addition, the intangibility and perishability of services, government regulations, and traditional professional and ethical practices challenge and restrain service marketers in their pricing freedom. To further confuse the issue, many service industries do not even use the word *price* when referring to the cost that the buyer must pay for receipt of a service. Consider, for example, educational services, medical services, brokerage services, and transportation services. Here, the terms *tuition, fee, commission,* and *fare* substitute for the mention of cost or price. Despite these complexities, a careful determination of pricing policies and strategies is essential to the success of a service business. In this chapter we explore pricing, the fourth and final element of the service marketing mix.

ESTABLISHING PRICING GOALS

The development of service pricing policies and strategies begins with the establishment of pricing goals. Most service businesses state their pricing goals in terms of profitability or return on investment. Usually, a service firm will set a goal of obtaining a reasonable profit or a fair and reasonable rate of return. These goals are expressed in precise quantitative terms. However, a service firm may also have to consider social and ethical constraints and its desire for a favorable public image when setting pricing goals. For utilities and other regulated service businesses, the maximum rate of return that is considered fair and reasonable is set by the regulatory agency, not the company.

When service businesses have more flexibility in pricing, goals are often stated in terms of the relationship of price to the service's marketing strategy. A prestige pricing goal, for instance, may specify that high prices are consistent with a restaurant's desired image of quality, gourmet food, and outstanding personal service. In contrast, a discount dry cleaner that emphasizes volume will establish a pricing objective to meet or sell below the price of local competitors. Other market-oriented pricing goals include maintaining or improving market share, stabilizing prices to focus competition on nonprice means, and meeting or selling below competitors' prices. These pricing goals must be consistent with the service firm's overall marketing goals and strategies.

Deregulation of the airline industry has brought pricing goals and strategies to the forefront. Because of increased fuel prices and the air traffic controllers' strike, nothing much happened when deregulation officially began in 1979. However, the last few years have seen dramatic price cutting and rapid expansion of route structures. New York Air, Continental Airlines, and People Express have emphasized low fares as a key element of their marketing mixes. These airlines have lower labor costs than the larger carriers such as United, American, and Eastern, and they have been able to pass these lower costs on to their consumers. The result has been an extremely price-competitive industry where consumers are faced with a confusing array of discount pricing strategies. This is so because the major carriers have been forced to lower fares selectively in an effort to protect their market shares.

PRICING STRATEGIES

Once its pricing goals have been established, a service firm must decide on an appropriate pricing strategy. Four major factors

EXHIBIT 12-1   Elastic Demand

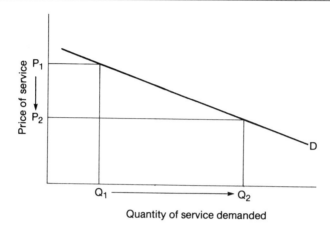

Quantity of service demanded

will affect the firm's pricing strategy: demand for its services, competition, costs, and buyers' perceptions of the value of its services.

Demand and Service Pricing

Demand is described by economists as a schedule of the varying amounts of a product or service that buyers will purchase at different prices over a given period of time. According to the law of demand, there is an inverse relationship between price and the amount, or quantity, of a product or service that will be purchased. That is, as price increases, the quantity demanded decreases; similarly, as price decreases, the quantity demanded increases.

Although it is difficult for many service businesses to estimate precisely the demand for their services, there is evidence that the law of demand holds true for services as well as for goods. As the costs of providing electricity rise, for example, consumers seek ways to conserve and reduce their consumption. Likewise, rising airfares will reduce air travel, especially among nonbusiness passengers. In contrast, lower airfares initiated by People Express and other discount carriers have increased the demand for air travel.

EXHIBIT 12–2 Inelastic Demand

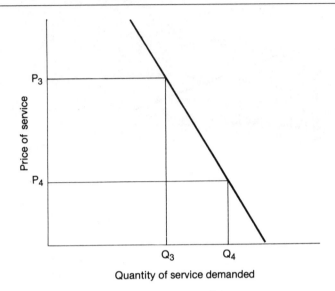

Quantity of service demanded

Elasticity of demand. An important concept for pricing is the elasticity of demand, or the responsiveness of buyers to changes in price. When demand for a service is elastic, a change in price will result in a significant change in the quantity purchased. Exhibit 12–1 shows the effect of a price change when demand for a service is elastic. A modest price decrease from P_1 to P_2 will result in a more substantial change in quantity purchased from Q_1 to Q_2. In contrast, Exhibit 12–2 indicates that, when demand is inelastic, even a significant decrease in price (from P_3 to P_4) will have little effect on quantity purchased (from Q_3 to Q_4).

The elasticity of demand for a service depends on three factors.

1. *Are acceptable substitutes available?* The demand for a service for which there are few, if any, acceptable substitutes will be inelastic. For example, the demand for most forms of medical care is inelastic.
2. *How important is the service's cost as a proportion of the buyer's budget?* The demand for an expensive service, such as a luxury vacation, will be more elastic than the demand for a less expensive service, such as a car wash.

EXHIBIT 12–3 Stimulating Demand by a Price Reduction

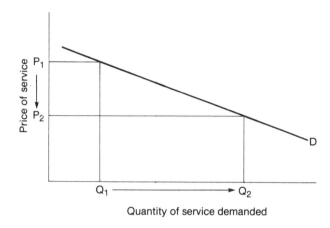

Quantity of service demanded

3. *Is the service perceived as a luxury by the buyer?* If a service, such as a vacation trip or a dinner in an expensive restaurant, is considered a luxury and therefore expendable, demand will be elastic.

The elasticity of demand has major implications for service pricing. Price is more likely to be an important part of a service's marketing mix if demand for the service is elastic. As Exhibit 12–3 illustrates, reducing the price of a service with elastic demand can greatly increase its sales. As noted, airlines have expanded sales and stimulated air travel by offering half-fare coupons, excursion fares, and other forms of price reduction. The demand for air travel is elastic because there are several substitutes; and, because the cost of airfare is substantial, many consumers still feel that air travel is a luxury.

There are many other examples of services for which demand is elastic, including tickets to a Broadway play and a midwinter Caribbean vacation. Attendance at Broadway shows has dropped steadily as ticket prices have increased, while half-price booths attract long lines of prospective theater patrons. Consumers can postpone or forgo purchasing costly luxury services. Accordingly, they will be much more responsive to changes in the prices of these services than to changes in the prices of services for which demand is inelastic. Service busi-

EXHIBIT 12–4   Stimulating Demand by Nonprice Means

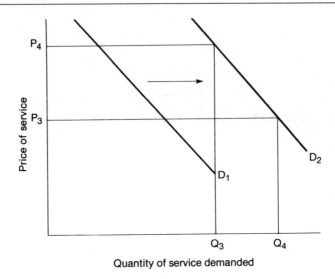

Quantity of service demanded

nesses may stimulate demand by offering a variety of "deals": a theater may offer half-price tickets for matinees; a travel agency may have lower-cost package plans for midwinter vacations or alternate economy tour arrangements; a professional sports team may have group rates for tickets.

For other services, however, demand is relatively inelastic. Services cannot be stored or inventoried for use on demand. Generally, there are few, if any, acceptable substitutes for the many services that are necessities. Medical care, utilities, and housing are major services for which demand is relatively inelastic. If demand for its services is relatively inelastic, a service business must use other marketing techniques, such as promotion and service differentiation, to stimulate sales. Through nonprice forms of competition, the service firm attempts to shift the service's demand curve to the right (see Exhibit 12–4). If these efforts are successful, buyers will either purchase a larger quantity (Q_4) at the same price (P_3) or the same quantity (Q_3) at a higher price (P_4).

The telecommunications industry provides examples of the impact of demand elasticity on pricing. Since the breakup of the Bell System, there has been greatly increased competition in the market for long-distance telecommunications services. AT&T

Communications now faces intense competition from MCI, Sprint, and other providers of long-distance services. As a result, demand has become more elastic and price is a more important part of the marketing mix of AT&T Communications and other carriers.

In contrast, local telephone service is still regulated as a public utility. Further, local service is perceived as a necessity while long-distance service is usually viewed as a luxury. The demand for local telephone service remains primarily inelastic. Although many consumers complain about higher prices, most have not discontinued their local telephone service.

Competition and Service Pricing

Until recently, competitive pricing had been less common in service industries than in goods industries. Inelasticity of demand for some services, regulatory guidelines, ethical restrictions, and limited numbers of competitors had diminished the importance of competitive pricing strategies. Today, however, deregulation, greater customer sophistication and price consciousness, and growing numbers of competitors have contributed to the increased importance of competition-oriented pricing. For instance, in a recent survey of business executives, 80 percent of the respondents said that they had switched auditors because of the lower fees offered by a competing public accounting firm.

Economists describe four models of competitive market structures: perfect competition, monopoly, oligopoly, and monopolistic competition. These are shown in Exhibit 12–5.

Perfect competition is an unrealistic competitive model. This market structure involves a large number of sellers all providing a standardized service. No major obstacles prevent firms from entering or leaving the market, and no firm is large enough to have any control over price. Furthermore, perfect competition assumes that each buyer has complete knowledge of all services offered for sale. As this brief description suggests, the model of perfect competition has value as an analytical tool only.

At the other end of the spectrum is a *monopoly,* in which complete control rests with one provider. Barriers to market entry, such as start-up and operating costs, and lack of access to

EXHIBIT 12–5 Range of Service Competition

	Perfect Competition	*Monopolistic Competition*	*Oligopoly*	*Monopoly*
Examples:	None in the real world	Most retail services: dry cleaning, fast-food restaurants, auto repair, barber and beauty shops	Most national service industries, telecommunications, airlines, insurance, auto rental	Regulated service industries: electric utilities, local telephone companies

resources or to customers are so severe that there are no competitors offering close substitutes. U.S. antitrust laws prohibit monopolies, except for a limited number of industries that are regulated by the government. Prior to deregulation, prices of transportation, communications, and other utilities were closely regulated by federal, state, and local agencies. Regulation often took the form of approving price changes and setting a maximum return on investment for the service industry. Local telephone companies and electric utilities still belong in this category today.

Most service industries fall between these two extremes into the categories of monopolistic competition or oligopoly. The *monopolistic competition* market structure involves sellers who differentiate their service offerings so that they may exercise some control over pricing. Such differentiation may be made on the basis of the seller's location, reputation, personal skills, or other attributes that make the service company's output unique in the minds of potential buyers. Most local retail service establishments, for example, dry cleaning, shoe repair, barber and beauty shops, fit this competitive model.

Oligopoly is a market structure that includes few sellers. To enter the market, a seller is often required to make a large initial investment, so that major entry barriers exist for new competitors. Large national service industries, such as insurance, auto rental, and broadcasting, are examples of oligopolies.

Medical, dental, legal, and other professional services may also exist as oligopolies in small communities. Because there are few competitors in this market structure, price is not used extensively as a marketing tool. In fact, one service firm usually serves as a leader in setting industry prices. Occasionally, however, price wars may erupt. Since the services of competing service providers are often considered interchangeable by the buying public, price changes by one competitor can affect sales and profits for an entire industry. Recent price wars sparked by dramatic price reductions on the part of major car rental firms bear testimony to the market volatility in an oligopolistic structure.

Another oligopoly that has undergone dramatic changes in pricing in recent years is the household moving industry. Before deregulation in 1980, it did not make any difference which mover a customer hired since the cost was the same. However, North American, United, and other major firms now offer consumers discounts of 10 to 15 percent below standard rates. Top corporate customers receive even greater discounts, ranging from 25 to 35 percent. All major carriers now offer their customers discounts based on distance and weight. This and other examples show that price competition will continue to gain importance as deregulation progresses and the competitiveness of various service industries intensifies.

Costs and Service Pricing

Costs are the most common basis for pricing most goods and services. Since many pricing decisions are based on costs, it is helpful to describe briefly the different types of business costs.

The two major types of costs encountered in a service business are fixed and variable costs. Fixed costs are those that remain the same regardless of sales volume. These are expenses that must be met, such as rent, fire and casualty insurance, depreciation, and salaries. Many service businesses have high fixed costs because of their investment in the facilities and capital equipment required to provide the service. Airlines, banks, hotels, and motels are examples. In many cases, most of the labor costs of service businesses are also fixed because of contractual agreements. A professional baseball team, for instance, will have to pay the million dollar salary of its star pitcher whether the team draws 500,000 or 3 million spectators.

Because these costs are fixed, they will be incurred regardless of sales volume. However, as sales volume increases, fixed costs per unit will decrease rapidly since the fixed costs will be spread over increased sales volume. For example, dividing the star pitcher's salary by 500,000 spectators yields a fixed cost per spectator of $2, but if the team attracts 3 million spectators, the fixed cost per spectator declines to 33 cents.

Variable costs, as the term implies, vary with production and/or sales. In a service business, these are often stated as a specific cost for each customer served. Examples of variable costs include direct labor, expendable supplies, and sales commissions. In general, these costs remain the same per customer served and increase in total as sales volume increases.

For example, for an airline that serves dinner on its evening flight from Boston to Chicago, the out-of-pocket cost of the meal to the airline is $3.75 per passenger. If there are 180 passengers on the flight, the total variable cost for the passengers' meals will be $675.

Total costs are the sum of all fixed and variable costs at a given level of sales volume. Of course, as sales volume increases, total costs also increase. Total costs per unit of output decrease, however, because the fixed costs are distributed over a larger number of output units.

Break-even analysis. Because many service businesses have high fixed costs, a useful service management planning and control technique is break-even analysis. Its applications include forecasting sales and expenses, cost control, and pricing.

The break-even point is the level of sales volume at which sales revenues of a service just cover all costs. The break-even volume can be stated in either dollars of sales or some measure of quantity (e.g., number of customers served, load factor, or occupancy rate). The relationship is shown in Exhibit 12–6. The break-even point is noted on the chart. At this particular point, the business realizes neither a profit nor a loss. As the name of the technique suggests, the business is just breaking even. If sales revenue and volume are above the break-even point, the business will earn a profit; if they are below, it will suffer a loss.

To illustrate the application of break-even analysis to a service business, take the case of a small country inn. The inn has 25 rooms that rent for $50 per night. The innkeeper's fixed costs,

EXHIBIT 12–6 Break-Even Chart

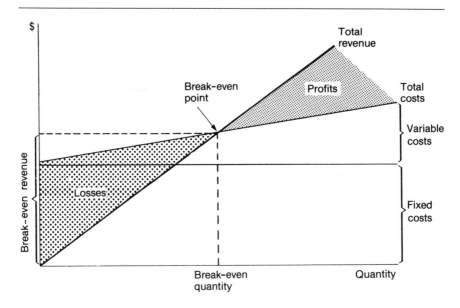

which include mortgage payments, insurance, salaries, and so forth, are $585 per day. The variable costs of cleaning each room after occupancy, supplying linens, soap, and so on, are $5 per room.

Computation of the break-even point involves two calculations. First, the innkeeper must calculate the unit contribution to overhead and profit. This is computed by subtracting the variable cost per room ($5) from the selling price, or rent, per room ($50). The second step is computation of the break-even point by dividing total fixed costs ($585 per day) by the unit contribution to overhead and profit ($45). This yields a break-even volume of 13 rooms. Thus, the required occupancy rate per night if the inn is to break even is slightly above half (52 percent).

This example can be extended further to illustrate the impact of a price change. If the innkeeper increased the room rental rate by $10 to $60, the needed occupancy rate to break even would decline to 11 rooms per night. As this simple example shows, break-even analysis can provide helpful insights to the service marketer who must contend with high fixed costs. It explains, for instance, why an airline that has reached break-even capacity for a given flight is willing to offer substantial discounts to other passengers. Even though these passengers are paying much lower fares, almost everything they are paying contributes to the airline's profits and overhead. Similarly, once the break-even volume was reached, the above innkeeper could theoretically rent a room for as little as $15 and still realize a profit of $10 per room due to the low variable cost.

Cost-plus pricing. Another cost-oriented pricing strategy is cost-plus pricing, used extensively by goods manufacturers and retailers as well as by many service industries. When employing this strategy, producers estimate total costs per unit and then add an amount ("plus") to cover any unassigned costs and to provide the desired profit.

Determining the cost of producing a tangible product is a fairly straightforward task. Costs of raw materials, the major cost components for many products, are relatively easy to estimate accurately. Also, there are standard techniques for allocating the costs of labor and overhead to the production of a good. For service producers, however, costs are more difficult to determine. Raw materials do not exist in the same sense in the production of services as they do in the production of goods. It is also often difficult to allocate labor and overhead costs directly to the production of a specific service.

Despite these difficulties, cost-plus pricing is employed to price services. Time spent in performing a service is often used as the basis for cost allocation ("billable hours"), but even this may be misleading. In professional service pricing, the difficulty of the assignment or the qualifications of the assigned professional may also enter into the equation. For instance, a management consulting firm may assign a relatively inexperienced consultant to a routine case at a rate of $50 per hour and a senior consultant to a complex case at $100 per hour. This example suggests that it is the quality, or value, of the service that is most important to buyers. Hence, value is the basis for the price they will pay for a service.

Value-Based Pricing

The establishment of a service's price is related most appropriately to two concepts: utility and value. Utility is the ability of a service to satisfy a customer's needs. This utility determines the value, or power of the service to command other services or goods in an exchange. Price is the common denominator, since it is the exchange value of a service expressed in monetary terms.

The prices of many services are more likely to be based on value than on cost. The value that a service represents is determined by customers' perceptions. As noted above, many professional service providers rely on perceived value to help determine their pricing structures. Customers will tend to pay whatever they feel a service is worth. If buyers feel that the price for a service is too high, they simply will not purchase the service. The service business must then lower its price or face the consequences of sales lost to competitors or do-it-yourself alternatives. Eventually, the value of a service, and thus its price, will be determined by the market. While the perceived value for the same service may be different for different providers, generally there will be only a certain range of pricing flexibility.

PRICING POLICIES AND PRACTICES

Pricing policies and practices in service industries are not substantially different from those in goods industries. As explained, a service business must consider the demand for its services; its production, marketing, and administrative costs; its perceived value; and the influence of competition when developing pricing strategies, policies, and practices. Recently, rising costs and increased competition have caused service companies to attach greater importance to pricing decisions than they did in the past. Also, service businesses are more concerned with relating pricing to other elements of the marketing mix because the price of a service is a major contributor to the service's image.

Pricing changes in commercial banking, fueled by deregulation, illustrate the growing importance of pricing to service businesses. Increased competition, higher costs of funds, and rising overhead costs have had a substantial impact on banks' profit margins. In addition, low-balance checking accounts, balance inquiries, frequent savings withdrawals, and other bank services and policies may, if not priced properly, severely drain a bank's profitability. These costs are now being passed on to consumers in the form of rising service fees. Consumers must now shop around for the right bank, since fees for such items as bounced checks, balances below prescribed levels, and the like may vary substantially from bank to bank.

Professional Pricing

Professional pricing practices have tended to limit price competition. Fees charged by lawyers, doctors, dentists, and similar professionals have traditionally been overseen by professional associations. Many business services, such as advertising and accounting, have also followed a traditional pricing structure. In recent years, however, antitrust concerns have forced professional service firms to reexamine their pricing practices.

Ethical considerations have been a major reason for the restriction of professional pricing practices. Because the demand for services such as medical and dental care is inelastic, professionals have an ethical responsibility not to overcharge their customers. However, cynics argue that ethical considerations are less a factor than the desire of a professional organization, such as a state medical association, to limit competition and assure adequate incomes for its members.

Another aspect of professional pricing revolves around the rationale that a professional should provide a needed service without concern for the fee received. A standard price may be established for the performance of a specific service. In a given community, for example, all dentists may charge $30 for an examination and cleaning; doctors may charge $35 for an office visit; and all lawyers may charge $200 for the preparation of a will.

Price Negotiation

Price negotiation is an important strategy consideration for some service transactions. Consumer services that sometimes involve price negotiation include auto repairs, foreign travel, and financial, legal, and medical assistance. Specialized business services, such as equipment rental, marketing research, insurance, maintenance, and protection services, are also priced through direct negotiation. In many business service purchases, the price negotiation is done by top executives.

The purchase of a sales training program by an insurance company illustrates the negotiation process. Several sales training consultants were asked to present proposals, including cost estimates. These proposals were reviewed by the vice president of sales and his staff. One sales training consultant was selected tentatively for the job, but she was asked to modify her proposal to lower the total cost. As a result, several changes were made in the proposal to reduce the cost before a final agreement was reached. Often, this give and take is a critical part of the pricing process for management training, consulting, and other business services.

Changing Service Prices

Changing the prices charged for various services is a challenging and uncertain task for service organizations. Organizations may wish to decrease their prices to stimulate demand, or increase their prices to accommodate increased costs of providing services. Regardless of the direction of the change, it will affect the firm, its customers, and its competitors. Further, as Braniff, Air Florida, and other airlines found out, lower prices are not always the way to profitability, or even survival. To the contrary, price cutting is an extremely dangerous marketing practice.

When considering price changes, it is wise to proceed with caution. Service businesses must try to anticipate the reactions of customers, since the market will ultimately determine the success of any price change strategy. Unfortunately, forecasting customers' reactions is a difficult task. One key is to estimate the elasticity of demand for the service. Services for which demand is inelastic will not be as greatly affected by price changes as services that have elastic demand characteristics. Finally, for regulated service industries, for which regulatory agencies serve as the market force, price changes require regulatory approval. The service business must submit to public hearing procedures before price changes are permitted to go into effect. Price change requests are often altered by regulatory commissions.

PROMOTIONAL PRICING TECHNIQUES

Pricing is a marketing tool used to stimulate sales in the same way that service differentiation, personal selling, and other marketing mix components are used. Promotional pricing involves the use of lower, or varied, prices to attract service buyers. Unfortunately, many service businesses have been reluctant to use pricing as a promotional tool. For service companies that have used promotional pricing, however, the results have often been very successful.

New Service Pricing

Pricing a new service is a key part of establishing its marketing strategy. Unless regulation restricts its pricing alternatives, a service business has two new service pricing options: skimming and penetration. The choice of one of these options will depend on the distinctiveness of the new service and, hence, its elasticity of demand.

Skimming is appropriate for a new service that represents a major innovation or is a unique service. Demand for the service is initially inelastic because there are no close substitutes. Skimming establishes a high price for the service, which enables the supplier to "skim the cream" off the market. Promoters of popular entertainers use this approach when they charge high admission prices for the entertainers' performances.

A major risk associated with the use of a skimming price for services is that buyers often have a do-it-yourself option. The car owner who feels that the price charged by a new automated car wash is too high may decide to wash the car at home.

If the expected demand for a new service is elastic, a penetration price is appropriate. This approach, which involves a relatively low price, is designed to appeal to all potential buyers so that the new service will become established quickly. New York Air, People Express, and Continental Airlines have used low fares to establish themselves in markets dominated by major airlines. For example, New York Air began its New York to Washington service at weekday and weekend fares that were substantially lower than Eastern's fare for its established shuttle service.

Loss Leaders

An effective form of promotional pricing is a "loss leader." Service retailers feature a loss leader when they price a specific service low, sometimes even below cost, to attract customers to the service establishment. The retailer is expecting customers to try the service, be satisfied with it, and buy other services at regular prices. Dry cleaners often feature low prices on specific garments or services as loss leaders. Fast-food restaurants follow a similar strategy when they offer a sandwich or soft drink at an attractive low price. An extreme example of a loss leader price was the 29-cent fare used by New York Air to attract attention to new routes between major cities in the Northeast corridor.

Odd Pricing

The odd pricing technique assumes that buyers will be more responsive to prices slightly under an even dollar amount. For instance, a vacation package priced at $799 might be more appealing to consumers than one priced at $800.

There is considerable disagreement over the value of this pricing practice, however. Proponents contend that buyers will feel that the purchase is a bargain. They also claim that many types of buyers are more attracted by odd prices. On the other hand, odd pricing's detractors view this practice as nothing more than a numbers game that has no significant impact on the buyer's decision. Regardless of which viewpoint is correct, one thing is clear: Odd pricing has become an accepted pricing practice. Odd prices are used much more than even prices in service marketing.

Price Discounts and Allowances

Price discounts and allowances are intended to make additional purchases of a service more attractive to potential buyers. Although some types of discounts and allowances, such as trade-ins and trade discounts, are not applicable to services, many service businesses are beginning to realize the value of price reductions.

Perhaps the best example of the use of this technique is provided by the airlines which have established quantity discount programs for passengers. Business executives, salespeople, and others who fly often accumulate mileage on a given airline. Points awarded for the accumulated mileage allow frequent fliers to become eligible for ticket upgrades, price discounts, and even free flights.

Special price discounts and allowances are also used to encourage customers to provide part of the service themselves. Fast-food outlets and cafeteria-style restaurants usually charge less for food than do full-service restaurants. AT&T Communications uses lower long-distance rates to encourage customers to dial directly. Many banks do not charge customers a fee to use an automated teller machine, but there is a fee charged for making a deposit or a withdrawal through a teller.

Nonpeak Demand Pricing

Nonpeak demand pricing is a strategy unique to service businesses. Since services are perishable and demand is variable, a major problem confronting many service marketers is how to increase demand during nonpeak periods. Vacant seats in a theater, idle bank tellers, and unused telephone equipment represent economic losses that can never be recovered. One way to increase demand and to maximize the use of service resources is to use differential pricing. For example, in recent years, electric utilities have given large discounts to encourage major industrial users to switch from daytime to evening operations.

AT&T Communications is another service organization that has used nonpeak pricing extensively. Lower rates are charged for long-distance calls made during evening hours and on weekends. Soon after divestiture, the carrier introduced a specific program, known as "Reach Out America," that provides customers with an hour's calling during late evening and weekend hours for a single low rate. This program also provides discounts for calls made during early evening hours.

Resort hotels and motels utilize nonpeak demand pricing, too. For instance, Cape Cod resort hotels feature special getaway rates during the winter months. They also promote their indoor pools, saunas, exercise rooms, restaurants, and the like at special weekend package rates. These lower prices stimulate nonpeak demand and increase the service firm's profitability by using otherwise underemployed facilities and/or personnel.

Prestige Pricing

Prestige pricing is a psychological pricing tactic that takes into consideration the service buyer's emotional reaction to prices. Because services are intangible, many buyers rely on the service producer's reputation and other emotional factors when they are evaluating buying alternatives. Price often is perceived as a prime indicator of a service's quality. Because of this perception, service marketers may use prestige pricing effectively. For instance, a two-day management seminar priced at $595 may be perceived by consumers as a better seminar than one priced at $295. Likewise, medical, legal, and other professional services that are priced high may have a marketing advantage over similar low-priced services.

Another aspect of prestige pricing is the status, or "snob" appeal, associated with a higher-priced service. The sensitivity to price may even represent an inverse law of demand. The higher the price for a particular event or service, the greater will be the demand. For instance, the more expensive ringside seats for a championship fight frequently are sold out before the less expensive seats.

SUMMARY

This chapter completes coverage of the marketing mix. Service pricing involves a careful review of economic factors, the characteristics of services, restrictions imposed by government agencies and professional associations, and the marketing mix. It is especially important that service pricing goals and policies are consistent with the service firm's overall marketing strategy. Break-even analysis, cost-plus pricing, and value-based pricing are three pricing approaches used by service businesses. In addition, promotional pricing techniques, such as new service pricing, discounts and allowances, and nonpeak demand pricing, are used to stimulate sales.

SELECTED REFERENCE FOR PART THREE

"Battling It Out in the Skies." *Time,* October 8, 1984, pp. 56–58.

Berry, Leonard L.; Charles M. Futrell; and Michael R. Bowers. *Bankers Who Sell.* Homewood, Ill.: Dow Jones-Irwin, 1985.

Braun, Irwin. *Building a Successful Professional Practice with Advertising.* New York: AMACOM, 1981.

Darden, Donna K.; William R. Darden; and G. E. Kiser. "The Marketing of Legal Services." *Journal of Marketing,* Spring 1981, pp. 123–34.

"Does the Frequent-Flier Game Pay Off for Airlines?" *Business Week,* August 27, 1984, pp. 74–75.

Donnelly, James H., Jr. "Marketing Intermediaries in Channels of Distribution for Services." *Journal of Marketing,* January 1976, pp. 55–57.

Doyle, Stephen; John Milne; and Karen Florman. "The Selling Effort in a Branch System." *The Bankers Magazine,* November–December 1982, pp. 76–78.

Dubinsky, Alan J., and William Rudelius. "Selling Techniques for Industrial Products and Services: Are They Different?" *Journal of Personal Selling and Sales Management,* Fall–Winter 1981, pp. 65–75.

Ficquette, Tom. "What It Takes to Transform Your Bank into a Vibrant Sales Organization." *Bank Marketing,* September 1983, pp. 10–14.

Fleagal, David W. "Planned Positioning: More than Window Dressing." *Bank Marketing,* November 1982, pp. 12–14.

George, William R. "The Retailing of Services—A Challenging Future." *Journal of Retailing,* Fall 1977, pp. 85–98.

George, William R., and Leonard L. Berry. "Guidelines for the Advertising of Services." *Business Horizons,* July–August 1981, pp. 52–56.

George, William R., and Claudia E. Marshall, eds. *Developing New Services.* Chicago: American Marketing Association, 1984.

Johnson, Eugene M. "Personal Selling: Key to Successful Marketing in the 1980s." *Review of Business,* Winter 1980–81, pp. 1–2, 22.

————. "Turning Them On to Selling." *Bank Marketing,* May 1980, pp. 20–23.

Kelly, Patrick, and William R. George. "Strategic Management Issues for the Retailing of Services." *Journal of Retailing,* Summer 1982, pp. 26–43.

Kinnear, Thomas C., and Kenneth L. Bernhardt. *Principles of Marketing.* 2nd ed. Glenview, Ill.: Scott, Foresman, 1986. See Chapter 20, "Marketing of Services," pp. 652–77.

Kotler, Philip. *Principles of Marketing.* 3rd ed. Englewood Cliffs, N.J.: Prentice-Hall, 1986. See Chapter 23, "Services Marketing and Nonprofit Marketing," pp. 679–97.

Kurtz, David L., and Louis E. Boone. *Marketing.* 2d ed. Hinsdale, Ill.: Dryden Press, 1984. See Chapter 12, "Services," pp. 335–56.

Lovelock, Christopher H., and John A. Quelch. "Consumer Promotions in Service Marketing." *Business Horizons,* May–June 1983, pp. 66–75.

Rathmell, John M. *Marketing in the Service Sector.* Cambridge, Mass.: Winthrop, 1974.

Richardson, Linda. *Bankers in the Selling Role.* New York: John Wiley & Sons, 1981.

Sasser, W. Earl, and Stephen P. Arbeit. "Selling Jobs in the Service Sector." *Business Horizons,* June 1976, pp. 61–65.

Schlissel, Martin R. "Pricing in a Service Industry." *MSU Business Topics,* Spring 1977, pp. 27–48.

Stanton, William J. *Fundamentals of Marketing.* 6th ed. New York: McGraw-Hill, 1981. See Chapter 21, "Marketing of Services," pp. 440–55.

Upah, Gregory D. "Mass Marketing in Service Retailing: A Review and Synthesis of Major Methods." *Journal of Retailing,* Fall 1980, pp. 59–76.

"Upheaval in Life Insurance." *Business Week,* June 25, 1984, pp. 58–61, 63, 65.

INDEX

This book has been set 202N, in 11 and 10 point Century Schoolbook, leaded 2 points. Part and Chapter numbers are 12 point Helvetica, while Part and Chapter titles are 18 point Helvetica. The size of the type page is 27 by 47 picas.